EAST, WEST, AND OTHERS

EAST,
WEST, *and Others:*
The Third World in Postwar German Literature

ARLENE A. TERAOKA

•

University of Nebraska Press

Lincoln & London

Publication of this book was assisted by a
grant from The Andrew W. Mellon Foundation.

Acknowledgments for previously published
material appear on page x.

The quotations from "A. von H. (1769–1859)"
on pages 62–65 originally appeared in *Mausoleum:
Thirty-seven Ballads from the History of Progress,* Hans
Magnus Enzensberger, trans. by Joachim Neugroschel
(New York: Urizen Books, 1976). Reprinted with
permission. Copyright: Hans Magnus Enzensberger,
MAUSOLEUM. Siebenunddreißig Balladen aus der
Geschichte des Fortschritts © Suhrkamp Verlag
Frankfurt am Main 1975.

The quotations from *The Sinking of the Titanic* on
pages 66–77 originally appeared in *The Sinking of the
Titanic,* Hans Magnus Enzensberger, trans. by Hans
Magnus Enzensberger (Boston: Houghton Mifflin,
1980). Reprinted with permission. Copyright:
Hans Magnus Enzensberger, DER UNTERGANG DER
TITANIC. Eine Komödie © Suhrkamp Verlag
Frankfurt am Main 1978.

Library of Congress Cataloging-in-Publication Data
Teraoka, Arlene Akiko, 1954–
East, west, and others: the Third World in postwar
German literature / Arlene A. Teraoka.
p.   cm. — (Modern German culture and literature)
Includes bibliographical references and index.
ISBN 0-8032-4431-2 (alkaline paper)
1. German literature—20th century—History and
criticism. 2. Developing countries in
literature. I. Title. II. Series.
PT405.T43 1997 830.9'321724—dc20
96-7446 CIP

To Heiner

CONTENTS

Acknowledgments

The completion of this book would not have been possible without substantial personal and institutional support. For the latter I am grateful to the American Council of Learned Societies and the Social Science Research Council for an East European Studies Grant in 1986–87. The University of Minnesota provided generous funds through a Graduate School Faculty Summer Research Fellowship in 1991 and a Bush Sabbatical Program Award in 1992–93. My work was further aided by the superb bibliographic skills of my research assistant Karen Storz. For support of another kind I owe heartfelt thanks to the former chair of my department, Gerhard Weiss. Without his integrity and humanity, and his many actions on my behalf, I could not have accomplished all that I have at Minnesota.

My greatest personal thanks go to Jim Parente, who gave painstaking attention to each version of the chapters of this book and who shares with me the joy, the challenge, and the humor of parenthood. I am grateful also to past and present friends who read significant portions of this work with intelligence and care: especially to Don Nonini, Azade Seyhan, and Leslie Adelson. My parents, Tetsuo and Doris Teraoka, deserve more appreciation than I can ever express. They taught me the value of education and did everything possible to help me realize my dreams. I only hope I might be able to do the same for Francesca and Sophia.

To Peter Hohendahl goes a special word of gratitude for his rare and inspiring professionalism. To Sara Lennox, my deep appreciation for detailed comments that led me to rethink my arguments. Finally, to the friends and colleagues whose lecture invitations allowed me to present my work to broader audiences, I give my sincere thanks again: Ehrhard Bahr, Angelika Bammer, Sigrid Bauschinger, Susan Cocalis, Ruth-Ellen Boetcher Joeres, Jeffrey Peck, Paul Roberge, Terence Thayer, Marc Weiner, and Hans-Jakob Werlen.

Acknowledgments

This book evolved over a number of years, and earlier versions of two chapters have appeared in print elsewhere. Chapter 1 was published under the same title as pp. 219–37 of *The Internalized Revolution: German Reactions to the French Revolution, 1789–1989*, ed. Ehrhard Bahr and Thomas P. Saine (New York: Garland, 1992), © Ehrhard Bahr and Thomas P. Saine. Chapter 5 appeared in *New German Critique* 46 (winter 1989): 104–28, in a special issue devoted to minorities in German culture; © New German Critique, Inc., 1989. Both were revised for this book and are published here with permission. Chapter 3 appeared in German translation by Isolde Müller as "Das Unbehagen in der Solidarität: Lateinamerikanische Revolutionen in DDR-Dramen," *"Neue Welt"/"Dritte Welt": Interkulturelle Beziehungen Deutschlands zu Lateinamerika und der Karibik*, ed. Sigrid Bauschinger and Susan L. Cocalis (Tübingen: Francke, 1994), pp. 201–21.

All foreign-language material in the following chapters is given in English translation. Page numbers refer to published translations when available, with emendations in square brackets. Bibliographic information on translations can be found following the original titles in the list of works cited. Material not previously translated has been expertly prepared for this book by Karen Storz.

EAST, WEST, AND OTHERS

Introduction

Reading the canonical works of white American authors in which black people appear, the black American author Toni Morrison came to realize "the obvious." The fabrication of the Africanist persona by writers such as Poe, Melville, Twain, or Hemingway "is reflexive; an extraordinary meditation on the self; a powerful exploration of the fears and desires that reside in the writerly conscious" (17). The chaos, madness, helplessness, and illicit sexuality associated with black figures in their works enabled the thematic development of freedom, authority, humanity, order, and individualism that were to define the essence of (white) American identity. "[T]he subject of the dream," Morrison reminds us, "is the dreamer" (17).

If founding fictions like *Moby Dick* or *To Have and Have Not* construct an image of the American as rugged male individualist through the mediating invention of a black Other, what constructions of postwar identity do leftist and socialist German writers enact in their texts about the Third World? Of course there are historical and cultural differences between the American and German literatures that I am juxtaposing here. But if white identity is characterized by sycophancy, as Morrison suggests (19, 57), how does this parasitical dialectic play itself out in works by Anna Seghers, Peter Weiss, Hans Magnus Enzensberger, Heiner Müller, or Günter Wallraff? If discourse about others is self-referential, how do the specific Third World constructions of these authors reflect reciprocal, imaginative constructions of Germany or Europe? To what First World German fears and desires do representations of the non-European world respond?

The work presented here explores the dialectic of self and other in an investigation of liberal, leftist, and socialist German authors who support the cause of political liberation in their texts about the Third World.[1] The chapters deal with literary works from the postwar period, reflecting different phases of interest in, and en-

I

counter with, the Third World: wartime exile in Latin America, the protest against Western imperialism in the late 1960s in West Germany, East Germany's traumatized reaction to American intervention in Chile in the 1970s, and the social and political tensions attributed to the presence of large immigrant groups in Germany today. It has not been my intention to offer a comprehensive survey of recent German writings dealing with the Third World.[2] Instead, I have chosen to present strategic readings of selected authors and texts, exploring problems that are relevant both theoretically and politically within a wider context. In the cases of Seghers, Weiss, Enzensberger, and Müller (chapters 1, 2, and 4), I work with major authors whose literary careers were deeply shaped by a concern with Third World politics. The East German authors Claus Hammel and Peter Hacks (chapter 3) and the documentary and ethnographic West German writers Max von der Grün, Günter Wallraff, and Paul Geiersbach (chapter 5), though not as significant individually, illustrate important bodies of writing about the Third World from each of the two postwar German states. Within a common framework of leftist progressive politics, a wide spectrum of aesthetic strategies and ideological positions is represented, ranging from an absolute, programmatic belief in universal reason and humanity (the continuing legacy of European Enlightenment ideals) to the paralysis of a fragmented, contradictory artistic self caught in the strictures of its cultural, political, national, and gender identity. At one end, there is the projection of a heroic persona, a champion of humanity, who combats ignorance and oppression and upholds the fundamental sameness and unity of peoples everywhere; at the other, we find the construction of a European self fraught with guilt and insecurity in its encounter with others perceived as categorically different.

Throughout the process of writing this book I have struggled with the possibility of constructing a discourse untainted by the ideologies of Western culture. In a way, there can be no pure encounter with the Third World in German literature—only a parade of constructions, impositions of privileged selves upon projected "others."[3] The analyses presented here, though written in as differentiated a way possible, have not escaped this judgment entirely (cf. Ihekweazu; Streese). Indeed, the seeming unavoidability of Eurocentric thought accounts for the often monotonous nature of analyses of Third World discourse, in which critics reveal and denounce the Eurocentric views embedded in literary texts (cf. Trinh, *When* 189–90; Todorov 178–79). I have learned, moreover, that the problem of hegemonic representation duplicates itself easily in the realm of scholarly interpretation. In discourses surrounding the Third World, there is nothing more Kantian than the notion of autonomy, nothing more Hegelian than the ideal of self-determination; even the goal of seeing the other as other appears fundamentally Western, articulated brilliantly in the dialectic of self-consciousness in Hegel's *Phenomenology of Spirit* (104–12). Although I try to justify my use of the term "Third World" as a label for a discursive rather than a material and political entity, all too often it carries unwanted connotations of inferiority, belatedness, and marginality. Taken to an extreme, self-interrogation of this kind can lead writers and critics to paralyzing modes of pessimism, claustrophobia, solipsism, or silence: unable to speak in a liberative way that is not eventually eroded by the legacy of our language and culture, we might feel forced, as our only remaining option, not to speak at all.

This methodological (and political) dilemma has dogged scholars of minority criticism for some time. Ülker Gökberk, for example, writing about scholarly approaches to minority literature, describes a "crisis of narration" in the current critical discourse, which knows "how *not* to talk about diversity" but not "how to *talk* about alternative forms of culture" (144–45). Robert Young asks the pointed question in *White Mythologies*, "But how to write a new history? When, as Césaire observed, the only history is white?" (119). How do we acknowledge the priority (the historical and institutional dominance) of our voices and yet speak persuasively for change? How do we promote the cultural interventions of others without reasserting our power and privilege in the process?[4] Deleuze and Guattari write of the collective, oppositional literature of minorities working within and against a dominating literary and cultural tradition (cf. Deleuze, "Manifest"). Minor literature, they assert, arises out of an "impasse" defined (quoting

Kafka) by "the impossibility of not writing, the impossibility of writing in German, the impossibility of writing otherwise" (16). Here we might ponder the similar predicament of a minority criticism defined in that necessary space between the impossibility of not writing, the impossibility of writing with categories of constraint, and the impossibility of writing otherwise.

Perhaps in response to this dilemma, authors and critics have claimed a critical edge by distancing themselves from the political "center."[5] But marginality (or Eurocentrality), whether we like it or not, is partially and permanently inscribed by the facts of one's class, race, gender, culture, language, and nation and is not entirely a matter of political choice.[6] (This, I show, is something the author Peter Weiss refused to accept.) Furthermore, these constituent facts of our identities interact in complex ways that defy any easy labeling of ourselves as minority or majority, marginal or central, critical or complicitous, liberative or repressive, "other" or "white." We are all, to varying degrees, both.[7] As Claus Hammel and Peter Hacks show us in their texts, the critique and demise of hegemonic institutions cannot be accomplished simply when white German writers and (mostly white) scholars abandon the center and gather, arms linked in solidarity, at the oppressed political margins. Thus, rather than seeking to promote the ways in which certain German authors and we as critics might belong productively to a critical minority, I believe it is equally important, if not more urgent, that we actively examine, in order to resist, our complicity in the systems of domination within which we live and work. It is not a matter of choosing between the center or the margin, or between oppression and resistance, so much as confronting their joint possession of us.[8]

I am vitally interested in the project shared by the authors discussed here, who write in support of the emancipation of Third World peoples from Western political, economic, and cultural domination and who criticize the imperialist attitudes and practices of Germany, Europe, and the United States. As a literary critic, however, I question the formulation, the motives, and the means of that project as it is depicted and circumscribed in literary texts. My task is not to embrace an ostensibly liberative mission on faith alone but to reveal and to interrogate the unspoken ideological tenets of its aesthetic expressions. Further, while Third World representations by European authors may never be free of Eurocentrism, the cultural biases of the European will appear in different ways, with varying degrees of self-reflection, and within evolving and competing agendas. The productive question is not whether what these authors say is Eurocentric—for that it inevitably will be in one way or another—but how and why they speak. That is, I would like ultimately to move beyond issues of content and expression to questions of strategy. More than recording the continued presence of Eurocentric, sexist, and racist images of the other, the invocation of a white Western European norm, the "residual imperialist propensities" (Said, *Culture* xx), in leftist postwar German literature, I hope to explore the ways in which these images are employed, the imaginative uses they serve, the cultural and political needs they meet. How do persisting Eurocentric stereotypes of the Third World (representing nature, sexuality, chaos, madness, revolution), especially in the work of well-intentioned, well-informed, politically progressive writers, construct a discourse, for example, on Europeanness?[9]

It will become clear that the authors addressed in this book write with a strong sense of themselves both as Europeans and as Germans. The experience of National Socialism in particular maintains its force as a foundational history, as major writers of the postwar era looked to the Third World for new possibilities of political revolution and emancipation. In the anticolonial and postcolonial decades following World War II, with West and East Germany allied with imperialist capitalist and totalitarian socialist superpowers, the Third World offered German intellectuals on both sides of the Wall an opportunity to reflect on the cultural and political heritage of fascism and on Germany's complicity in the continued rule of Europe and the West. Ultimately, my endeavor has been to trace ways in which certain German writers attempt in their literary work to envision a nonhegemonic mode of encounter with non-German others. Their task, as the following chapters demonstrate, has not been easy. The examples of Seghers, Weiss, and others illustrate in detail the complex (and often unconscious) nature of hegemonic thinking and the fundamentally conflicted, contradictory quality of a European identity that allows for the coexistence of progressive politics and dominating modes of representation. Nonetheless, we can strive to promote the conditions for new encounters, in our interactions with others and in our contributions to scholarship, in which the inherently hegemonic nature of our texts and our disciplinary discourse can be openly acknowledged and confronted. My hope is that this work will contribute productively to that project.

I

RACE, REVOLUTION, AND WRITING

Caribbean Texts by
Anna Seghers

The Jewish Communist writer Anna Seghers (1900–1983) left for Paris in 1933, after Hitler's electoral victory and the rising fascist climate had made it impossible for her to remain in Germany. When Hitler's army entered Paris in 1940, she began another journey that took her first to a small town in unoccupied France, then to the port of Marseilles, where she embarked, in the hold of a freighter, to Martinique. After further stopping points at Santo Domingo, Ellis Island, and Veracruz, she arrived, some ten months after she had fled Paris with her two children, at her final destination, Mexico City (Seghers, "Briefe"). A renowned author—Seghers had received the prestigious Kleist Prize for her first book, *Aufstand der Fischer von St. Barbara* (1928; *The Revolt of the Fishermen*)—a member of the German Communist Party since 1928, and a founding member of the Association of Proletarian-Revolutionary Writers (Bund Proletarisch-Revolutionärer Schriftsteller), Seghers remained in Mexican exile until her return to Soviet-occupied Germany in 1947. There, after the founding of the German Democratic Republic (GDR) in 1949, she became a literary icon of the socialist regime. Head of the GDR Writers Association (Schriftstellerverband) from 1952 to 1978 and dedicated to world peace, Anna Seghers was probably the most honored literary figure in the East German state.

Seghers's works, with few exceptions committed to furthering party goals, deal largely with developments in Germany—with the origins of fascism and forms of resistance against it, and the social and political history of the GDR—as the lived experience of

ordinary people. *Das siebte Kreuz* (*The Seventh Cross*), published
in 1942 in English and an instant bestseller in the United States,
presents a panoramic view of life in Nazi Germany in the story
of an escape from a concentration camp. *Transit* (1943; *Transit*),
another wartime work, is devoted to the nightmarish uncertainty
of refugees waiting to leave Nazi-occupied Europe. Seghers's trilogy from the postwar period, *Die Toten bleiben jung* (1949; *The
Dead Stay Young*), *Die Entscheidung* (1959; The decision), and *Das
Vertrauen* (1968; Trust), offers a broad history of class struggle in
Germany and the development of socialism in the GDR.

But alongside this sweeping socialist oeuvre of modern Germany, a number of shorter works reflect a persistent interest in
Latin American history and culture. Mexico, Seghers's exile home
from 1941 to 1947, provides the backdrop for "Crisanta" (1951),
"Die Heimkehr des verlorenen Volkes" (1965; "The Return of the
Lost Tribe"), and "Das wirkliche Blau" (1967; "Benito's Blue");
another work, *Überfahrt* (1971; Crossing), tells the love story of a
German Communist man and a Brazilian woman. But more impor-
tant are the works that treat the theme of revolt in the Caribbean.
Three texts, *Die Hochzeit von Haiti* (1949; The wedding of Haiti),
Wiedereinführung der Sklaverei in Guadeloupe (1949; The reintro-
duction of slavery in Guadeloupe), and *Das Licht auf dem Galgen*
(1961; The light on the gallows), the focus of this chapter, comprise
Seghers's "Caribbean trilogy" on the revolt against slavery led by
Toussaint L'Ouverture in Haiti in 1791. A second and shorter trilogy, published in Seghers's eightieth year, portrays instances of
women's resistance in Haiti from the time of the conquistadors to
the present day (*Drei Frauen aus Haiti*, 1980; Three women from
Haiti).

The reasons that have been offered for Seghers's preoccupation
with Latin America are numerous and complex, and probably
none is alone sufficient to explain her writings about the region.
Seghers spoke of the task of the writer, returning from exile, "to
present foreign peoples as the earth's contribution to humanity"
(qtd. in Gutzmann, "Lateinamerikanische" 156) — to heighten Germans' awareness and appreciation of other cultures and to instill
a sense for international class struggle in a society that had been

8

drilled in fascist ideology. There was an emotional and moral debt to be repaid to the continent that had saved her, her husband and children, and hundreds of other German Communists, a need to maintain bonds of solidarity and remembrance as they returned after the war to build a socialist Germany. Mexico and the Caribbean, recreated in nostalgia, served also as the locus for the author's projections of ongoing revolutionary process and an open socialist art intimately connected to its mass audience, as a subtle vehicle for critique against real existing socialism in the GDR (Gutzmann, "Lateinamerikanische" 168–70). In each of these projects, laudable as they were, Latin America was discursively "made" to serve Seghers's purposes.

Seghers was fascinated by the continent and culture of her exile home, but she did not write her Latin American texts on the basis of intimate knowledge. Before her arrival in Mexico, she had, in fact, repeatedly expressed her strong preference for a visa to the United States ("Briefe"). Her years in Mexico were spent within the insular community of fellow Communist exiles, who devoted their efforts to forging an international alliance of intellectuals against fascism in Europe. The Heinrich Heine Club, active from 1941 to 1946, which Seghers headed, pledged itself to the preservation of the humanistic European art defamed and deformed by the National Socialists. *Freies Deutschland* (Free Germany), the monthly magazine published in Mexico City from 1941 to 1946, to which Seghers was an essential contributor, provided the major print forum for German exiles throughout the world to analyze developments in Europe and to plan Germany's renewal after the defeat of Hitler.[1] The emotional, intellectual, and political focus, for Seghers as for nearly all of the hundred German Communist Party members in exile with her in Mexico City, was Europe, not Mexico.[2] With the exception of "Der Ausflug der toten Mädchen" (1946; "The Excursion of the Dead Young Girls"), in which the country provides the setting for recollections of the protagonist's school days in Mainz, Seghers looked to Mexico in her literary texts only after returning to Germany.

The same holds true, but in an even more drastic way, for Seghers's stopping points in the Caribbean. Two anxious months on Martinique were spent in a primitive refugee camp while Seghers and her family waited for further visas and money; another two weeks in Santo Domingo found her exhausted and depressed, unable to absorb much of her new surroundings. Only in Mexico and later in Europe did Seghers learn about Haiti and its history. Her research with mostly Western sources, supplemented by sketchy personal memories of Santo Domingo, became the basis for numerous literary texts on the Caribbean.[3] Drawn from an imagination guided by political interests, they provide rich material for uncovering the ideological structures governing Seghers's vision of a Third World culture.

In each story of Anna Seghers's Caribbean trilogy the main characters are Europeans. Michael Nathan in *Die Hochzeit von Haiti* is a Jewish jeweler from Paris and an enthusiastic supporter of the French Revolution. Called upon by the black Haitian leader Toussaint L'Ouverture to assist him in his correspondence with the French commissioners, Michael becomes inextricably involved in the Haitian slave revolt. When Toussaint dies years later in a French prison, Michael, nurtured by the same humanistic ideals, dies at the same time in London. In *Wiedereinführung der Sklaverei in Guadeloupe*, the Frenchman Beauvais and the French-educated mulatto commander Berenger work to restore economic prosperity and to secure the new social order on Guadeloupe by reorganizing agricultural labor among the freed slaves. When slavery is reestablished by Napoleon, both men resist: Berenger blows up his fort and with it himself and his family; Beauvais dies in a local battle against French troops, the single white body in a pile of black corpses. Finally, *Das Licht auf dem Galgen* records the story of three French revolutionaries, Galloudec, Sasportas, and Debuisson, who are sent by the Directory to free the slaves in Jamaica. When Napoleon comes to power, the former slaveowner Debuisson forsakes the revolutionary mission and betrays his two comrades. Sasportas is hung on the gallows and Galloudec dies in a prison hospital, both loyal to the end to the ideals of the French Revolution and to the slave revolt.[4]

Such narratives practically interpret themselves. If one focuses on the major figures and events of Seghers's texts as I have just done and as most interpreters of these texts do, one is led simply to add another voice to the scholarly chorus. Solidarity between black and white, individual commitment and loyalty to revolutionary ideals, the survival of the revolution even in defeat, the universality of the fight for freedom, and the moral and political significance of any individual's death in that fight—these principles are what Seghers's Caribbean texts forthrightly and eloquently demonstrate.[5]

What interests me more, however, is what is left out: not those heroic European or Europeanized revolutionaries who die noble deaths fighting for freedom in the Caribbean, but the shadowy figures in the background who play no recordable role; not the main figures who are vehicles for some more or less explicitly stated political lesson, but those minor ones who are politically unengaged, unaware, and inarticulate. Seghers's revolutionaries and their fates are documented in traditional histories (Seghers, *Aufsätze 1954–1979* 256–57). These others, blacks known only as "Ann," "Suzanne," "Douglas," or "Angela," are Seghers's invention and, along with descriptions of the marketplace and the tropical weather, help to create the Caribbean setting of her stories.[6]

Local color in Seghers's Caribbean texts is presented with vivid sensuality. There are torrential rainstorms, the tropical sun, the wild and exotic vegetation of islands whose products—coffee, sugar, rum, cacao, pepper, precious wood—indulge the European nose and palate. The white observer is overwhelmed by the sights, sounds, and smells—the fruits and fish, the colors, the medley of human voices, the screeches and grunts of the animals for sale—in the marketplace of Port Républicain (*Licht* 152–53).[7] The seductive sensual power of the Caribbean world emerges thematically in *Das Licht auf dem Galgen*, where Debuisson, drawn by the physical beauty of the land, loses sight of his mission of revolution (184).

But this pervasive sensuality is also specifically sexual, and it is here that it becomes most interesting. In the fictional tropical world, black skin seems intimately tied to sexuality. Further, as this world is one seen and experienced by principal figures who are without exception male, it is the black woman who unambiguously exudes the promise of sex.

Two examples come to mind, both striking for their gratuitousness in the narratives. The housekeeper, Angela, is "no longer very young but also not old enough to break off her chain of lovers, which she strung together as need, whim, or chance would have it" (*Hochzeit* 39). The mother of several children with different fathers, Angela has no political convictions of her own but rather adopts the opinions, however contradictory, held by her lovers. Lucy, another black housekeeper, here seen through the eyes of the black servant Douglas, is "plump and oldish, but with a cheeky look in her eyes and still wild about dancing." Douglas is expected by his master to marry Lucy, but, as he sees it, "[h]e hadn't the least desire to do this. What there was to enjoy in Lucy's skirts and kitchen had always been at his disposal" (*Licht* 231). Neither female figure plays a functional role in the revolutionary narratives. Rather, their stories exist as self-contained vignettes illustrating the presumably typical lives of slave women. Lucy and Angela are not unusually beautiful or unusually promiscuous; they are in fact not presented as unique in any way. The black woman is simply available for sex: much like the climate and the indigenous flora of the islands, she appeals by nature to the senses.

More importantly, the inherent Caribbean sensuality becomes a crucial element of plot in each of the three stories in the sexual relationship between a white male revolutionary and a black female slave. The point of intersection between master narrative and local color is richly articulated in the following, first encounter between Michael Nathan and the black slave Margot, who is to become his lover and the mother of his child, in *Die Hochzeit von Haiti*. The weather sets the stage for sex. It is night, in the hot, rainy season, during a heavy downpour. Michael returns home and is intercepted at the door:

> He wanted to enter. Just then a small black woman pressed through under his arm into the doorway. Her young, healthy scent was so strong from the dampness that even Michael

could not escape it, although he otherwise avoided temptations of this kind. This same small woman had brushed by
him three times already in the past weeks with a slight signal
of her hand that probably indicated readiness for love. . . .
Now, as he became aware of the small breasts in the wet
calico dress, it was clear to him that he had seen correctly.
The girl was exceptionally beautiful. The furious jealousy of
white women at the sight of her was understandable; understandable, the cruelty that they vented on their female slaves
through unthinkable punishments (more imaginative than
men) for small offenses. Michael cursed himself for a moment because he couldn't even look at these long legs and
hips, this little belly in the slippery dress, these breasts that fit
into two cupped hands, without thinking at the same time of
the general condition of humankind. She grasped the edge of
his sleeve between her thumb and forefinger with a shyness
that could not be shyness about love; that much he already
understood about this island. (28–29)

Shedding hat and coat, Michael follows Margot in the pour-
ing rain through a maze of empty streets, alleys, and courtyards.
Finally, just when he hopes that they have reached some kind of
culmination ("one was at a kind of goal" [31]), Margot disappears
and is replaced by a black man who steps out from the shadows.
When Michael is told that Toussaint L'Ouverture needs him to
draft a confidential letter of momentous import, Margot and the
sexual pleasure she promises are immediately, completely, forgotten: "[Michael] felt the pleasure of intellectual adventure, which
had a vast expanse and was more enticing than that young thing,
whom he had already stopped thinking about" (32).

The passage is remarkable in a number of respects. The young
Michael Nathan, who usually resists temptations of the flesh and
who is, we learned early in the story, "ugly" and "pensive" (11), suc-
cumbs instantly to the power of the small, almost childlike black
woman, following her with abandon into the night. The sight
and smell of Margot's body, enhanced by the rain that plasters her
dress to her skin, seem to exude sex, just as her every gesture offers

a signal of her "readiness for love." But Michael is unable to look at Margot's body without thinking of the treatment that blacks suffer from their white masters: the sex of the black woman is the vehicle for considerations of a very different sort; it demands the attention of the man only to draw it elsewhere. This is then reinforced at the end of the chase where, at "a kind of goal," Michael is rewarded not by the expected act of intercourse with Margot but by an abrupt meeting with a messenger of the slave revolt.

We learn later that it was Margot's task to deliver Michael to Toussaint's messenger. But Michael, who is already predisposed to the black cause and who finds the "intellectual adventure" of the revolt intrinsically more attractive than the adventures of the flesh, did not need to be—literally—seduced to follow. The sex as such, therefore, is gratuitous. Or, rather, in a fascinating and fundamental way, sex and revolution are so intimately connected that one functions as an extension of the other. Michael is drawn to the black woman as to the revolution and follows one as the other; it is telling that he is not attracted to just any woman, or to white women, but specifically and powerfully to Margot. Thus the seeming interchangeability, actually a strange identity, of the two goals: significantly, the meeting with the revolutionary leader Toussaint becomes Michael's eagerly anticipated "nocturnal rendezvous" (37).

In *Wiedereinführung der Sklaverei* there is the brief affair between the Frenchman Beauvais and the black Suzanne. In order to maintain his commitment to the abolition of slavery, Beauvais finds that he must renounce his promises to his fiancée, Claudine, in France. When Suzanne nurses him during a self-induced illness, one that is meant to prevent him from sailing to Europe and that thereby marks his irreversible choice to remain in Guadeloupe, Beauvais's emotional focus turns from the white fiancée to the black Suzanne:

All at once the memory left him. He strained to hold onto something blond and white; then it slipped into darkness as if into water, into a time that was no longer his. Suzanne remained, hard and shiny like the pit of the fruit that she peeled for him. The fruits of the land. Red, yellow, violet, and green, now and then with black pits. He loved the pink palms of her hands more than the blond and white vapor. (101–02)

Again we see the peculiar link between the revolution and the black woman, so that Beauvais's commitment to one is experienced simultaneously as passion for the other. Suzanne grows intense like the tropical colors of the island while Claudine fades into "something blond and white"; the two women represent opposing aesthetic sensibilities as well as conflicting political commitments. Thus when Beauvais decides to remain on the side of the freed slaves in Guadeloupe, the black woman enters his dreams and phantasies to replace the particular erotics of the white.[8]

Even in *Das Licht auf dem Galgen*, written some twelve years after the first two Caribbean stories, the relationship between Sasportas and the slave girl Ann follows the familiar pattern. At a crucial point after Napoleon's takeover in France, an event that places the mission on Jamaica in serious jeopardy, Sasportas must decide either to withdraw from the band of blacks who are organizing revolt or to keep his appointed secret meeting with his black liaison. Predictably, it is at this juncture that the black slave Ann is introduced.

We have been told that women find Sasportas attractive (139–40) but also that he is generally unresponsive: "[Sasportas] was not interested in girls" (155; cf. 143). Suddenly it seems certain that he and Ann will sleep together. We hurriedly learn her name, her physical qualities, her life story (187–88); Ann and Sasportas have met before, but only now do we hear of the earlier encounter and their immediate, mutual attraction (191–92). The act of lovemaking occurs without suspense or hesitation: Sasportas lifts up the mosquito net surrounding his bed; Ann climbs in (192). What is a matter of suspense, however, namely Sasportas's decision to suspend the mission or to continue with the slave revolt, is silently resolved in the hours spent with Ann. We learn nothing of what goes through Sasportas's mind, a narrative silence emphasized by the dash in the text that breaks off the account of the night in bed. Or does the sexual act itself connote Sasportas's answer to the revolution?

Once again the sexual bond occurs simultaneously with the bond to the revolution. Later Sasportas will leave Ann's bed and climb out the window to keep his meeting with the black slaves, enlisting Ann's help in covering up his absence (193). The woman too becomes committed to the revolution as she commits herself to the man: Ann, previously fearful of being punished by her masters (192), is now suddenly unafraid as she aids Sasportas's escape. Indeed, this is only the first of many actions she will perform for the sake of the slave revolt, at increasingly greater personal risk and with such increasing boldness that she becomes in the end "completely fearless" (241). The change in her character and actions is abrupt and irreversible and linked undeniably to her sexual encounter with the white revolutionary;[9] loyalty to the slave revolt is loyalty to her lover, just as for Sasportas the commitment to the black woman represents simultaneously a commitment to continued revolution.

What I have presented lies beneath the main action of the texts, with their undebatably clear political and ideological intentions. The relationships between white men and black women, in contrast to the primary stories of revolution, appear sketchy, unfinished, confusing, and disturbing. The three instances of white-black relationships share the curious consistency that the white men, the revolutionaries, are dispassionate and sexually uninterested. (One might be tempted in this regard to speculate on the hidden meaning of Michael Nathan's lower lip, which hangs characteristically "limp" from his mouth [*Hochzeit* 11].)[10] It is always the black woman who is attracted to the white man, who is at first oblivious to her signals of interest. What attracts the black women, and why are the men so annoyingly passive?

In all three texts the women gain their identity, which is always their place in the revolution, through their men. Margot brings Michael to Toussaint, Suzanne nurses Beauvais back to health, Ann helps Sasportas to escape and becomes a valued messenger. Two of the women are named only when the sexual relationship with the white man is about to be established: before that time Margot is only "a small black woman" (*Hochzeit* 28), while Ann is not even present. The very existence of the women in the narratives is determined by the need for their services in the revolution. Accordingly, when separated from the men, the women fade away as narrative figures: Margot dies, and Suzanne and Ann are sold—that is all we are told; apparently that is all we need to know. A further similarity is their explicitly childlike character. Margot's smallness and youth are continually emphasized; Suzanne is perceived as "something that suffered and was threatened and that needed more love than a human being was capable of giving" (*Wiedereinführung* 102). Ann, "a very young, small, almost frail Negress," "a child," is "somewhat retarded in physical and mental development" (*Licht* 187, 190). All await a process of physical, intellectual, and political maturation to be initiated by the white male and his revolution.[11]

With the white men the situation is different. Already revolutionaries, they are drawn to the black women (and explicitly not to the white) as extensions of their political commitment. Thus when separated from their lovers the men do not become lost to the revolution. For them, in fact, the women are forgettable, and indeed this happens in just so many words: twice Michael Nathan is called to Toussaint, and both times he forgets Margot completely.[12] Beauvais forgets his white fiancée, so that he cannot recall her even in his dreams. Seghers's texts show that the women are seduced into embracing the politics of their lovers, while the men are committed to their politics through (one supposes) principles. Essentially asexual, the men can and do do without the women: the women lack political identity, while the white men are presumably already whole.

The specific "whiteness" of this view of things is emphasized in *Wiedereinführung der Sklaverei* through the contrasting story of Paul Rohan, an exemplary black revolutionary who, like the white Beauvais and the mulatto Berenger, remains loyal to his ideals to the very end. Yet the men are not three of a kind. Beauvais and Berenger become increasingly distanced from their white bride and mulatto wife as they come to terms with their unqualified commitment to the principles of the revolution. As Beauvais puts it, in the choice between happiness with a woman and the problems of the slave population of a Caribbean island, the woman dissipates like vapor (92). For the black Paul Rohan, in contrast, there is no choice between the principle of freedom and the woman he loves.

In his last years of slavery Rohan was not able to marry his lover, who had been sold to another farm. Subsequently, freedom for him does not entail forgetting one's wife or bride in times of revolutionary crisis but exactly the opposite—freedom means being with the woman one loves: "[f]reedom for generations to come—that had fused together for him with the girl whom the administrator of the Rohan estate had sold to the Noailles estate" (77). While the white Beauvais must learn to sacrifice his "earthly happiness" (92), the black Rohan, in becoming part of the revolution, learns to recognize the importance of his personal desires: "[i]t had taken him a long time to set himself apart as one who had within the common sorrow a particular sorrow, and a separate happiness . . . and a particular, separate love that concerned him alone" (81). For the whites revolution entails self-sacrifice; for the blacks it requires self-assertion. This makes a difference for their women as well: Claire, unlike the lovers of the white men who tend to disappear from view, dies fighting alongside her husband, Rohan, even more vicious in battle than he (121).

What emerges in these various stories is a sense of difference between a white and a black dynamic of revolution. The difference is reinforced by curious statements in the texts regarding a characteristically black sense of time. When Michael Nathan is in Toussaint's camp we read: "[h]e had been up here for days now already, maybe even weeks. It had become the time of the Negroes, the boundless, weightless time of drifting sand" (*Hochzeit* 55).[13] A black experience of time as a kind of timelessness, such that one does not experience its duration measured by days, weeks, or months, is articulated also in *Das Licht auf dem Galgen*: Sasportas, once he has committed himself without reservation to the black revolt, "had almost as little understanding for the meaning of time, its measure, its passing, as did his beloved" (206). And toward the end of the story he loses all sense of time whatsoever: "[o]ne could see that Jean didn't know how much time had passed in the meantime. One could see that he had ceaselessly waited, listened, hoped for something. . . . [W]as it days, was it weeks ago?" (220).[14]

Limitless and undefined, the black world exists in silent contrast to the primary world of the whites with its historical clarity and chronology.[15] Not surprisingly, images of darkness and light work to strengthen the difference. Beauvais's memory of his white bride, once he decides to join his fate to that of the blacks on Guadeloupe, disappears not only into black time, "a time that was no longer his," but into "darkness" as well (*Wiedereinführung* 101). There is also the "light on the gallows" that serves as a beacon for future (European) revolutionaries and that symbolized for Seghers enlightenment, historical memory, and reason.[16] But as the concepts of light and darkness suggest, black and white worlds, while contrasted, do not stand in absolute opposition. Rather, their relationship appears to be one of an ideologically laden continuum, a process by which blacks move on several levels from "blackness" to "whiteness"—from slave labor to European culture, from emotions to thoughts, and from illiteracy to literacy.

Crucial here is the depiction of the black leader Toussaint L'Ouverture, whom Seghers considered one of the most important historical figures in the time of the French Revolution.[17] In *Die Hochzeit von Haiti* Toussaint's rise from slavery to become the leader of the black revolution and the military governor of the island is presented rather shamelessly in terms of his becoming "white." Toussaint, having learned to read (which means reading the works of white men), acquires an unqualified admiration for European culture: "[t]he white culture seemed to him a radiant, immense castle. A reflection of it had fallen upon his poor boyhood years, making life worthwhile for him. It should not be despised because it had been thought up by the whites. In a better life all people would be allowed to take part in it. The same reflection would be allowed to fall upon all lives" (34). Emancipation in Toussaint's view is thus the process of making white culture universal—not of preserving difference in equality but of instituting sameness.[18] Skin color therefore does not matter (34); since Christ suffered for all men, the only real difference at stake, in Toussaint's view, is the one between good and bad Christians, between a sufficient or insufficient, complete or incomplete participation in the cultural value of whiteness (35).

In a number of ways Toussaint himself provides the role model. He has learned from white books. His governor's palace is adorned with lamp shades, carpets, silk wall fabrics, and uniformed servants in the best French tradition (47). He earns the servant Angela's respect through his "courtly" demeanor toward her and his connoisseur's eye in choosing among the various delicacies she offers him (48). And he has developed a genuine aesthetic appreciation for the fine jewelry of the European aristocracy (49). The black slave Toussaint, in short, has grown to become a master of white culture.[19]

Much the same holds true for Paul Rohan, who, like Toussaint, learns to read from a sympathetic clergyman: "[h]e had finally overcome the most difficult obstacle in learning: to pull together into words the single letters that he long since knew" (*Wiedereinführung* 90). Learning to read resembles learning to think, in that exceptional blacks who previously recognized only isolated fragments of their world, "single letters," slowly gain the ability to synthesize them into meaningful "words." Rohan is singled out in the narrative as a black who, through his relationship with the whites, has acquired revolutionary insight; "the favorite of one of these whites," Rohan has learned to think politically, that is, like a white revolutionary, often falling into disagreement with other blacks who are presented as less advanced in their understanding of events in Guadeloupe (*Wiedereinführung* 96–97).[20]

In contrast, "black" blacks cannot read or even think clearly, as Debuisson's loyal servant Douglas demonstrates when he slowly comes to the realization that his master is a revolutionary on the side of the slave revolt:

> [Douglas] did not understand much of the talk. He understood nothing of being free and becoming free. But one thought was fermenting in him, he didn't even know where it came from: it swelled and swelled and tormented him, almost made his head burst. . . . Douglas sensed suddenly that the foreign young gentleman, Master Debson's friend, was

suspicious, and if he was, then so was Master Debson. Douglas sensed this. He didn't astutely put together the details; it was all mixed together in this feeling he had. (*Licht* 232)

A page earlier we are told that Douglas usually forgets what he does not see or hear (231). Now he strains to piece together the fragments he remembers, isolated details of his interaction with Debuisson and Sasportas, in order to arrive at the difficult thought fermenting inside him. In what reads like a caricature, we see the inveterate slave trying to think! The process even gains tragic overtones, as the thought that Douglas formulates after so much effort leads him to betray the very men who are trying to liberate him.

The final consequence of such intellectual underdevelopment is graphically illustrated by the demise of an illiterate black in *Wiedereinführung der Sklaverei*. Learning of the French order to reinstate slavery, Jean Rohan returns to the jungle, a decision that results from his lack of political understanding: "[Jean Rohan] didn't have . . . the bold and wild mind that seldom shrinks back (but when it does, then in despair) when the realization of its unlimited imagination is made impossible in the limited world" (108). In the jungle Rohan in fact ceases to think at all—here the (European) narrator must step in to tell us what his thoughts would have been "had he still had thoughts at all in the hot, whistling darkness" (110; cf. 111). Hunted down by a pack of dogs, he is finally shot from his hiding place in the branches of a tree; referred to in the text as the "dead man," then as the "prey" of the dogs, the dead Rohan, who has long since been deprived of his reason, is now stripped rhetorically of his humanity. The dogs must be torn away from the body, and the narrative concludes with images of the corpse slowly being devoured by jungle animals and insects: "[i]n their wake a migration of insects fell upon the remaining flesh; then came small creatures with teeth and beaks. Finally a large, bushy beast of prey came with its young one, calmly and heavily, frightening off the others, the mother hungry, the young one hungry" (111).

We are made to see that it is only the rare, "white" individual who possesses the reasoning power and the strength to recognize what is actually attainable at a given historical moment. Shortly before his arrest and deportation Toussaint's deep sadness is described, "such waves of melancholy, as if he had just measured once and for all the gap between the boundary of everything attainable on earth and the boundlessness of thought" (*Hochzeit* 54). Michael Nathan expresses a more pessimistic (and, according to the narrative, realistic) view of the situation than Toussaint: "Michael understood that these people could not see the situation in the same light as he did. He also understood that the gap between what is attainable on earth and the boundlessness of thought, which Toussaint had just brooded over, was a few eons shorter for these people than for himself" (*Hochzeit* 54). For Michael Nathan, the only real white in these excerpts, the distance between what one is capable of imagining in thought and what one is capable of achieving in reality is greatest—"eons" greater than for the blacks. Toussaint, the "whitest" of the blacks, understands the tragedy of this distance.[21] The literate Paul Rohan has some sense of it as well, as do, to a lesser extent, Toussaint's followers. But the illiterate and black Jean Rohan, who lacks any understanding of the challenge of ideals, is made to die a horrifying death in which he is returned—fittingly—to animal flesh in the world of nature.

The embellishment of the revolutionary narrative with local color in Seghers's Caribbean stories reveals the encounter of two worlds, black and white, characterized by familiar Eurocentric dichotomies. The white world represents the epitome of civilization, reason, and thought; the black world, in contrast, is a world of brutal nature, confused emotions, immediate sensations that do not add up. Whites are sexless men of ideals and principles; blacks are represented by oversexed women or by men with befuddled minds, all of whom act on emotion and instinct. The white world is an ordered history of struggle and progress; the timeless black world is one of endless waiting and senseless death.

The most fascinating and disturbing moments in Seghers's narratives occur when these worlds meet. This happens in two typical ways. The white revolutionary becomes sexually involved with a black slave woman; alternatively, blacks learn to read and to think, which means they read the works of white culture and come to think like white men. The Eurocentric and sexist attitudes underlying this conceptual framework are obvious: the blacks enter the world of the whites, which is presented as politically advanced and culturally superior; further, sex is the means of entry for the black women while reading and writing are reserved for the men.[22] It is only a small consolation that Seghers intends to demonstrate not any inferiority of the blacks in the Caribbean but their committed struggle for emancipation: the black slaves, as Seghers would have it, overcome the color barrier both in their erotic-emotional and in their intellectual lives, to fight for the freedom that belongs to men and women everywhere.[23] The unfortunate paradox of Seghers's writing is that it reasserts the superiority of the white world and the inferiority of the black, despite its own intentions.

Supreme as their ideals may be, a striking sense of emptiness and impotence marks the white revolutionaries. Except for Margot's daughter, who dies of yellow fever, the men in question father no children with their black lovers, leaving nothing, no one, behind.[24] Failure characterizes also their activities as revolutionaries: Michael Nathan dies in London as Toussaint dies in his French prison in the Alps; Beauvais and Berenger both die in a symbolic attempt to resist the counterrevolutionary Napoleonic army; Sasportas is hanged on the gallows, his efforts to aid the slave revolt betrayed by Debuisson. The black Haitian republic is left in ashes, slavery is reestablished on Guadeloupe, and the revolt on Jamaica never occurs. Yet if the white revolutionaries leave no legacy in the way of natural heirs or political achievements, they are remembered—this is Seghers's point, and her example—through the stories, oral and written, of those who come after. For these men, (black) sex is replaced by (white) writing as a means of binding oneself and others to the revolution.

In the end writing emerges for the whites in the Caribbean narratives as the revolutionary act *par excellence*. It is the means by which the revolution first triumphs in *Die Hochzeit von Haiti*: Michael Nathan, as Toussaint's secretary, writes a letter that joins

Toussaint's slave army to the commissioners sent by the revolutionary French government, an alliance that leads eventually to the abolition of slavery. In *Das Licht auf dem Galgen* Sasportas, Debuisson, and Galloudec coordinate their efforts to organize the slave revolt by means of written messages that Douglas delivers (but is unable to read). On a more important level, writing occurs in the third story of the cycle in the letter that Galloudec sends to Antoine, the French official who had dispatched the initial order to organize the Jamaican slaves. The letter, which is finally delivered to Antoine in hiding from Napoleon, provides the narrative frame of the story (which is all about passing messages) and thematizes directly the significance of writing. Antoine reflects:

> A letter is worth a lot. Even if it was intended for an office that no longer exists, for a person who no longer holds an office. Such a letter is a true testimonial. The young person [Sasportas] can be easily forgotten. As I had almost forgotten him. How many have already been forgotten! Monuments are built for lesser men. Not for him. Only this bit of paper remains. (*Licht* 131)[25]

In a strange way, the act of writing assures that one is remembered, regardless of which former official of which abandoned office ultimately reads the document. The "bit of paper" suffices, though its readership may be unknown or uncertain.[26] The act of writing is important in itself as an act of personal and revolutionary affirmation. Thus even with just one reader, Sasportas's death on the gallows is inscribed in memory as an inspiration to revolutionaries everywhere: "[t]hus Jean Sasportas had a legacy of sorts, faint and cautious, after so many years. Your memory and mine—it is no salute, but it honors him, it sustains him, it preserves him" (*Licht* 245). In the end, revolutionary passion is incited by seduction through the eyes and ears of an audience; the white world produces no children of the revolution but only its own readers. Through writing, and perhaps only through writing, the failure of the revolution is subsumed and overcome, and the deaths of the revolutionaries gain meaning again. Europe's revolutionaries are saved through words on a page; revolution survives, as text.

Historically the figure of Toussaint L'Ouverture and the events of the Haitian revolt marked a major turning point in European colonialism. For the first time, slaves organized not to correct particular injustices within the system of slavery but to abolish the system of slavery itself (Stavrianos 369–70). Toussaint's overthrow of slavery on Haiti in 1791, his victory over Napoleon's army in its attempt to recover the colony, and the declaration of an independent black state in 1804 represented the first successful acts of resistance by a Third World colony against a European nation. With these events came a crisis in the literary discourse of colonialism, as the violent revolt of the Haitian slaves destroyed forever Europe's fantasy of colonies that were willing partners in their subjugation. Contemporary German writers such as August von Kotzebue and Heinrich von Kleist, for example, struggled to replace or recast the dominant narrative of colonialism that had taken the form of a love story between the European male conqueror and the native, virgin woman-land (Zantop; Hulme).

Seghers's Caribbean texts attest, however, to the continuing force of the traditional colonial narrative. Their story of sexual seduction, simultaneously a story of political conquest, takes place not between a white male colonialist and the native woman but between the black female slave and her white male liberator. Yet this is a difference that maintains much of the original inequality of power: the male-gendered cultural and intellectual values of Europe are still presented as normative and universal; the beloved native woman (land) only exchanges one white "savior" for another. More interesting is the difference between the male protagonists: whereas the typical colonialist's narrative ended with procreation and production on fertile colonial soil, the revolutionary's story that Seghers writes is one of biological and political impotence. Or, rather, the white men's power over the blacks exists and is exercised within different realms altogether: the colonialist's, within the reigning political sphere; the modern revolutionary's, within an ideal, ideological, and future realm guaranteed by his readers. By moving from the real-political to the symbolic, Seghers attempts to refashion the inherited model of colonialist seduction and conquest into a revolutionary one of projected political emancipation. But because political, moral, and intellectual authority is still anchored in European traditions, her texts remain ultimately as oppressive as they are potentially liberative.

The normative, Eurocentric core of Seghers's works stems not simply from her commitment to orthodox Communism but, more deeply, from an intellectual debt to the European Enlightenment. It is not coincidental that Seghers's interest in the Caribbean focused on the thirteen-year period of the Haitian revolt (1791–1804) that coincided with the period of the French Revolution and the Napoleonic era; not coincidental but symptomatic that she stressed the ideals of the French Revolution and the Enlightenment as Toussaint's inspiration. Rather, as Gutzmann argues, it was exactly because of Seghers's orientation toward the ideals of the Enlightenment that she was unable to appreciate the unique qualities of a foreign culture; the humanitarian ideals of freedom, equality, and fraternity inscribed in Seghers's texts served to level rather than to foreground differences of culture and race ("Eurozentristisches" 190). According to Gates, a kind of systemic racism lies embedded in the very discourse of reason that defined the Enlightenment: once reason was privileged above all other human characteristics, he argues, blacks were seen as "reasonable" and thus human ("men") only if they mastered "the arts and sciences," that is, became literate. "So, while the Enlightenment is characterized by its foundation on man's ability to reason, it simultaneously used the absence and presence of reason to delimit and circumscribe the very humanity of the cultures and people of color which Europeans had been 'discovering' since the Renaissance" ("Editor's" 8).[27] As we see in Seghers's Caribbean texts, blacks earn distinction and respect and emerge as viable actors in revolutionary history only when they become "white"—when they learn to read, to write, and to think as "we" do. The Third World, in this perspective, gains recognition only as a poor and undeveloped form of Europe.

2

"WORLD THEATER" VS.
"EUROPEAN PERIPHERY"

Third World Paradigms in Peter Weiss
and Hans Magnus Enzensberger

The Third World became a political issue in West Germany in the protest climate of the late 1960s. Where the decade of the 1950s had seen the economic and political rebuilding of the German state under the leadership of Chancellor Konrad Adenauer, the generation of citizens who came of age in the 1960s began to question the foundational values of Adenauer's policies and of the society they had created. Rigid anti-Communism, an unwavering alliance with the West, particularly with the United States, and an overriding commitment to the growth of a free market economy had forged a prosperous West German society anchored firmly in capitalist politics and consumerist culture.[1]

In the midsixties unease began to mount. Recession slowed the expanding postwar economy, and support for Adenauer's Christian Democratic Union (Christlich-Demokratische Union, CDU), which had enjoyed an absolute majority since 1957, weakened. In 1966 the Grand Coalition was formed between the CDU and Willy Brandt's Social Democratic Party (Sozialdemokratische Partei Deutschlands, SPD), moving the SPD decisively into reformist politics and, in the eyes of many, eliminating the possibility of effective opposition from within the parliamentary system.

The first radical critics of West Germany's government and society at this time were West Berlin's university students. Their protest was directed first against the authoritarian university structures inherited from the Weimar Republic and the Third Reich but moved quickly to other targets: the unexamined heritage of National Socialism in the postwar era, particularly the promotion of former Nazis into high government positions, an earmark of the Adenauer regime; West Germany's complicity with the military involvement of the United States in Vietnam, which had escalated in 1965 with continuous air strikes and the massive mobilization of ground troops; the impending passage of Emergency Laws that would allow the suspension of constitutional principles in times of national crisis, seen by many as totalitarian abuse; and the machinations of the Springer publishing empire, which disseminated anti-Communist propaganda under the guise of news. The protest movement soon organized as the Extraparliamentary Opposition (Außerparlamentarische Opposition), which programmatically rejected the established system of electoral politics. The police murder of Benno Ohnesorg, a relatively unpolitical student, at a demonstration against the visit to Berlin by the shah of Iran in June 1967 and the attempted assassination in April 1968 of the student leader Rudi Dutschke led to the rapid radicalization of students in every university town in Germany.

Most of West Germany's leading writers had been longtime supporters of the SPD.[2] Group 47, the legendary association of nonconformist authors and critics, among them most of the great literary talents of postwar Germany, had always defined itself in opposition to Adenauer and the CDU. But with the formation of the coalition between the Christian and Socialist parties in 1966, dormant political differences within the group raged to the fore. While writers like Günter Grass and Siegfried Lenz remained staunch supporters of the SPD, others took positions farther to the left. Scarred by the acrimonious political debates that ensued among its members, Group 47 disbanded in 1967.

Among Germany's prominent authors in the late 1960s, Peter Weiss (1916–1982) and Hans Magnus Enzensberger (b. 1929) were the most radical. Despite their differences, both aligned themselves wholeheartedly with the Extraparliamentary Opposition and with the revolutionary student movement; no other writers campaigned so fiercely against the passage of the Emergency Laws or against the Vietnam War; no others wrote so extensively about anticolonialist and antiimperialist struggles in the Third World (cf. Bohrer, "Revolution" 99). The revolutionary atmosphere of the late sixties would prove to be shortlived. The radical students never succeeded in forming a stable alliance with Germany's working class and thus remained isolated in their protest. After the leftist-liberal coalition of the SPD and the Free Democrats in 1969, many students could again align themselves with established parties. Those who remained in the movement were paralyzed by sectarianism, while a few, Ulrike Meinhof among them, turned to terrorism. By the mid-1970s, the student revolt had become a thing of the past. But at no other time were West Germany's authors more aggressively engaged in political battles than in the heyday of the movement. Whereas Weiss maintained his commitment to revolutionary politics until his death in 1982, Enzensberger would never again be as active in West German political life as he was in the late sixties.

In these protest years Peter Weiss enjoyed professional success and critical acclamation for the first time in his career. His father, a Hungarian-born Jewish textile manufacturer who had converted to Christianity, had emigrated with his family from Berlin to London in 1935, then, in pursuit of better business opportunities, to Prague in 1936.[3] With the occupation of Sudetenland in 1938, the family moved again, to its final home in Sweden. Weiss, introverted and emotionally withdrawn from his bourgeois parents, studied painting and worked with bitter reluctance in his father's factories. His first attempts at a career in the visual arts met with little financial success. After some early publications in Swedish, Weiss placed his first German book, a surrealist novel, with the prestigious Suhrkamp publishing house in West Germany and soon afterward devoted himself completely to his writing. With the premiere of his most famous drama, *Marat/Sade*, in 1964, the Swedish citizen Peter Weiss, nearly fifty years old, seemed to emerge from nowhere to attain international stardom. His next play, *Die Ermittlung* (1965; *The Investigation*), a documentary drama on the trial of Auschwitz guards and officers, premiered in Berlin under the direction of Erwin Piscator and was produced simultaneously in fifteen other theaters in East and West Germany. By this time firmly committed to Marxism, Weiss joined the Swedish Communist Party in 1968. In the late 1960s, Weiss was indisputably West Germany's most prominent playwright.

Born to a bourgeois family in Bavaria in 1929, Hans Magnus Enzensberger spent his childhood in the city of Nuremberg. Fifteen years old near the end of the war, he was drafted briefly into Hitler's Volkssturm. In 1955, at the age of twenty-six, he earned a doctorate degree with a dissertation on the German Romantic poet Clemens Brentano. His first publications, anthologies of poems and essays sharply critical of West German capitalist culture and the political establishment, earned him a reputation as Germany's "angry young man." By 1956 he had won his first literary prize; in 1963 he received the Büchner Prize, the country's most prestigious literary award; and in 1964 Theodor Adorno was hailing Enzensberger as the equal of two of Germany's greatest writers of the eighteenth and nineteenth centuries, Gotthold Ephraim Lessing and Friedrich Schlegel (Grimm, "Introduction" 12–13).

Although never loyal to the politics of any party, Enzensberger wrote and edited a number of works that demonstrate his interest in revolutionary Marxism. The essay "Las Casas oder Ein Rückblick in die Zukunft" (1966; "Las Casas, or A Look Back into the Future") accompanies Enzensberger's German edition of the report written by the sixteenth-century Spanish priest Bartolomé de Las Casas on the decimation of the West Indies by the conquistadors. *Freisprüche: Revolutionäre vor Gericht* (1970; Acquittals: Revolutionaries on trial) brings together courtroom speeches by revolutionaries from the last two centuries. The three-volume *Klassenbuch* (1972; Class book) collects documents on class struggle in Germany from the mid–eighteenth century to the present (Enzensberger et al.). The novel *Der kurze Sommer der Anarchie* (1972; The short summer of anarchy) is dedicated to the life of the Spanish revolutionary Buenaventura Durruti; there is also the voluminous edition of *Gespräche mit Marx und Engels* (1973; Conversations with Marx and Engels). In addition, *Kursbuch* (Train schedule), the Berlin journal that Enzensberger founded in 1965 and edited until the midseventies, provided the major forum for leftist discussions of the Third World and oppositional politics in West Germany, reaching a circulation of 50,000 by 1968.[4] A prolific poet, playwright, novelist, essayist, translator, and editor, Enzensberger was, already in the late 1960s, unmatched among West German writers in his political acumen, his literary versatility, and his linguistic virtuosity.

As with Seghers, the literary treatment of Third World material by these authors was based more on political conviction than on personal experience. Weiss, who hated to travel, visited Cuba for a month in 1967 and North Vietnam for a month in 1968, after the completion of his plays on the Third World. While remaining supportive of revolutionary movements in other countries, he lived and worked throughout his adult life in neutral Sweden (Ellis 55). Enzensberger, an inveterate traveler, lived for prolonged periods in Norway, Italy, the Soviet Union, and the United States, as well as in West Berlin and Munich. In 1968, in a famous incident, he resigned a fellowship at the Center for Advanced Studies at Wesleyan University to spend the next year in Cuba, but there is little to suggest that he did more there than live the life of a privileged intellectual.

As Lennox has noted, the constructions of the Third World on the part of sixties leftists in Germany "had much more to do with [their] own political needs than with the realities of particular non-Western countries" (185; cf. Spivak). The two decades since the end of World War II had seen the dismantling of European empires, the growth of nationalist movements throughout the world, and, perhaps most importantly, the emergence of a generation of non-Western revolutionary intellectuals knowledgeable about Europe's traditions and critical of its institutions (Stavrianos 624–25). Representative of these new revolutionaries was Frantz Fanon, a black psychiatrist from Martinique, who became a leading spokesman for the Algerian revolution and one of the most influential theorists of the Third World. Notably, Enzensberger first brought Fanon to a German audience: the special Third World issue of *Kursbuch* from August 1965 contained the opening chapter of Fanon's *Les Damnés de la terre* (1961; *The Wretched of the Earth*) on the necessity of revolutionary violence on the part of colonized peoples ("Von der Gewalt"). Unlike Seghers's vision of a non-European world waiting for European enlightenment

31

and leadership, the anticolonial and antiimperialist Third World struggles of the 1960s were defiantly waged without a European vanguard. What revolutionary role could Weiss and Enzensberger imagine for themselves in such campaigns, and what political ideals and ideological structures governed their divergent imaginative constructions of the Third World?

The most revealing remarks concerning the political and personal tension between Peter Weiss and Hans Magnus Enzensberger were offered by Weiss in his notebooks from 1978. The forceful rhetoric of his words betrays deep animosity even as they describe an attempt to mend bridges more than a decade after the authors' heated exchange in the pages of *Kursbuch* in the mid-1960s. Not wanting to remain "angry or antagonistic," Weiss claims to be ready to forgive the "malicious, venomous things" that Enzensberger had once said of him. He continues, "[P]erhaps he never saw his attacks as perfidious. . . . I just always wanted to know: where do you stand. But that was precisely what he despised; he detested these commitments, these definitions of his position, which I desired" ("Aus den *Notizbüchern*" 102).[5]

When Enzensberger—the only colleague to express concern—later calls long-distance to inquire about Weiss's ill health, Weiss is moved to meditate further on the differences that separate them: *"[r]egarding Enzensberger.* . . . [H]e thinks I take everything too seriously, [I] take myself too seriously, I'm an idealist, I make prognoses, I 'believe' in something. The fact that I believe at all in concepts such as 'class,' 'class struggle,' etc., that I don't doubt enough, that I'm not cynical enough, that revolutionary history is not yet over for me—this is naturally a great mistake" ("Aus den *Notizbüchern*" 103). Finally Weiss launches a tirade against himself in the imagined voice of his rival: "[y]ou can't parody, always want to put yourself in the foreground, that's it, you're a kind of prophet, yes, there is something unctuous about you, that's what I can't stand about you, if you were only more composed, more easygoing, but these emphatic tones, you believe you know everything, can speak about everything, above all about politics—I believe in nothing" ("Aus den *Notizbüchern*" 103–04).

Crucial for Weiss is the act of stating his commitments, while Enzensberger never renounces his sovereign irony. Weiss believes in class conflict and revolution; his counterpart stands for critical doubt and parody. Negative alter egos bound inextricably to one another (as is evident in the passion of Weiss's entries and in Enzensberger's unique concern for Weiss's health), Weiss and Enzensberger in their work enact opposing models of aesthetic and political activism. Critics have viewed their conflict as representative of the 1960s in West Germany and as an important contemporary chapter in Marxist aesthetics (Bathrick 135–36; Gugelberger, "Them" 93). In what follows I argue that the debate and the differences that raged between them are also specifically paradigmatic for their Third World discourse.

The discussion of the Third World in Peter Weiss begins and ends with Dante. In 1964, having completed *Marat/Sade* and started work on what would become *Die Ermittlung*, Weiss began to attend the Auschwitz trials in Frankfurt. The experience precipitated a personal and poetological crisis that the author recorded in two short works dealing with Dante's *Divine Comedy*: "Vorübung zum dreiteiligen Drama divina commedia" (1965; Preliminary exercise for the three-part drama divina commedia) and "Gespräch über Dante" (1965; Conversation about Dante).[6]

The preoccupation with Dante is intimately tied both to Weiss's struggle to come to terms with Auschwitz as material for literary treatment and to specific details of Weiss's biography. The poetic crisis Weiss faced, which in his view Dante had resolved six centuries earlier, was the rational analysis and artistic representation of what seemed to be sheer madness and monstrosity. "Was this material for a play?" the authorial voice asks ("Vorübung" 128): "I lost the capacity of speech even as I struggled to capture the impressions of this [Auschwitz] tribunal and to imagine the events that formed the basis of this hearing. My thoughts failed me when I contemplated the scope of what was being touched upon here"

("Vorübung" 135). Dante's work offered inspiration and proof that it was possible to speak the unspeakable, that words would prove adequate to the horror; in Dante's wake Weiss formulated the ambitious plan that was to guide his subsequent work but that he would complete only in part: "the plan . . . to take this amorphous material, which expanded in all directions, and put it into place in Dante's three-part composition" ("Vorübung" 136).[7]

To be sure, there was much that Weiss could not adopt, and in fact had to reject, in the "unified worldview" of Dante's *Divine Comedy* ("Gespräch" 144). The absolute moral conviction, the appeal to transcendent authority, and the divine closure of Dante's world, in which worldly wrongdoing and suffering met with afterworldly punishment and salvation, were no longer tenable in Weiss's wholly secular reality. Nonetheless, the spirit of Dante's project continued to govern Weiss's poetic endeavors: the search for meaning and truth; the conviction that the artist would prove able to comprehend his world, however ugly and chaotic it might appear; the belief in the power of language and art to convey truth in its totality; in short, the possibility of a clarifying "world theater" ("Gespräch" 142) remain essentially intact.

More importantly, it was not Dante the poet but Dante the man who provided the object of Weiss's identification: the Dante who escaped death by fleeing into exile ("He is a fugitive. He has a death sentence hanging over him. He is sitting somewhere in exile and writing" ["Gespräch" 150]) and the Dante who betrayed Beatrice and who remains forever guilty of his youthful "sin of omission" ("Gespräch" 153). In both Dante texts Weiss writes of his parallel failure in lines that border on the obsessive. In "Gespräch über Dante":

Who is Beatrice for me? A young love whom I never dared approach. Then came the political terror. The war. I was driven out, ended up in exile. Beatrice remained there. I heard nothing more from her. Had I been courageous, I would have taken her with me when I fled. What happened to Beatrice? Would I ever have wanted to live with her? Beatrice died. Perhaps she was beaten to death. Maybe gassed. She had long since turned to ashes, and I was still imagining her beauty. (154)

In "Vorübung":

> He had betrayed Beatrice, who died in our world. Fearful of any commitment, he had turned away from her and had glorified only himself when he glorified her, the disembodied girl, as art. He had not dared to touch her, to take her with him when he fled. He left her where she was, and there he could pray for her, while her body bled to death. This was his defeat. And this insight—that everything he had done up to that point was false and a failure—could become the impetus for embarking on a new path. (141)[8]

We hear in these passages the immense guilt of the young Peter Weiss who had escaped his rightful "place" in Auschwitz (Weiss, "Meine Ortschaft"), who had done nothing to save the person he loved, who had fled instead to a safety that enabled him to pursue his artistic interests. Sitting and writing somewhere in exile like Dante, Weiss realizes his ethical failure as an artist: the aesthetic isolation and all that it afforded him are bought at the price of his moral responsibility to other human beings. The recognition of the fundamental guilt and the personal inadequacy lying at the core of an earlier art devoted solely to "beauty" and "prayer" leads to the modern Dante's denunciation of his life and work as false and to a poetic, personal, and political rebirth.

This new beginning is located in, and defines, the Purgatory of Weiss's world theater. In the author's vision, Inferno is reserved for the oppressors who—in contrast to Dante's sinners—continue their lives unpunished, comfortable, even admired; Paradise is home for the oppressed who await the salvation that can come only from concrete actions in the material world. While both regions present situations of stasis, Purgatory offers the possibility of change and resistance: "[i]n Purgatory, however, they can defend themselves. They have the freedom to take a stand on the hostilities" ("Gespräch" 166; cf. Gerlach and Richter 55–56, 59).[9] The definition of a Purgatory that promises "the hint of an alternative" ("Vorübung" 139) grants Weiss the chance to undo his past failure, to recast himself in terms of an alternative—namely, to engage this time in active resistance rather than fleeing into a sublime, aesthetic isolation. "[H]ere one ought to be required to show one's colors; here questions should be asked that demand a decision" ("Vorübung" 138).[10] The "new way" demands aggressive questioning, analysis, and unswerving commitment: "[m]y Dante, the Dante with whom I speak today, quickly turns his ability to love into understanding for the conditions of life, into sympathy with human efforts to make life on earth bearable. And thus he enters into the domain in which all hostility is stored up, in which everything that hinders these efforts is gathered. He enters into it in order to examine it" ("Gespräch" 158). Instead of leaving the beloved Beatrice to die, Weiss's Dante proclaims his solidarity. Specifically, for the reborn Weiss, the cause of the lost love in Auschwitz is replaced by, and regained in, the commitment to the cause of Third World revolution: "[Dante] could go into the back alleys of the cities and wander through the countries and continents that are ruled by dictators and colonizers" ("Gespräch" 168).

The main outlines of Weiss's overtly political aesthetics thus begin to emerge in the preoccupation with the *Divine Comedy*. Faced with a crisis situation caused by the apparent literary untameability of the horrors of Auschwitz and by the author's guilt in allowing the death of a prisoner, Weiss finds his way first by asserting his faith, inspired by Dante's example, in the power of reason to analyze and to comprehend violent oppression and in the power of language and art to represent adequately the discovered truth. Second, there is the related conviction that the truth represented in art entails the author's—and reader's—active commitment to effect change in the world. Intellectual examination is directly connected to participation in political struggle; change is predicated upon, and guaranteed by, the rational analysis of the world offered in the work of art and the unproblematic efficacy of the human will, of free political choice, that follows upon it.[11]

The speech given at the 1966 meeting of the Group 47 in Princeton, entitled, significantly, "I Come Out of My Hiding Place," reflects Weiss's new vision and marks his explicit turn to the politics of the Third World. Here we find for the first time the equation that becomes a litany in Weiss's subsequent work: German fascism continues to exist, its oppressive practices now spread throughout the world.[12] "[M]assacres continued—10,000 were thrown into the prisons of Greece, 80,000 were murdered by the colonizers in Madagascar, innumerable were the dead in Vietnam, in the Congo, in Angola; millions were kept as slave workers in South Africa and Siberia; millions were suppressed in Latin America. The great robbery was going on all the time" ("I Come Out" 655). The specific historical event of Auschwitz is literally globalized in Weiss's developing vision of a world theater, with the result that Weiss, who had once withdrawn from any action, can make a different choice in the situation of a worldwide Holocaust: choosing solidarity with the Third World, Weiss thereby performs the missing act of resistance against fascism.[13] Again the rigor of analysis provides the simple key to revolutionary activism; in Weiss's text verbs such as "studying," "exploring," and "understanding" chart an unproblematic transition from the purely inner freedom of an isolated art to active solidarity with the world's oppressed ("I Come Out" 655).

Not surprisingly, political enlightenment constitutes one of the central themes as well as the guiding formal principle of Weiss's *Gesang vom Lusitanischen Popanz* (1967; *Song of the Lusitanian Bogey*), conceived as part of an extended *Divine Comedy* project and the first major literary text written after Weiss's relocation in the "Auschwitz" of the Third World.[14] The issue of education announces itself in the opening scene of the play, where we witness the mechanical Lusitanian bogey, symbol of Portugal's colonial rule over Angola and Mozambique, being dressed before our eyes. Although one of its stage props is a professor's cap (translated as "a hat of dignity" [5]), the bogey's continued existence rides on the fixed, contrary belief that people (here: the colonized Africans) are incapable of intelligent self-governance:

> Repeatedly it is shown in history
> that man is not capable

of guiding himself
He needs the direction of an authority

the bogey proclaims (6). The decidedly paternalistic colonial state, we are told, requires as its foundation the ignorance of its subjects (7). Immediately, any resistance or revolt against the Portuguese is associated in the logic of the play with the overcoming of political ignorance and illiteracy. Education thereby becomes revolutionary, an act of breaking away from a state defined in terms of patriarchal authority and "[c]unning gall deceit and lying" (5). As in Seghers's Caribbean narratives, the revolutionary power of the people is thus directly tied to the level of their political understanding.[15]

The connection between knowledge and resistance recurs throughout the text in a number of ways. It serves as the thematic core of the opening scene of the second act, the sixth scene of eleven in the German text and the structural center of the play.[16] Here again we hear the lies of the state, whose civilizing mission is said to consist ironically in a kind of education:

None the less with relentless
Civilizing patience we slowly
guide the people from the darkness
where long ago
we discovered them. (35–36)

But the hypocrisy is immediately exposed by the conflicting testimony of one of the natives, who offers facts in place of rhetoric: after five centuries of Portugal's civilizing mission, only one out of every hundred Africans has learned to read and write in rudimentary fashion; of one and a half million children, only ninety thousand are enrolled in missionary schools (36–37). Through this technique, the African natives (the "speakers" of such texts in the dramatic fiction of the play), as well as actors and audience, are drawn into a didactic process in which their ignorance or lack of reflection about Angola is dispelled. The clash between the claims of state ideology and concrete facts attesting to the contrary activates the critical capacity of both dramatized natives and dramatic audience and serves the function of political enlightenment.[17] The result is tangibly represented on stage in the development from early individual speeches to mass choruses formulating revolutionary insight and program later in the text. In scene 7 (scene 8 in the original German), for example, the entire cast joins for the first time to articulate the revolutionary vision of the now highly politicized natives:

> That the land should belong
> to those who work it
> That the houses should be lived in
> by those who build the houses. (43)

In keeping with the structural logic of the text, total comprehension is achieved in the play's concluding scene. There reports of indigenous revolt and of tortured political prisoners clash with descriptions of Portugal's growing economic prosperity and of increased foreign (European and American) investments in Angola that work to maintain the colonial state (57–59). In the end we see the natives with insight not only into specific colonial practices in Africa but into the global system of imperialism that stands behind them; their education (and ours) reaches the point at which the workings of the entire capitalist system, extending far beyond the political and cultural borders of Angola, become clear.

Just as we had once heard that the bogey's domination over Angola was justified because the natives were unable to govern themselves, we hear in its final speech in the play that

> . . . within 10
> to 15 years
> the so-called
> sovereign Africa
> shall disappear in chaos
> for it is not capable
> of governing itself. (60)

From start to end, the absence of self-determination among non-Europeans is used to legitimize the interests of the colonial state. Yet the new revolutionary native population, having completed the historical and educational process enacted in the intervening scenes of the play, displays the results of its political maturation. "Well look at this old man," "Look how his face is thin," "Look at this man of straw," "Strike hard this pallid man" (60), they cry. Once the immature, ignorant child requiring the state as father and paternal authority, the people now constitute, as an enlightened populus, the mature adult rising up to threaten an old and incompetent colonial regime. The child incapable of self-governance becomes, through the process of political education depicted in the text, the historical subject capable of revolutionary action. In the final moments of the play the once-mystifying bogey is dismantled before our eyes, the duplicitous "insinuating [obsequious] melody" of a peaceful and harmonious life in the colony answered by harsh speech (61–62) that calls for clear critical thinking and an unwavering commitment to the revolutionary cause. Thus the play ends with a united chorus, the visible and verbal symbol of revolutionary solidarity and global insight, proclaiming continual struggle and promising sure victory against oppression.

This illustrates a number of assumptions about the process of political education that are key for Weiss's dramatic work at this time. Thematically the text exhibits the connection between knowledge on the one hand and revolutionary consciousness and action on the other; revolution requires understanding, just as the process of understanding guarantees the simultaneous development of revolutionary consciousness. Accordingly, with regard to the play's formal aspects, it is the word above all that serves to transmit political insight. Despite the use of pantomime, shadow plays, and songs, unanimously lauded by theater critics who found the strength of the play to lie in its dramaturgical diversity, the revolutionary process in the text is carried by its speeches, individual and choral, which provoke critical reflection on the part of natives and audience.[18] The play remains, despite its musical and visual elements, declamatory theater; in it, in keeping with Weiss's Dante reception, the power of language alone proves adequate for the representation of political and historical truth.

Much has been made of the mutual independence of actors and roles in the play. Rejecting theatrical convention, Weiss insisted in his stage directions that all seven cast members portray both blacks and whites with minimal costume adjustment and without masks or makeup: "[w]hatever the color of their skin, the actors speak interchangeably for Europeans and Africans" (3). Scholars have pointed out that such a procedure, which keeps skin color (whether natural or the result of stage makeup) separate from role, shifts the focus of the text's analysis from race to class.[19] But there is another consequence, one that suggests a particular view toward the process of political understanding enacted in the play: the actors, in speaking the roles of both blacks and whites, oppressors and oppressed, are implicitly granted a position outside the dramatic action from which they can judge, and call forth judgment upon, the colonial struggle they depict. The play thereby projects through its dramaturgy the existence of a neutral position untouched by race, class, political alliance, or nationality, a place beyond or above loyalties to any particular "role." Critical evaluation and the knowledge it produces, the text implies, can be free, unbiased, and universally available to all who can similarly disengage themselves from their various interested positions.

For his part Weiss makes the following pronouncement in an interview given a year after the publication of *Gesang vom Lusitanischen Popanz*:

> I believe that you can free yourself; I believe that I, for example, am no longer burdened by bourgeois thinking. It's clear that you're in solidarity with the so-called Third World, you're in solidarity with oppressed peoples, you're in solidarity with the working class . . . and it's clear that you don't belong to them by birth—but your own sympathies lie there. It's clear that you're biased, but at the same time, you have a tremendous privilege by virtue of the fact that you had the opportunity to acquire so much knowledge. (Gerlach and Richter 118)[20]

In Weiss's view, with himself as a prime example, it is possible if not imperative to escape one's biased and culturally burdened identity and to achieve an emancipated stance from which to make correct political decisions, namely, for solidarity with the oppressed (cf.

Große and Thurm 154, 170–74). The possibility of attaining this emancipated position, indeed, enables and legitimizes the claim of the author in this text and elsewhere to speak on behalf of those victimized.[21] Political knowledge and the writing based upon it thereby become the privileged weapons of the author, recast as a resistance fighter, in the anticolonial campaign.[22]

The equation of enlightenment and revolution reaches its extreme in Weiss's next play on the Third World, commonly referred to as *Viet Nam Diskurs* (1968; Vietnam discourse). The full title of the text reveals much about Weiss's view of his task; the genre label, borrowing from and appealing to the Enlightenment tradition, proclaims that there is a clear lesson to be demonstrated in the ensuing text: *Diskurs über die Vorgeschichte und den Verlauf des lang andauernden Befreiungskrieges in Viet Nam als Beispiel für die Notwendigkeit des bewaffneten Kampfes der Unterdrückten gegen ihre Unterdrücker sowie über die Versuche der Vereinigten Staaten von Amerika die Grundlagen der Revolution zu vernichten (Discourse on the Progress of the Prolonged War of Liberation in Viet Nam and the Events Leading Up to It as Illustration [Example] of the Necessity for Armed Resistance [by the Oppressed] against Oppression [Their Oppressors] and on the Attempts of the United States of America to Destroy the Foundations of Revolution*).[23] The "discourse" on the specific historical case of Vietnam treats it as an "example of the necessity" of armed struggle against oppression: the particular stance announced by the title presupposes that the examination of a single case will reveal aspects that can be generalized or universalized, so that firm conclusions about necessary truths may be drawn. Implicitly the text asserts its (or the author's) superior vantage point, a position of supposed objectivity and rational judgment, from which the events of a history two thousand years long can be explained according to universally valid categories of "liberation" and domination, "oppressors" and "oppressed"; it is also a position from which political and moral imperatives can be identified and asserted.[24]

As in *Gesang vom Lusitanischen Popanz*, the text presents not individual characters but representative figures who collectively enact the lawful process of history. Hegelian in his philosophical view, Weiss promises to illuminate the broad, universal movement that eludes the insight of the anonymous actors caught in the grip of their private individual experience. Weiss explains in the foreword to the play:

> Each actor . . . represents a number of figures whose statements and behaviour as a whole typify a particular historical development. . . . The aim is to present figures bound up in historical processes, even when it is a matter of historical developments of which the participants were themselves not aware. An attempt is made to present a succession of social stages, with all their essential features and discrepancies, in such a way that they throw light on the conflict existing today. (67; cf. Weiss, "Peter Weiss")

With stage positions corresponding to compass directions, a strict and intricate choreography of movement depicting historical events and encounters, and the categorical use of black and white to mark oppressed and oppressors, the stage of Weiss's play becomes the visible representation in miniature of a world governed by identifiable rational principles. Actors take on a variety of roles throughout the play, with identities indicated not by costume but primarily by stage location: the staging of the play suggests that political alliances can be abandoned or exchanged according to a shift in physical (as a cipher for ideological) viewpoint—"through a change of position" (Weiss, *Viet Nam* 67)—without regard to differences of race, class, culture, or nationality. The discovery of lawful order in the world, despite the impression of chaos and circularity that the sequence of events might create, lies completely open to the power of reason; and political change, the shedding of roles as oppressor and oppressed, becomes a matter of individual will based on rational insight.[25]

Thematically as well the play maintains its focus on the political significance of human reason. As in the Angola play, the text on Vietnam begins in its first scene by isolating a (if not the) key factor in the relationship between rulers and ruled: political power is related to superior knowledge. If the peasants produce by their physical labor the material goods required for the state's survival and prosperity, they are promised in return a share in a culture perceived to be (or presented as) more advanced and civilized: in exchange for rice, fish, lumber, and weapons, the rulers offer "the discoveries of our sciences" and "the arts / of poetry and painting" (79–80). Of course, the promise of knowledge is never fulfilled. Instead, as the next scene announces, the state chooses to educate only the sons of families who are loyal supporters, in order to assure the continued smooth functioning of the oppressive system (83; cf. 96–97, 110). No education is intended for the masses; their subordinate status is insured—so the implication—by their being kept in deliberate ignorance.

In the world of *Viet Nam Diskurs*, the path of history retraces a single, categorical conflict, that between "oppressors" and "oppressed," in nearly endless variation. A striking pattern of conquest marks the various historical periods depicted in the text, leading many critics to claim that—Weiss's intentions aside—history seems nothing more than an inescapable cycle of oppression.[26] Time and again, those who guide the Vietnamese people to their emancipation emerge themselves as the next tyrants. The actors who play the defeated and executed feudal lords rise up before our eyes to join the new set of conquerors, thus enjoying continued rule over Vietnam (85); it is one of Vietnam's rulers who takes on the role of Le Loi, the leader of an insurrectionary peasant army (95); the brothers Tay Son, who lead the peasants to overthrow the state, become its new and equally demagogic rulers (104–05); the French who offer help in the war of liberation do so only in order to win economic control over the country (111); and so forth.

The repetition, however, slowly gives rise to the insight on the part of the Vietnamese peasants that they are continually fighting the wars of one set of oppressors against another while the domination they suffer remains constant. The learning process that both audience and dramatized peasants undergo reaches a high point toward the end of the first half of the play, with Vietnam in the colonial grip of France. The chorus chants:

Again and again they rose up
against enemies who invaded the country
and against oppressors in their own land
. . . .
All that changed in thousands of years were
the names of the rulers
. . . .
But the peasants could never remove
the causes of their oppression. (127)

The statement that the structural causes of oppression, and not just the oppressors of a given moment, need to be eliminated formalizes the political insight that has been gained and calls at the same time — characteristically — for the necessity of yet further learning: "[n]ow is the time for learning," the chorus continues (127). Learning and more learning, and the power of reason that it presupposes, seem the necessary and the sufficient response to violent oppression. In this way Weiss's text enacts, thematizes, and absolutizes the process of education, such that once again emancipatory knowledge is granted an inherently (and exclusively) revolutionary function.[27]

By the end of scene 11, the concluding scene of the first half of the text, the conflicts between the Vietnamese peasants and their various rulers over two thousand years culminate in the highly generalized war "of the robbed and betrayed . . . / of the third world" (143), with the Vietnamese peasants having achieved an understanding of their world-historical role.[28] Part 2 of the text is devoted to the struggle between Vietnam and the United States of America as the prime example of this war, a specific situation to which Weiss's presentation attributes global significance. As the chorus of American advisors asserts, "We are trying / to strike at the root / of revolution" (208–09). Both the role of the United States and that of Vietnam are universalized, so that the Southeast Asian country becomes the very embodiment of "revolution," while American power defines the epitome of capitalist oppression and the essence of all former invaders and conquerors (227). The struggle represented in Weiss's text grows heavily schematic, the depiction of Vietnam so romanticized as to seem wholly detached from any realistic political assessment. Resistance is conveyed, for example, in the penultimate scene of the play by the image of indomitable peasants planting rice with guns slung over their shoulders (225; cf. Schmitz 136–37); and the last lines of the play identify the source of oppression simply as "the great power / of [the oppressors'] wealth" (228–29). In its final analysis the discourse on Vietnam constructs a view of the world stripped of all ambiguity and specific historical circumstances, divided with absolute clarity but little analytical insight between oppressors and revolutionaries, rich and poor.[29]

But if education is the overriding goal and organizing principle of Weiss's *Viet Nam Diskurs*, it also constitutes its chief fault. The almost maniacal single-mindedness of Weiss's Dantesque project demonstrates in this text its serious limitation: namely, the project to illuminate the workings of the world, to enlighten an audience regarding laws that should govern the struggle between oppressors and oppressed, proves to be excruciatingly boring.[30] In fact, the problem can be connected directly to the enlightenment project, for Weiss, by insisting exclusively on the power of human reason to penetrate the chaotic or repetitious events of history, refuses to engage, excite, or entice the reader in any way other than through the exercise of that isolated capacity.

Gone are the rich instances of pantomime and song of *Gesang vom Lusitanischen Popanz*, gone the symbolic bogeyman on stage. Weiss works instead solely with declamatory speeches (by anonymous or representative figures, or by a chorus) and stage movements corresponding to directions of the compass. The black and white color scheme aptly captures the sense of Weiss's sensual reduction—"ascetic" is the author's description for the virtue of his text.[31] The extreme sparseness of the stage and of the craft of the actors forces the audience to focus on the words being spoken; nothing else is offered for our viewing. As a result, the only motivation for readers to persevere through two hundred pages of text, or for audience members to endure the performance of the play in its entirety, is their preexistent political conviction. The text does not seduce but rather tires us out (cf. Karnick 225; Blumer

190–93, 205–07). The play will impart its lessons through the word
alone: its ascetic form reflects and reinforces the singular belief
in human reason as *the* revolutionary agent, thematized throughout the work. The pseudoreligious or moral "conversion" Weiss
undergoes through the belated experience of Auschwitz and of personal guilt thus results in the extreme of ascetic self-abnegation:
art (and revolutionary action) becomes a realm of purely rational
contemplation.

It is noteworthy that Weiss turned down all invitations to visit
North Vietnam until he had completed his Vietnam play, claiming
that "local color" was of no concern to him.[32] Nothing illustrates
better the status of Vietnam as a paradigmatic, not a historically
specific, country in Weiss's text. Ironically, the methodological and
categorical denial of specificity and the author's exclusive focus on
reason as the capacity for artistic and political analysis exact their
toll once Weiss puts pen and paper aside to experience Vietnam
firsthand.

The private account in *Notizbücher 1960–1971* of Weiss's trip in
May and June 1968, conducted at the height of U.S. bombardment,
describes a severe crisis resulting from the overwhelming physical
experience of the Third World country. The day after Weiss's arrival
in Hanoi in May 1968, the author is hospitalized by a sudden attack of kidney stones precipitated by insufficient fluid intake in the
tropical heat (579). Weiss is "filled with shame" (580), and the dis-
comfort restricts his activity through the first week and a half of his
visit. Seven months later, on 31 December 1968, Weiss relives the
Vietnam trip in a self-chastising, melancholic review of the year:

> The trip to Viet Nam full of difficulties, the almost hysterical
> preparations, the boundless fear of flying. The deep psycho-
> logical dimension beneath the whole *learning process* there.
> My state of health undermined by the suffocating conditions.
> *Still need to describe sometime all the sickness, fear, and inner
> sense of loss that emerged there*. The thoughts of death, the
> weakness, the dejection. The night in Hai Phong. The nights

of colic in Hanoi. And everything covered up by *unflagging work*. Then the preparation of the material. Worked without a break straight through until September, the pamphlet on the air raids, the book on cultural life. (617; emphasis in original)

Significantly, the painful and highly personal nature of the illness that Weiss recounts contrasts sharply with the sovereign, didactic tone of the published interviews, essays, and book that result from his subsequent "preparation of the material." The *Spiegel* interview "'Amerika will den Völkermord'" (America wants genocide) from July 1968, the interview given earlier that month in Swedish in *Dagens Nyheter*, the *Notizen zum kulturellen Leben in der Demokratischen Republik Viet Nam* (1968; *Notes on the Cultural Life of the Democratic Republic of Vietnam*), and Weiss's and Gunilla Palmstierna-Weiss's *Bericht über die Angriffe der US-Luftwaffe und -Marine gegen die Demokratische Republik Viet Nam nach der Erklärung Präsident Johnsons über die "begrenzte Bombardierung" am 31. März 1968* (1968; *"Limited Bombing" in Vietnam: Report on the Attacks against the Democratic Republic of Vietnam by the U.S. Air Force and the Seventh Fleet, after the Declaration of "Limited Bombing" by President Lyndon B. Johnson on March 31, 1968*) reveal little if any of the physical and emotional trauma suffered by the author in Cambodia and Vietnam.[33] We are given statistics and dates, eyewitness accounts of bombings, even euphoric or romanticized images of the resistance of the Vietnamese people but virtually nothing concerning the physical impact of the land on its European visitor. This striking transformation, perhaps more properly viewed as an act of repression, illustrates one of the major qualities, if not the essential one, of Weiss's *Divine Comedy* concept: the mastery of chaotic and overwhelming experience through the discipline of reason and its forceful articulation in words inspired by high moral and political ideals. The author in his published texts presents himself strictly as objective witness, reporter, and judge.

Two years later Weiss, still haunted by the memory of his vulnerability in the Third World climate, begins in characteristic fashion to distill an abstract political and philosophical truth from his experience of physical collapse. He writes again in *Notizbücher 1960–1971*:

[T]his representative of rich countries, of highly developed industry, of hygienic packaging—this spoiled and satiated man
arrives at the showplace denigrated as the Third World. And
precisely there, where he, a declared enemy of the system that
had produced him, should have engaged in effective actions
of solidarity and demonstrated in practice his alliance with
those who have been plundered—there the ground fell out
from under him after just a few days. . . . [E]ven though he
was able, after laborious trips through the ravaged land, to
put together the results of his investigatory expeditions and
publish them in pamphlets, articles, and books, the real experience of his visit was the realization of his frailty, of his own
limitations, the irrefutable fact of not being able to move
forward. (794–95)

Now the kidney ailment is transformed and elevated into a lesson
regarding the limitations of the European and of his cultural and
social traditions in the Third World context, "a lesson about the
inferiority of the one who is overloaded with material goods in relation to the impoverished representatives of an authentic culture"
(795). In the process the details of his illness are recounted in obsessive detail (795–98): Weiss was treated as a highly privileged guest
for whom even precious X-rays were not spared. Restricted because of his condition, the author sat in a comfortable hotel room
reading books about Vietnamese history and culture and receiv-
ing visits from prominent writers and government officials. When
Weiss was able to travel again, his experience of the country remained colored by a sense of physical and personal moral failure
(799). Even when back in Europe and formulating the documentary accounts intended to publicize the American bombings in
Vietnam and to elicit support for the Vietnamese peasantry, Weiss
was tortured by fears of personal weakness and, concomitantly, of
the political inadequacy of his work (799–800).

Here it is crucially important that Weiss—who was unable to
cope with the tropical climate and who, despite having been
treated with the utmost privilege, felt deprived of the comforts of
his "affluence" in the foreign "wilderness" (800, 801)—experiences

above all the inadequacy of the "European" when faced with the reality of Third World combat. The essence of the Vietnam experience for the author culminates in the recognition, couched in characteristically (and simplistically) binary terms, that Europeans are guilty, weak, insignificant, and spoiled, with the Vietnamese "infinitely superior to us in determination, consistency, knowledge, and humanity" (802; cf. Weiss, "Che" 558–59; Polacco 90–91). In the final analysis, the breakdown in Vietnam signifies nothing less than the weakness of "European civilization" in the face of the Third World. Notably, Weiss overcomes his moral guilt and political confusion once again through abstractions provided by the faithful exercise and saving discipline of reason. Both thematically and formally, reason represents the means and, in its causal identification with revolution, the definitive goal of Weiss's "world theater," guaranteeing political enlightenment and moral certitude to both author and audience. All of this is radically different in the case of Hans Magnus Enzensberger.

The famous debate between the two authors in the pages of *Kursbuch* in 1965 and 1966 was sparked by Enzensberger's essay "Europäische Peripherie" (1965; European periphery).[34] Published in an issue devoted to the topic of the Third World, the essay divided the globe into highly developed industrial societies on the one side and colonies and colonial enclaves on the other. In Enzensberger's view, the Cold War division between East and West had been replaced by an international class struggle waged between rich and poor. Such a division recognized essential differences of inequality within each of the traditional capitalist and Communist blocs and aligned Washington and Moscow alike against the developing countries of the Third World: "[t]he line drawn in the new class struggle separates poor from rich communists, poor neutrals from rich neutrals, poor from rich members of the 'free world.' . . . In the face of every 'yellow,' 'black,' or other colored 'danger,' a solidarity is proclaimed that extends from the big banks to the last union functionary" (162, 163). Enzensberger argued, further, that a nation's internal class conflicts dissipated in the face of sharpened international struggles (163).[35]

This reconfiguration of the political map held serious repercussions for the possibility of Third World solidarity on the part of Western intellectuals. In what could be read as a critique of Weiss, Enzensberger attacked the "doctrinaires" who followed the international class struggle with close attention, possessed a "coherent system" with which to judge its progress, and, above all, took sides against the privileged world to which they belonged and in which they continued to live (171). Enzensberger derided the fact that their adamantly oppositional stance did not result in political action: "[t]hey remain at home; they go to poor countries only on study trips. Their activity remains verbal; it exhausts itself in agitation" (171).[36] In his view, all attempts at solidarity were destined to fail, because it was impossible for First World intellectuals and political activists to shed their privileged and thus already compromised skins. In Enzensberger's much-quoted formula, "[n]o power of action or imagination is sufficient to put oneself in the position of a black mine worker, an Asian rice farmer, or a Peruvian Indian" (172). The European was thereby relegated to an inescapable position on the periphery of revolutionary struggle; no shared consciousness was possible between rich and poor; the solidarity of the European sympathizer was illusory only.[37]

Interestingly enough, Enzensberger too falls back on the ideal of reason to save himself from his intellectual, political, and personal quandary, calling for a politics "based on knowledge" (175) that would combat a hegemonic politics founded on "ignorance" (174). Enzensberger appeals, however, to a notion of rational enlightenment different from that of his counterpart Weiss. In the opening discussion of his essay, he describes in negative terms a "non-public opinion that isolates itself from all discussion and that immunizes itself against enlightenment by evading any public confrontation" (152). The implied ideal of a rational public discourse that ensures the correction and "enlightenment" of individual personal opinion contrasts markedly with Weiss's adherence to the individual exercise of reason.[38] The essay's conclusion goes on to suggest that the reason attained through public discourse is only a heuristic ideal; Enzensberger doubts that there can be any morally or politically unassailable position to be reached, only various degrees of ignorance that should be recognized and eliminated (174). If, for Weiss, reason leads to moral and political truth, for Enzensberger the exercise of reason takes the form of active doubt, so that its result is only a progressive lessening of dogmatic error, never absolute certainty.

In "Enzensbergers Illusionen" (1966; Enzensberger's illusions) Weiss insists not on the political and cultural limitations of the intellectual, as does Enzensberger, but on the seemingly limitless capacity of his reason to penetrate and to understand even distant, foreign events. While European intellectuals do not work as slave laborers in African mines, "we have," according to Weiss, "the ability to discover the causes that have led to these situations, and in discovering these causes, we come very close to those who are destroyed by them" (36). The tool of the intellectual, his superior reason, is thereby turned into a viable, if not powerful, political weapon. The intellectual's definitive task is to analyze the situation of oppression; further, the exercise of his capacity of reason leads necessarily to the establishment of a relationship of political solidarity between intellectual and mine worker. Indeed, rather than signal his limitation, this investigative function becomes the unique privilege and the special moral and political obligation of the European. "In some cases," Weiss ventures to claim, "we . . . can even understand more about the situation and develop more of an overview than those who, lacking any opportunity for education, are crushed by it" (36). Enzensberger's disqualifying privilege thus becomes Weiss's unique authorizing talent. It is not surprising, furthermore, that the response to Enzensberger, coinciding with Weiss's study of the *Divine Comedy*, reveals traits of Weiss's reception of the Italian poet. Specifically, the analysis of the Third World situation, like the analysis of the Holocaust, which seemed so incomprehensible, demonstrates for Weiss that "even what is most horrifying still has human proportions, and that everything that is brought about by human beings has a cause and an explanation" (36). Throughout the essay the author remains unwavering in his belief in the power of reason to penetrate human phenomena and to unite rational beings in a fight against fascist oppression in its multifarious forms.

The idea of unity is key for Weiss, as we find in his arguments a pervasive tendency to seek out what is the same, not what is different. Whereas for Enzensberger no action or act of the imagination can put us in the place of an African mine worker or an Asian rice peasant, for Weiss such cultural and class differences can without question be overcome: "[w]hat happens far away among those without means and what happens here among us, who have acquired a certain standard of living, *is fundamentally the same*. We find ourselves in the same social struggle, even if we are able to view this struggle in an objectionable state of leisure, while the others risk their lives at every moment" (39; emphasis added). By pointing out the continuity of industrial interests under Hitler and postwar German investments in South Africa, Weiss in a familiar move equates the exploited peoples of the Third World with the prisoners of Nazi concentration camps; the struggle of the Third World against oppression becomes thereby essentially "also ours" (44).[39] In the author's worldview, we can and should recognize ourselves as being the same as, and on the side of, others who are oppressed. And as always for Weiss, the means for that process of recognition is reason, with sufficient knowledge leading directly and necessarily to active solidarity: "[b]y acquiring as much knowledge as possible about conditions in the countries most heavily oppressed by the 'rich,' we can bring these countries close to us and develop our solidarity with them" (40). The same intellect that brings Enzensberger to a position of radical doubt leads Weiss to an unshakable certainty about the nature of the world and his oppositional role in it.

Enzensberger extends the debate in a sharp rejoinder to Weiss's idealization of reason as a universal category of revolutionary unity. In the essay "Peter Weiss und andere" (1966; Peter Weiss and others) he polemically asserts that it is indeed "fundamentally two different things"—the contrast to Weiss's formulation is deliberate—"whether one dies in a mine in Angola or reads a statistic about Angolan mine workers" (251). In Enzensberger's view, Weiss's notion of reason as the expression and the vehicle of universal humanity and global solidarity lacks any specific content, goals, or strategy: "[h]e has neither a program nor a strategy to propose. But a political decision that has no precise goals remains empty; a political decision without a precise strategy remains blind" (247). Not coincidentally, the formulation mimics Kant's dictum in the *Critique of Pure Reason* that "[t]houghts without content are empty, intuitions without concepts are blind" (A 51); the Kantian language that Enzensberger borrows reveals that at the crux of the political debate between the two authors lies a fundamental disagreement concerning the meaning of enlightenment.

If for Weiss the exercise of reason in the realm of politics results in the overcoming of cultural and class differences in the stance of universal solidarity, for Enzensberger the critique of reason leads inexorably to the recognition of inalienable difference. As he insists, an "abyss" separates Kreuzberg from Calcutta (247). Interestingly enough, Enzensberger's characterization of himself and Weiss parallels Kant's attempt to situate his philosophy vis-à-vis that of his dogmatic predecessors:[40] Weiss's position is grounded on "confessions" and "sentiments"; Enzensberger, in contrast, holds to "arguments" and "doubt" (251). The word "doubt" occurs frequently throughout the essay as a telltale label for Enzensberger's critical stance: while Enzensberger calls for a "critical theory" for which doubt constitutes the essential component, Weiss is painted as the "doubtless," that is, unquestioning, colleague with a penchant for normative judgments (247). In essence Enzensberger claims the classic Kantian "enlightenment" position of radical doubt, casting Weiss in turn as the religious dogmatist.[41]

While Weiss's reason brings him to solidarity, Enzensberger's rational doubt leads to the recognition of a fundamental European self with privileges and limitations that cannot be shed by acts of will or by decisions of the intellect. This raises the uncomfortable question of the European's complicity in the global system of oppression that he means to combat—of exactly that sense of guilt and inadequacy that Weiss expressed privately in his notebooks but suppressed in his political and dramatic writings. Enzensberger presses the point with biting irony:

They show their colors. We on the other hand sit in our five-room apartments. We just write after all. Maybe we make a trip at some point to Cuba or to the Soviet Union, but only as tourists; maybe we do a reading at some point in Leipzig, but then we get on a train that takes us back to the West. That's nothing but theory. That's just bare words. . . . By contrast, Peter Weiss and others! They put themselves in danger. They fight. They have nothing to do with the society in which they live. They have dropped out. They stand shoulder to shoulder with the black miner in the copper mines of the Transvaal, with the Asian rice farmer in the fields of South Vietnam. . . . There they stand, shoulder to shoulder, and fight. Peter Weiss and others are not, as we are, accomplices of the rich world. (250)

Enzensberger's critical reason, which seeks to maintain differences rather than to erase them in an ideal universality, holds insistently to his identity as European in contrast to the rice peasants of the Third World. Weiss's reason works to define a sense of right and wrong in the realm of politics and to establish an unwavering ethical guide for revolutionary action. In Enzensberger's view political change does not consist of a simple decision to commit to "The Good Cause" and to place oneself above material interests (248). Rather, political enlightenment is a matter primarily of self-knowledge, of the merciless examination of unfounded beliefs and ideals; reason thus leads not to solidarity but to relativism, to a critique of one's privilege and cultural-political limitations—to a position, as inalienably European, on an epistemological and political "periphery." For Weiss, reason serves above all as the source of an absolute moral certainty; for Enzensberger, reason requires the radically destabilizing critique of all belief. If Weiss speaks of "showing one's colors" as the imperative of choosing political sides, the phrase for Enzensberger can signify only the self-conscious recognition of one's inescapable whiteness.[42]

The unmitigated rejection of Europe (and, by extension, of the

United States) as a potential source of revolutionary energy is soon brought to dramatic life in *Das Verhör von Habana* (1970; *The Havana Inquiry*), Enzensberger's play on the public trial in Cuba following the failed Bay of Pigs invasion in 1961.[43] In his introductory essay to the play Enzensberger characterizes the American effort to overthrow Castro by mercenary force in unqualifiedly negative terms: those who followed Batista into exile (and who comprised part of the invasion army) constitute, Enzensberger writes, "that portion of the Cuban people which could be described objectively as Cuba's dregs: a useless, parasitic elite of corrupt politicians, military brass, large landholders, together with such hangers-on as professional murderers, goons, and police informers" (5). The rhetorically charged language is maintained throughout the introduction, producing the effect of an unequivocal denunciation of the American invasion.[44]

Reminiscent of Weiss is the depiction of the televised interrogation of selected members of the counterrevolutionary forces as a representative investigation of larger philosophical and world-historical conflicts. Enzensberger stipulates that he was not interested in the "parochial [local] aspects" of his material but rather in its historical and political generalizability: "[t]he structure that we see . . . reemerges in every class society" (15; cf. 22, 51).[45] Like Peter Weiss, who offered in his works on Angola and Vietnam not analyses of the two countries in their historical and cultural specificity but depictions of their universalized struggle against oppression generally, so too does Enzensberger in his play on Cuba present a structural and ideological examination of class society anywhere: "[t]he prisoners are interchangeable. You can find them in every American, West German, Swedish, or Argentinian city. . . . In addition, the questions that were asked and the answers that were given were not directed at individual situations or characteristics, but instead at conditions of a collective nature [the behavior of a collective group]. With the utmost clarity, they reveal the character of a class" (16). The universal conflict dissected here rages between "the ruling class" and "the People" (16–17) — both categories, like Weiss's "oppressors" and "oppressed," emptied of specific historical content.[46]

While Enzensberger appears like Weiss to insist on a Manichaean morality in which oppressors are equated with evil and the oppressed with moral goodness ("The moral circumspection [superiority] of the Revolution is obvious," he proclaims [19]), it is at this point that the similarities end.[47] For despite the author's insistence on moral clarity and on a universal struggle against imperialism and the oppression of class society, and despite the unambiguous stance he announces with regard to the Cuban revolution and the American attempt to overthrow it, the text, taken as a whole, seems disturbingly ambivalent.

It is an important fact of the work's appearance that the volume bearing the title *Das Verhör von Habana* includes much more than the text of the documentary play. The author's introductory essay constitutes an integral part of the work, as do the bibliography of the author's sources, the photographs that close the volume, and its five substantial appendices: the transcript of Castro's discussion with a group of captured soldiers, testimony describing the milieu of the exile community in Miami, the radio text of a Catholic priest calling for a general uprising against Castro, the final judgments of the revolutionary court, and biographies of the interrogators. Taken as this larger whole, the "text" offers a much more varied view than the rhetoric of the introductory essay alone would suggest.

In fact, the essay contains important inner tensions that bear on its arguments. At odds are the claim that the play offers the "self-portrait of a group" (19), on the one hand, and the author's persuasive and rhetorically charged interpretation of that counterrevolutionary collective, on the other. Enzensberger's virtuoso analysis of the ideological premises and self-delusion of the bourgeois class as articulated in the testimony of its members, the exposé offered in the introductory essay, leaves little to literary scholars of the dramatic text than the varied repetition of the author's brilliant insights (Berghahn 279–80). Indeed, the essay is so compelling that the dramatic text seems to offer only the anticlimactic documentary verification of the main points of Enzensberger's analysis. The authoritative gesture of interpretation performed by the essay, reinforced by the formality of supporting footnotes, thus undermines the claim of its title to allow a self-portrait of counter-revolution (4). The counterrevolution is not allowed to present itself to us; rather, our judgment is shaped even before we are allowed access to the testimony of the trial.

The force of Enzensberger's analysis, which compels its recapitulation by others, thereby places the reader (and the critic) in a position ironically similar to that of the mercenaries in the invasion army, who parrot the language of the Enlightenment and of the French Revolution in their testimonies (22–23). Enzensberger views the exiled Cuban aristocracy, too, as manipulators who are themselves manipulated by their roles and rhetoric; their social function is disguised not merely to those they oppress but to themselves as well (25). At the core of their failure lies the uncritical acceptance of received wisdoms (roles, functions); this "immaturity" (*Unmündigkeit*), to use Kant's term from his essay on the definition of Enlightenment, amounts to a total paralytic stalemate—the inability to arrive at independent judgment (29–30). Enzensberger's exposé of such blind adherence to perceived authority should therefore alert the reader to the possibility that the claims of Enzensberger's masterful introductory excursus are not to be taken at their word. Not the results of Enzensberger's analysis should be our generalizable model but his method; the dissection of political testimony to reveal its ideological tactics needs to be performed on Enzensberger's discourse as well.[48]

Indeed, the testimony offered is anything but unequivocal or homogeneous. For Enzensberger, as it turns out, deliberately includes statements from three participants in the invasion who do not belong to the rich bourgeois class of prerevolutionary Cuba. The anomaly is announced, significantly, in a "postscript" to the introductory essay: "[a]dded . . . are three dialogues which do not fit the proposed interpretive formula. It is a myth that the invading forces were exclusively composed of property owners, industrialists, and their intellectual supporters and strong-armed goons" (49). The essay, which presents a monolithic "formula" for the literary text it precedes, thus appears at the last minute to question its own powers of abstraction and generalization by promising to offer counterevidence and by admitting that certain aspects of its analysis are actually only myth.

The gesture of self-questioning is repeated once again at the volume's end. The second appendix, on the situation of the Cuban exiles in Miami, for example, describes the economically and politically desperate, confused state that allowed many to be manipulated by U.S. government agencies—controversial information that belies any easy categorization (or denunciation) of the invading army as a parasitic elite or as police informants and murderers. Further, in the fifth appendix and thus the concluding "last word" of the volume (omitted from the English translation) we receive not a reconfirmation of the revolutionary commitment expressed in the introductory essay and in the dramatic text but rather a disconcerting glimpse into the historically arbitrary nature of the revolution. The biographical information offered about the revolution's representatives, who confront the bourgeois prisoners as morally and politically exemplary figures in the play, cause us in fact to question their political legitimacy. The interrogators appear ambiguous in the light of later historical developments, as does, by extension, the character of the revolution they once represented: of the eight interrogators, two live in exile from revolutionary Cuba, two others were stripped of the offices they had once held. The appendix provides details of various compromises and conflicts, facts and cursory summaries offered without explanation or historical or political analysis. The impression we are left with is one of irony and unease. The documentary evidence gathered in the volume as a whole, in short, questions much more than it proves; the interpretive formula presented so authoritatively and convincingly in the introduction is fraught with contradiction.

The unexpected move to unsettle what was previously thought to be secure becomes the central aesthetic principle of *Der Untergang der Titanic* (1978; *The Sinking of the Titanic*), Enzensberger's second dramatic work on the topic of the Third World. The way is paved by a number of important texts that develop the ideas of difference, contradiction, and the unconscious as necessary aspects of political and poetic experience. The essay "Zur Kritik der politischen Ökologie" (1973; "A Critique of Political Ecology"), for example, launches an attack against the popular ecological metaphor of the "spaceship earth" as promulgating a "false consciousness" concerning the distribution of the world's natural resources (201).[49] The globalizing platitude "We are all in the same boat," in Enzensberger's view, serves an ideological function: "[t]he aim is to deny once and for all that little difference between first class and steerage, between the bridge and the engine room" (201).[50] The denial of class differences in the rhetorical gesture of global unity legitimizes those differences and the exploitation that underlies them. As Enzensberger sees it, ecology is a unique concern of the middle class (196), and its purely ideological metaphors should be abandoned in favor of a sensitive analysis of "social variables" (223), the "abstract statement" replaced by an "examination of [the] concrete situation" (207).

The emphasis on the category of difference reemerges in *Der Weg ins Freie* (1975; The way out), a collection of five biographies, two on Latin American figures, that describe attempts to escape from situations of domination, including slavery, the insane asylum, the military, and prison. In his afterword to the volume Enzensberger delivers an insightful meditation on the methodological, philosophical, and political problems of documentary literature. The concept of the document, he argues, reflects a vague desire to recover a lost authenticity, "as if, by means of the microphone or the camera, it could be recovered just like that" (114). In effect, such an ideal of authenticity is inevitably tainted by the intervention of technical recording apparatus and by the necessary and oftentimes unacknowledged choices of the interviewer. In Enzensberger's view, the researcher's language, gestures, and class background (I would add race, culture, gender, and age) influence profoundly what his or her interlocutors reveal and conceal (114); further, the ethnographer is "not an authority but himself a mediator, contaminated by exemplary precursors and expectations, models, regulations, strategies of intimidation . . ." (114; ellipsis in original). Given such multileveled complications, the aim of documentary truth amounts to nothing more than a methodological "dead end" (113).[51] In fact, Enzensberger continues, the worst error that the documentary writer can commit is to "plan" his material, to rob it of its contradictory nature or to subsume it under an abstract theory in the interest of scientific presentation (115). Alternatively, the only possible solution for the writer who has recognized his complicity and limitation is to produce a text deliberately riddled with contradictions: "[t]he alternative to this would be . . . to pay attention precisely to the ruptures and rifts in the text, to the discontinuities and inconsistencies, to what is skipped over, left out, and contradictory" (115).[52]

Where *Das Verhör von Habana* offered an apparently monolithic interpretive model and presented an attempt to subsume its material under programmatic theory, the author now insists on those aspects of reality that refuse to be tamed—on discontinuities, contradictions, ruptures that remain unmended in the final literary product. "Zwei Randbemerkungen zum Weltuntergang" (1978; "Two Notes on the End of the World") launches further arguments for the move away from a projected rational mastery and toward a recognition and acceptance of the essential unruliness of experience. Here the author enumerates the philosophical beliefs, grounded in the traditions of the Enlightenment and German Idealism, that no longer obtain:

> that there is no world spirit; that we do not know the laws of history; that even the class struggle is an "indigenous" process, which no vanguard can consciously plan and lead; that social evolution, like natural evolution, has no subject and is therefore unpredictable; that consequently, when we act politically, we never manage to achieve what we had in mind, but rather something quite different, which at one time we could not even have imagined; and that the crisis of all positive utopias has its basis precisely in this fact. (158–59)

In stark contrast to the purported ideological certainty of *Das Verhör von Habana*, we hear now that there are no easy answers: no formulas for historical progress or for revolutionary change, no viable leadership, no guaranteed goals, and no transcendent truth.

Enzensberger chides the "customary ideological critique" (158) for its inability to deal directly with the apocalyptic visions that accompany the disintegration of social utopias and links this inability to an all-too-rigid adherence to the ideal of reason. "Has it not struck you," he asks, "that [ideological critique] has long since ceased to explain things that do not fit its schemas, and started to taboo them instead? . . . Their maxims are: (1) never concede anything; (2) reduce the unfamiliar to the familiar; (3) always think only with the head; (4) the unconscious must do what it is told" (158). With Enzensberger's critique arises an adamant recognition of the existence of "the unfamiliar" and "the unconscious" as necessary, hitherto exorcised sociopolitical (and, I would add, poetic) forces. Visions of the future, the wishful or fearful projections of society, are no longer the products of a sovereign political reason but rather the involuntary expressions of a collective fantasy, a social unconscious (157).

If these essays on political ecology, apocalypse, and the aporia of documentary literature record Enzensberger's intellectual shifts from *Das Verhör von Habana* to *Der Untergang der Titanic*, a brief poem devoted to Alexander von Humboldt marks an emotional change ("A. v. H. [1769–1859]"). Significantly, Enzensberger houses his tribute to the German explorer of the New World in a textual edifice characterized by ambivalence: the volume of poems entitled *Mausoleum* promises a gallery of ballads devoted to scientists, artists, and political and religious figures who have served the "history of progress" (subtitle), yet the individual texts question the actual progressive nature or effect of their contributions. The invention of the guillotine, for example, can hardly be seen as an unequivocal case of social progress. Humboldt's project of research on the natural and cultural phenomena of South America is thereby immediately cast in a dubious light. Indeed, the poem in its opening lines evokes the same epistemological and political paradox expressed in different form in the afterword to *Der Weg ins Freie*:

> Outside, painted in oil and very blue, the faraway peaks,
> the palms,

the naked savages: inside, in the shade of the leafy hut,
the walls hung with skins and giant ferns, a gaudy macaw
perched on the pack-saddle, the companion in the
    background held a blossom
under the magnifier, orchids were strewn on the crates of
    books,
the table was covered the plantains, maps, and instruments:
the artificial horizon, the compass, the microscope, the
    theodolite,
and shiny brassy, the reflecting sextant with the silvery
    limbus;
bright in the middle, on his camp-chair, sat the celebrated
    geognost
in his laboratory, in the jungle, in oil, on the banks of the
    Orinoco. (62)[53]

Interesting is the stance of the scientist toward his objects of in-quiry. The opening description of a painting establishes a contrast between the landscape and the wild natives, who are "outside" and painted in oil, and the "inside" of the researcher's tent, which con-tains scientific instruments and selected fragments of the foreign world that surrounds it—pelts and ferns, flowers and birds. The indigenous world of South America remains—or is kept—safely at a distance and is, it appears, only artificially present ("painted in oil") to the scientist, while the presumably "real" world of the Eu-ropean is isolated, sheltered, and ordered through the skilled use of scientific tools. But the poem goes on to point to the aestheti-cized nature of the scenario of the researcher in the wild: in the end, it is not just the landscape in the far background but also the geographer in his laboratory who is rendered "in oil." The dispas-sionate scientist, no less than the strange New World he charts, is an artistic construction for our contemplation, a cultural fiction.

Furthermore, not only does Enzensberger question the in-tegrity of the scientific project that seeks to study another culture in such mechanical and isolated a manner. The project is imbued with colonialist overtones. The rhetoric of conquest can be heard, for example, in the sovereign tone of Humboldt's investigations, ultimately a project of mastery: "[t]he terra incognita melted like snow under his gazes. / He cast his net of curves and coordinates over the last glaciers, / the bleakest mountains" (62). What remains conspicuously missing is the very sense of the unknown and unconscious, aspects of experience that defy rational mastery, that Enzensberger recognized in his essays around this time. The colonialist ethnographic project, like the attempt in *Das Verhör von Habana* to dissect the ideology of the bourgeois class, envisions rational analysis as always perfectly adequate to the task of understanding (thus taming) the social and natural world, no matter how foreign it may be.

The parallel between Humboldt's initial stance as represented in the poem and the stated project of *Das Verhör von Habana* gains force through the connection in both texts to the idea of social revolution. It is not coincidental that Humboldt's clothing bears the mark of the French Revolution and of times during which the French Republic hoped to export its revolution to the Caribbean (65). The gesture of reasoned analysis and emancipation in both texts is associated closely with a larger revolutionary project. But while *Das Verhör von Habana* (through the inclusion of ambiguous or contradictory material at its margins) allows only slight disturbances of this normative endeavor, the poem "A. v. H." moves on and beyond to a time when revolution has been abandoned.

In contrast to the omnipotent gesture of the poem's opening lines, the image of Humboldt at the text's conclusion strikes a tone of personal defeat and resignation:

Then the reactionaries won. Back to German wretchedness.
  A gentleman-
in-waiting, a reader, i.e., flunky at Potsdam's court.
. . . .
. . . In this heavily policed
sandy waste, he often thought about the Tropics. Why
  were they so bewitching?
. . . . / . . .
. . . A healthy man he, an unwitting carrier
of the disease, a selfless harbinger of plundering, a courier

who didn't realize he had come to announce the
  annihilation
of what he lovingly painted until ninety, in his *Views of
  Nature*. (65–66)

Gone is the confidence of the earlier time when the German scientist exercised a supposedly unchallenged rule over his new world. In a period of political reaction and retreat into the misery of a complicitous life in Berlin, all that is left is nostalgia for the tropics and the painful realization that the earlier project, fueled by naive illusions, served to record and to prophesy the end of its exotic other world. This describes exactly the emotional position of the authorial consciousness in *Der Untergang der Titanic*.

Interestingly, Enzensberger's work celebrates its own literary debt to the author of the *Divine Comedy*: *Der Untergang der Titanic*, subtitled "A Comedy" (Enzensberger's English translation reads: "A Poem") and composed of thirty-three cantos, announces formal ties to Dante in unmistakable terms.[54] Thematically as well, the link is explicit and intricately woven: in the final canto, for example, the warnings of the authorial "I" regarding impending catastrophe fall on uninterested ears, including those of a man dressed in white (the author as Dante reincarnate) carrying the lost first version of the *Titanic* text (97). While Weiss's writings on Dante resolved a personal crisis and initiated the period of his documentary plays on the Third World, Enzensberger's preoccupation with the Italian poet effectively ends his involvement with Cuba and signals a new dilemma: in Enzensberger's text, Dante, a passenger on the *Titanic* (43), is not among the list of survivors aboard its last lifeboat (72).

The text incorporates the complex history of its making, a history that moves, in a striking reversal of Weiss's development, from a time of revolutionary euphoria to a present situation of isolation and resignation. Cuba, as a Communist island of the Third World defying the ideological and economic dictates of its powerful northern neighbor (one thinks of the unsuccessful Bay of Pigs invasion and Castro's handling of the counterrevolutionaries that Enzensberger seemed to celebrate in *Das Verhör von Habana*), provides the background against which the author's changed positions are registered.

Crucial are the third and fourth cantos, in which the author (following the text's fiction that identifies "I" as Enzensberger) locates himself at two distinct moments of history: the revolutionary atmosphere of Havana in 1969; and the present, 1977, in a cold and nonrevolutionary Berlin. In the earlier time, caught up in revolutionary passion and in the zeal of his ambition, the author engaged in discussions with other European intellectuals on the tropical island about Horkheimer, Stalin, and Dante (9–10). Back then, in the context of socialist victory in Cuba and with high expectations for the future, the idealistic poet began a text on the sinking of the *Titanic*, symbol for the capitalist world:

> . . . I worked at *The Sinking of the Titanic*.
>
> . . . .
>
> . . . I remember us thinking:
> Tomorrow things will be better, and if not
> tomorrow, then the day after.
>
> . . . .
>
> . . . Yes, everything
> was going to be quite different.
> A marvelous feeling. (8)

Now, from his later vantage point in a wintry Berlin, an older author looks back on his youthful self and on his earlier faith in revolutionary progress with bemusement, irony, and nostalgia.[55] The text we read is not the one begun in 1969 but one written in the narrative present, not in a revolutionary Cuba but in a Berlin that smells (as does the fictional author) of its progressive decay, "of old cartridge cases, / of the East, of sulfur, of disinfectant" (8). The older Enzensberger writes out of the painful realization that the earlier euphoria and ambition were misplaced—"We did not know / that the party had finished long ago" (9)—and appends a melancholy lyric interlude acknowledging the loss of hair, nerves, time, innocence, and desire (11).[56]

It is significant that the Enzensberger of 1977 looks back on, and tries to reconstruct, the lost text of 1969. The poem maintains the claim that the earlier version, written in pencil in a black oilcloth notebook, disappeared in the mail en route from Havana to Paris (13). Literally lost at sea, the earlier text (and the revolutionary ideals that provided its inspiration) becomes a mythical *Titanic* that the author struggles, in halting and self-reflective manner, to salvage. The present poem on the sinking of the *Titanic* is thus simulta-neously a text about the loss of an original creation, its youthful idealism, and the naive authorial persona of the earlier time: the author of *Der Untergang der Titanic*, in a wintry Berlin that is it-self a sinking European *Titanic* (it is two degrees below zero both in Berlin and on the luxury liner at the time of its sinking [18, 26]), writes nostalgically of the author of *Das Verhör von Habana*, who had basked in the warm certainty of his beliefs.[57]

In both its form and thematic content the text addresses the possibility of philosophical or political certainty and the ability of the poet to capture truth in his writing. Notably, Enzens-berger's project disputes the very qualities that Weiss perceived and thought to emulate in Dante; the evocation of Dante as a passen-ger on board a sinking ship creates the occasion for a reevaluation of the poet's claim to a total vision of the world. For Enzensberger writing in 1977, in contrast to Weiss, who began his Third World projects in the late 1960s, the times are decidedly nonrevolutionary, and an apparently resignative vision of impending doom displaces the earlier belief in the inevitability of political revolution.

The key image is that of the iceberg, which asserts its presence from beginning to end. Already in Havana the poet records the prophetic image of the white mass:

> I saw the iceberg, looming high
> and cold, like a cold fata morgana,
> it drifted slowly, irrevocably,
> white, nearer to me. (10)[58]

Years later in Berlin, he writes to distract himself from thoughts of the impending end. Like the passengers of the *Titanic*, the poet is (or imagines himself to be) unmoved by the fate that awaits, yet the shared subzero temperature links him firmly to their plight. His wishful and emphatic denial, "There is no iceberg in sight" (18), is belied by the following lyric interlude, "The Iceberg," which explores the meaning of the unseen ice: it approaches "irrevocably," it has "no future," "[i]t does not make progress," "it has no off-spring"; "[i]t leaves nothing behind. / It disappears to perfection" (19–21). Perfect in the absolute quality of its disappearance, leaving no change behind, much less change of a positive kind, the iceberg as an image of complete and total end contradicts any notion of progressive enlightenment. Significant here is the rising water that invades even the isolated Berlin apartment at the end of the text (89, 95). The text evokes, or seems to evoke, a sense of imminent and inescapable disaster, of slow, silent, and torturous death. There was and will be no revolution, not on the *Titanic*, not in Cuba, not in Berlin.

Yet like *Das Verhör von Habana*, which offered a facade of absolute certainty only to have it erode, the later text harbors its own anomalies. Against an overwhelming impression of disaster and despair, the poem records instances of resistance—anecdotes of small, individual acts of defiance, and the presence of an enigmatic "Third World" that refuses to go down with the ship. Figures of the Third World emerge prominently just after the sinking of the *Titanic* at midpoint (cantos 16–18). In canto 19 a Japanese man, strapped to a door, is saved. Canto 20, sung in verse with strong dialect overtones and based, according to the author's footnote, on American black narratives from the streets of Philadelphia (55), tells the story of the black man Shine who abandons his post in the boiler room as soon as he is in danger of drowning. Refusing to stay on board either for money or for sex, Shine abandons ship and swims to safety. Similarly, canto 24 describes the inexplicable invasion of stereotypical Third World figures on deck—barbarically painted olive faces, women with gold armbands, naked children, old men in turbans carrying sabers and silver daggers—who come alive out of the exotic paintings that adorn the ship (66) and who disappear, in equally mysterious fashion, on the morning of 14 April, just before the final catastrophe (67). Finally, five mysterious Chinese, stowaways on the *Titanic*, emerge in the next canto on the floor of the last lifeboat (73).

While in Enzensberger's vision of a present-day *Titanic* the lower decks of the ship are filled with Turkish guest workers (Jamaicans and Chicanos in the English translation), Eskimos, Palestinians, Asians, Arabs, and the unemployed (63, 77, 78, 80), the figures representing a "Third World" are also tenacious survivors who, positioned in the belly of the ship and unlike the European intellectuals, who remain euphorically ignorant (8–9), are the first to notice signs of danger (4). From the point of view of the respectable white passengers, their presence is inexplicable, yet their strength is unquestioned; in contrast to the doomed Europeans, they appear in the poetic imagination of their epic narrator to escape the inevitability of the disaster.[59]

Other unincorporated, anomalous images are offered in the tenth and seventeenth cantos. In canto 10 the reader is made to peer into the portholes of the *Titanic* to observe a heated exchange between a Russian émigré, "B.," who preaches "the gospel of revolution" while remaining oblivious to icebergs and shipwrecks, and a British textile manufacturer who argues for the necessity of discipline and authority (32). Again the text insists on the nonrevolutionary situation on board the sinking ship: the discussion ends without resolution, neither interlocutor is seen on a lifeboat, nothing further is heard from them (33). But again, against a dominant impression of European incapacity, the lyric interlude between the tenth and eleventh cantos interjects a puzzling image of resistance: "The Reprieve" tells of an old man who turns his garden hose upon a wall of approaching volcanic lava, inspiring a mass action of neighbors and schoolchildren, who stop the flow of molten earth, symbolically halting for a time "the Decline of Western Civilization" (34). Canto 17, occupying the structural center of the text, offers a related image and counterimage. The canto documents the sinking of the ship, which proceeds with chilling order, discipline, and decorum ("We are sinking without a sound. . . . / No disputes, no squabbles. Muted dialogues. / After you, sir" [45]). But the lyric text that follows, "Cold Comfort," offers enigmatic examples of resistance in a time of widespread social strife and injustice: the waiter who listens patiently to the lamentations of an impotent man, the bigoted spinster who shelters a deserter, the kidnapper who unexpectedly ceases his criminal activities (47). The failed idol of reason is replaced by simple, individual, and ultimately inexplicable demonstrations of humanity; grand revolutionary ideals, by spontaneous acts performed by everyday people (cf. Götz Müller 264–65):

> Unfortunately we cannot refrain
> from rape and from ravishment,
> from nailing each other down
> to the nearest crosswalk
> and from gobbling up the remains.
> To find out why would be nice,
> balm on the wounds of Reason.
>
> We are annoyed but not surprised
> by our daily atrocities.
> What we find puzzling
> are mild ministrations,
> groundless generosity
> and angelical sweetness. (47)

That both the Third World figures and such small acts by nameless individuals remain unexplained is deliberate. Remaining stubbornly beyond the reaches of an ordering, disciplining reason, such images represent a realm of unincorporated life that is in principle "puzzling" — the "unfamiliar" and "unconscious" that Enzensberger acknowledges in the essays that separate *Der Untergang der Titanic* and *Das Verhör von Habana*. This forces a reexamination of the poetic project, modeled after Dante, articulated by Weiss, and apparently emulated in Enzensberger's Bay of Pigs drama, of the sovereign author who offers a complete picture of the world in which, given the correct perspective, everything is illuminated and nothing hidden.

Enzensberger addresses the identity and function of the poet throughout his text on the sinking of Western ideals. The evocation of Dante is not coincidental. But while the Italian poet exposed the workings of his world with linguistic elegance, moral certainty, and unassailable integrity, Enzensberger's poet stam-

mers, jabbers, mixes, and contaminates (42), proving himself
artistically and politically untrustworthy. Immediately following
the three cantos in the center of the text that record the actual sinking of the ship, a poem offers, disconcertingly, "Further Reasons
Why Poets Do Not Tell the Truth":

> Because words come always
> too late or too soon.
> Because it is someone else,
> always someone else,
> who does the talking,
> and because he
> who is being talked about,
> keeps his silence. (50)

Poets lie necessarily and inescapably, because their words cannot
speak for or render the experiences of others; in this view, the poet
is bound by his private experience and identity and cannot attain a
sovereign stance from which to survey the world. Thus the text disputes even its ability to speak of the *Titanic* and casts any attempt
to do so as bad faith and deception.[60]

Significantly, the idea of the poet as deceiver is developed at
two places in the text that construct a frame for the fragmented
depiction of the *Titanic* catastrophe. Cantos 6 through 7 and 24,
offering discussions of paintings, thematize their status as poetological meditations within the text. In the sixth canto the poet
(as the older Enzensberger in his Berlin apartment) is at work
remembering and reconstructing the earlier text that has been ir-
retrievably lost: "it is my pleasure to recover a text / that probably
never existed. I fake my own work, / I restore my images" (18).
Notably, not only the existence of the earlier text but also the
present poetic work is put into question; the poet does not create an original text but is a restorer, a forger of sorts.[61] Indeed,
if all art comprises an act of restoration or forgery, the notion of
any "original" truth falls equally into jeopardy. The lyric text following canto 7 makes exactly this point. "Last Supper. Venetian.
Sixteenth Century" records the thoughts of a painter who, in order

to escape persecution from the Inquisition, renames and secularizes his all too pleasureful *Last Supper* (23–25). In his painting the artist creates a fanciful turtle on the marble floor that, with imagined criticisms and sophistic interpretations ringing in his ears, he then hides under carefully painted black, green, and pink tile. In both cantos the finished work of art does not reveal but conceals and thus distorts its poetic truth; the artist does not uncover but rather covers up.[62]

The corresponding poem following canto 24, "The Rape of Suleika. Dutch, late 19th Century," iterates the concept of the artist as restorer and forger in the figure of Salomon Pollock. In Pollock's view there are no "Old Masters" (68), only works that have been reconstructed "by means of resin, / wax and saliva" (69). Pollock's artistry lies in his paradoxical ability to recover "things that never existed"; his works, "a fraud, sublime," display his genius on the walls of the Rijksmuseum (69). The similarity is deliberate to the aging Enzensberger, who recreates (restores) a lost text that perhaps never existed (18). And like the sixteenth-century painter who takes subversive delight in his unseen turtle, Pollock too allows himself a small corner of his works in which his private "truth" is offered, like a cryptic signature. Significantly, this truth is the blurred, soiled, indistinguishable "original" that is left unrestored and unrecreated:

> a tiny square left untouched in a corner,
> showing off the filth of the centuries,
> the muddle, the ever imperfect remorse
> of posterity, which is beyond redemption.
> I used to spend hours and hours
> pondering this dark remnant,
> which exposes me and my manipulations. (70)

Poets and painters lie, and "[t]he truth, a dark window down there / in the corner, the truth is mute" (71) — such an understanding of the nature of art and the role of the artist overturns completely the Dante ideal emulated by Peter Weiss.[63]

Given the text's fundamental philosophical and political ambivalence, it is surprising to note, nonetheless, its rigid formal structure. Indeed, we find the outlines of an unmistakably symmetrical order. The first and last cantos of the text (cantos 1 and 33) enact the emergence and continued survival of the poetic "I" that is both Dante and Enzensberger, signaling the centrality of notions of the poet and of poetic creation. The text is organized internally by the placement of four lyric descriptions of paintings (following cantos 2, 7, 24, and 29), paired thematically. The paintings "Apocalypse. Umbrian Master, about 1490" (canto 2) and "The Rest on the Flight. Flemish, 1521" (canto 29) thematize the common, deeply ingrained obliviousness to signs of disaster: in the first, daily life goes on unaffected while the painter renders his vision of the end of the world (6–7); in the second, the figures of the painting, as well as the viewer, are unable to see the one element that spells their imminent death (84–85). The inability to perceive, much less to contemplate or comprehend, the absolute end is amplified in the cases of the *Titanic* and of the European intellectuals who bask in a revolutionary Cuba.

The second pair of poems, the "Last Supper" of canto 7 and "The Rape of Suleika" of canto 24, focuses on the concept of the artist as restorer-forger. Within the space of the text framed by these poetological meditations (cantos 8–24) we find passages on impending death and the wait of the *Titanic* passengers (cantos 11–13), on the sinking of the ship (cantos 16–18, the structural center of the text), and on the isolated escape of Third World figures from the general disaster (cantos 19, 20, 24). The overall structure of the text reveals a set of internal frames, defined by the descriptions of paintings and focused on key thematic issues, that surround the symbolically central event of the sinking of a ship (the *Titanic*, Cuba, Berlin) with weighty ideological cargo.[64]

But despite the complex and almost mathematically precise structure of the text (and this is the very point of its rigidity), cracks and crevices develop and remain visible in the edifice. For one thing, the lyric passages interjected between cantos seem consistently to undermine and to ironize the power of the Dantesque form: the poem "The Iceberg," to take a jarring example, follows immediately upon the statement at the end of canto 6 that "[t]here is no iceberg in sight" (18). More importantly, the text is replete with unexplained, inexplicable images of foreign exoticism and resistance, images that remain stubbornly unincorporated, in thematic as well as structural terms, in the main narratives of the sinking *Titanic* and the loss of the poet's revolutionary ideals. Figures of the Third World, small and generally overlooked acts of individual resistance, the turtle that comes to life only to be hidden under painted marble tile, or the smudged corner that is deliberately left unclarified and unrepaired—such riddles and rifts in the text signal the existence of things beyond the reach of rational comprehension and artistic mastery. Enzensberger's *Der Untergang der Titanic* becomes, in this perspective, a text of ambivalence, uncertainty, and self-doubt, in spite of—perhaps by the very virtue of—the facade of Dantesque order and organization that it so carefully constructs.[65]

The fundamental difference between Weiss's overwhelming sobriety and seriousness—his unwavering ability to perceive the world according to universal categories—and Enzensberger's destructive self-irony—in which all idealism is undermined by radical doubt—is reflected not only in the terms of their political debate but also in the themes and forms of their literary texts. From the preoccupation with Auschwitz and Dante to the monumental *Viet Nam Diskurs*, Weiss's work seeks above all to establish and to assert the author's identification with victims of worldwide oppression in their struggle for political emancipation. Arising out of a private crisis brought on by a belated confrontation with Auschwitz, Weiss's proclamations and gestures of solidarity serve to revise and recreate the author's identity as one based not on aesthetic withdrawal but on political opposition: with Auschwitz projected into a global, Manichaean confrontation between oppressors and oppressed, Weiss gives himself a second chance to assume the role of resistance fighter that he had eschewed earlier in life.

This relocation or recreation of the authorial self in the context of the Third World, understood as a globalized Auschwitz, reflects the centrality of the notions of sovereign consciousness and will for Peter Weiss. In his view, it is possible for a human being to overcome the history and the prejudices that have formed his or her self and to adopt a new identity and history, all through the equivalent processes of rational analysis and political education. Through the exercise of reason alone one arrives, as the example of Weiss's life and his *Gesang vom Lusitanischen Popanz* and *Viet Nam Diskurs* are meant to demonstrate, at the morally and politically correct vantage point from which individual (cultural, historical, racial) differences are transcended and universal humanity and solidarity embraced. Thus the author's identification with the victims of history is nothing less than an expansion and transcending of his previously limited and guilty self. The author stands shoulder to shoulder with the mine workers of Africa and the rice farmers of Asia; the vast differences that separate Europe from the continents of the Third World prove negligible in the face of universal ideals of humanity and reason.

While the Third World becomes in this manner the open, global arena for correct political and moral action for Peter Weiss, its role in Enzensberger's work is deliberately limiting. Weiss's self expands to embrace the struggles of oppressed peoples throughout the globe; in contrast, images of the Third World in Enzensberger's oeuvre serve to reduce, not to amplify, the scope and identity of the European self. If Weiss projects an authorial identity that encompasses literally the entire world and that finds itself everywhere at home in struggles of liberation, Enzensberger's work moves in the opposite direction, to focus increasingly on the painful reality of one's inescapable perspective, one's boundedness, one's complicity as European in the process of victimization against which Weiss so rightfully rages.

Even the apparently unequivocal support of the Cuban revolution expressed in *Das Verhör von Habana* and in the author's vehement and rhetorically powerful introduction to that text does not bear out, as contrary or ambivalent testimony in the interrogations and in the documentary appendices to the volume suspend any easy acceptance of the text's programmatic claims. Enzensberger's later questioning of the validity of documentary literature in general, on the grounds that documentation is always already distorted and skewed by the author's interests, articulates the highly problematic nature of the literary text when conceived as the attempt to render the world with complete accuracy. "Truth" for Enzensberger can be approached only by means of contradiction and discontinuity within the text. Thus the "Third World," rather than providing the stage for the enactment of morality and truth as is the case for Weiss, is represented in Enzensberger's *Der Untergang der Titanic* as a puzzle, a blank or smudged spot in the corner of the canvas, as small and almost unnoticed acts of possible resistance, or as mysterious figures that enter and exit without apparent reason. While the Third World in Weiss offers the opportunity to join and to identify completely and harmoniously with a larger world, the same realm of images in Enzensberger stands stubbornly outside and beyond the reach of the self, unincorporated into its system of rational understanding, deliberately unexplained, categorically inexplicable. For Weiss the Third World *is*, given sufficient political enlightenment, one's true self; for Enzensberger, it remains always mysterious and incomprehensible, evidence of one's inescapable limitation and bad faith.

Weiss's general stance vis-à-vis the Third World finds its ultimate expression in his project of a "world theater." In the attempt to offer a comprehensive and analytical portrait of the world-political situation (specifically, in dramas devoted to colonial struggles on each of the three continents of the Third World), Weiss is necessarily bound to certain beliefs or ideals that ground his Dantesque project. Underlying his vision is a faith in grand historical narratives, or grand dramatic conflicts, that set good against evil and oppressors against oppressed—a view of history and of political reality in which, given the proper insight, everything can be distilled into two clearly identifiable positions. As was the case for Anna Seghers, fronts can be drawn, allegiances unequivocally sworn. An unwavering belief in the power of human reason as the instrument of political and poetic analysis is simultaneously implied, a sovereign position to be attained through political education, from which all that seemed chaotic can be rendered with absolute moral and political certitude.

Enzensberger, in contrast, has located his position (and that of Europe as well) on a "periphery." Refusing to claim, much less to occupy, the center, Enzensberger's work in effect moves toward a renunciation of all historical and moral certainty: the revolution has not and will not take place; there is no world-historical subject moving toward the realization of its freedom; history does not develop toward particular ends that can be perceived and guided by astute intellectuals; reason guarantees nothing but rather serves to disfigure and distort truths that are rooted in the unconscious, in social fantasy, in contradictions and discontinuities, and that cannot and should not be excised in an effort to obtain an unobtainable clarity. Weiss finds in his Manichaean world of black and white, good and evil, and oppressors and oppressed the opportunity for identification with, and alignment on the side of, the victims of history who will eventually, necessarily, triumph. Through a process of identification that erases differences of race, class, and nationality, Weiss crafts a new authorial identity defined solely by its political commitment and its stance of resistance. For Enzensberger, in contrast, the self is slowly, inexorably reduced in stature. Excluded epistemologically, politically, and culturally from ever attaining a sovereign mastery of its world, the European self remains inescapably bound and limited by its interests and heritage and is left only the task of survival in decidedly nonrevolutionary times. Thus *Der Untergang der Titanic* ends not with a call for revolt and solidarity, as do Weiss's texts on colonialism in the Third World, but with a whimper:

> Business, I wail, as usual, everything lurching, everything
> under control, everything O.K., my fellow beings probably
>   drowned
> in the drizzle, a pity, never mind, I bewail them, so what?
> Dimly, hard to say why, I continue to wail, and to swim. (98)

There is no sovereign stance to be attained, no world-historical role to be played out.[66]

"World theater" versus "European periphery": Weiss locates in the realm of a revolutionary "Third World" a universal drama of good and evil in which all can participate. He becomes a freedom fighter, his Hölderlin in tune with the spirit of Che Guevara (Weiss, "Interview" 148; cf. Bohrer, "Revolution" 95). There is room for

heroism and courage, idealism and political commitment, solidarity and action in the world drama of oppressors against oppressed.
In contrast, Enzensberger claims not only that Europe and its authors belong on the periphery but that there is no center: as forger
and restorer in one, Enzensberger writes, reconstructing and remembering a text that perhaps never existed or that survives only
in smudged, indecipherable fragments or in mysterious presences
from a world of European fantasy. Seen as the text of Third World
revolution (or as the ideal of revolution projected onto the Third
World), the nonexistent original of Enzensberger's project remains absolutely irreconcilable with Weiss's world theater. Much
is at stake in their differences: for Weiss the Third World provides
the stage for the grand drama of history in which postwar Germany
can redeem its fascist past and forge its new identity for the future; for Enzensberger it is only the incomprehensible, hopelessly
smudged site that offers a slate for yet new forgeries and fantasies.

3

SOLIDARITY AND
ITS DISCONTENTS

Latin American Revolutions
in East German Drama

While West German authors wrote and debated about the Third World in the politically tumultuous years of the late 1960s, it is not until the early 1970s that a comparable engagement can be found among writers of the GDR. The year 1973, which marked the end of the Vietnam War and the publication of Peter Schneider's *Lenz*, offers a convenient date for the widely noted shift within West German literature from the political battles of the late 1960s (and the interest in anticolonialist and antiimperialist struggles in the Third World) toward subjectivity and introspection (Sareika, *Dritte* 9–10).[1] Remarkably, the Third World emerged as a major literary topic in the GDR in this same year in response to the overthrow of socialist Chilean president Salvador Allende.

As was the case for West Germany, the GDR's relationship to countries of the Third World had everything to do with its political and ideological identity. This underwent an important change in the early 1970s. Initially, East Germany's foreign relations with non-Communist countries were aimed at achieving official recognition of its status as an independent nation. In this endeavor, the GDR was severely hampered by West Germany's Hallstein doctrine, formulated in 1955, which called for the severing of economic and diplomatic contact with any country (with the exception of the Soviet Union) that established such ties with East Germany (Turner 87–88). The signing of the Basic Treaty (Grundlagenvertrag) with the Federal Republic of Germany in December 1972, however, normalized relationships between the two states and opened the door to legitimizing the GDR on an international scale. That same month, twenty-two countries, mostly from the Third World, established diplomatic relations with the East German state; forty-six countries followed the next year. In 1973 East Germany was admitted to the United Nations with status equal to that of the FRG; in 1974 formal diplomatic recognition was granted by the United States. With its political status secure and its international prestige enhanced, the GDR entered into a phase of active involvement with nations of the Third World (Sodaro 106–09).

Among Third World regions, Latin America held special significance for East Germany. Equipped with natural resources, an established infrastructure, and a skilled labor force, Latin American countries were emerging in the postwar era as economically and politically independent states with a growing influence in international politics. Strong nationalist movements and pro-Soviet Communist parties in every country made the region fertile ground for resistance against Western imperialism. Furthermore, Cuba's presence served as a reminder of the greatest defeat of U.S. foreign policy in the region (Uschner 42–44, 49; Bischof 641). With the apparent weakening of American economic and political influence in the area, as the GDR saw it, came the expanded neo-colonialist engagement of the GDR's ideological rival, the FRG — at stake in Latin America, in short, was the credibility of the Western capitalist system represented by the United States and by West Germany in its stead (Uschner 52–54; Bischof 642).

Of the Latin American nations, Chile earned a special place in the hearts of East Germans. After the electoral victory of Unidad Popular in the fall of 1970, diplomatic relations were established between Chile and the GDR, making Chile one of fewer than two dozen countries at the time that defied the Hallstein doctrine. Contacts were nurtured at all levels and to an extent that surpassed that of any other Third World tie. Reciprocal visits between East German and Chilean party officials, military delegations, trade unionists, and students and youth groups gave East German citizens of every age and occupation personal experience with socialist Chile (Bischof 645–47). Only in the case of this Latin American country did political rather than economic motivations determine trade relations: exports to Chile rose from 3 million marks in 1969 to 32 million in 1973; imports in the same period soared from 200,000 marks to over 69 million (Bischof 649). When the Allende government was overthrown in 1973, the putsch induced a national trauma for the GDR so intense that Erich Honecker characterized East Germans' solidarity with Chile as one of "the greatest social movements in the history of the GDR" (qtd. in Krüger 63). For months solidarity actions were organized on a massive scale in factories, cities, and universities (Bischof 653). Fourteen million signatures and 15 million postcards (in a country of 17 million) expressed protest against Pinochet; fifteen hundred Chilean exiles were granted asylum (Krüger 63–64).

Culturally, the early 1970s was a time of "thaw," when restrictions on artistic expression were loosened. The political stability that resulted from normalization and the hard-won economic achievements of the GDR in the 1960s, which had established it as tenth among the industrial nations of the world at the price of a depressed standard of living and severe restrictions on civil liberties, sparked expectations of domestic changes as well. When Erich Honecker succeeded Walter Ulbricht as first secretary in 1971, the promise seemed to be met: at the Fourth Plenary Conference of the Central Committee of the Socialist Unity Party (Sozialistische Einheitspartei Deutschlands, SED) later that year, Honecker announced that "[i]f one proceeds from solid premises of socialism, there can . . . be no taboos in the realm of art and literature" (qtd. in Huettich 151). Despite the vagueness of the requisite socialist tenets, the slogan of "no taboos" was taken as a signal of political and aesthetic openness on the part of the SED. Indeed, Honecker's proclamation was followed by the publication of one of the GDR's most critical literary works, Ulrich Plenzdorf's *Die neuen Leiden des jungen W.* (1972; *The New Sufferings of Young W.*). The atmosphere of aesthetic freedom, coupled with a stable sense of national identity and international status for the first time, generated optimism. The climate for GDR authors was aptly described by the scholar H. G. Huettich, whose book on East German theater ends at the onset of the "liberal 'Honecker era'": "[t]here seems to be a new dialogue, a give and take among the party, their authors, and the public, the extent of which is quite novel in the GDR" (153–54).

The dialogue, as it turned out, would be shortlived. But the brief period of liberalization coincided with, and allowed for, the beginning of a provocative and complex literary engagement with Third World issues.

In the German Democratic Republic, international solidarity in the fight against imperialism was, in the words of the general secretary of the Solidarity Committee, "both state politics and a matter of the heart for all citizens" (Krüger 64).[2] Firmly established in the GDR constitution and in the program of the SED as a fundamental principle of the East German state (Krüger 52; *Kleines* 777), active support for revolutionary struggles in Africa, Asia, and Latin America included direct financial assistance; mass letter-writing campaigns; contributions of food, equipment, and supplies; services such as hospital care and teacher and technical training; and political asylum.[3]

Under the banner of antiimperialism and international solidarity, the GDR lay claim to a progressive tradition of German humanism and antifascism, while the Federal Republic was painted as an imperialist, neocolonial power representing the interests of monopoly capital. The rhetoric was especially vehement with regard to involvement in Latin America. Here, for example, a typical statement taken from a journal on foreign policy from 1979: "[t]he imperialism of the FRG is the second largest foreign exploiter of the Latin American peoples today. . . . While the Latin American policies of the FRG have an imperialist, expansionist, and antiprogressive character, the relations of the GDR to the Latin American states have been defined for thirty years by the principles of equal rights, mutual advantage, and antiimperialist solidarity" (Uschner 54).[4] A historical continuity was asserted between the Federal Republic and the colonial and imperial endeavors of Germany up through World War II (Uschner 53; Bischof 642); with regard to Latin America the GDR claimed for itself, in contrast, the "progressive" tradition of German-Latin American relations "from A[lexander] von Humboldt, to the émigré generation of 1848 and the victims driven out by Bismarck's antisocialist legislation, to the effects of antifascist emigration" (Bischof 651).

For GDR writers, solidarity with the Third World became a political and literary program of major proportions following the American-backed military overthrow of Allende's socialist government in Chile in September 1973.[5] Immediately the Writers Association published an unconditional, impassioned denunciation of the putsch (Präsidium). Expressions of outrage, grief, and solidarity marked speech after speech at the Seventh Writers Congress in November 1973,[6] and the issues of the association's journal, *Neue Deutsche Literatur*, were filled the following year with literature from or about Chile by writers such as Alejo Carpentier, Julio Cortázar, Christa Wolf, Stephan Hermlin, Fritz Rudolf Fries, and Volker Braun (January, July, September, November 1974; February 1975). *Sinn und Form*, the journal of the GDR Academy of Arts, devoted an issue in 1973 to Latin American literature, including works by Neruda, Cortázar, García Márquez, Octavio Paz, and Ernesto Cardenal, as well as political songs, myths, and Quechuan lyric (*Sinn und Form* 25.3); in early 1974 the journal published responses to the military putsch in Chile and to the death of Pablo Neruda (*Sinn und Form* 26.1).[7] In 1979, in reaction to events in Nicaragua and El Salvador, both journals produced special issues on Latin American literature and politics featuring literary works and essays on the revolutionary Christian commune founded by Ernesto Cardenal in Solentiname, the Chilean singer Victor Jara, the new Chilean folksong movement, and the development of the Latin American novel, as well as the text of Heiner Müller's *Der Auftrag: Erinnerung an eine Revolution* (*The Task*) on revolution in the Caribbean (*Sinn und Form* 31.6; *Neue Deutsche Literatur* December 1979). The commitment to solidarity was still strongly visible two years later, when *Sinn und Form* presented major contributions by Alejo Carpentier and Carlos Fuentes on the Latin American novel, and *Neue Deutsche Literatur* published yet another special issue on Chile (*Sinn und Form* 33.6; *Neue Deutsche Literatur* December 1981).

During this period from 1973 to the early 1980s, the subject of Western imperialism and Third World revolution is treated with noticeable regularity in East German dramatic literature. Forming the common concern of texts as different as Rainer Kerndl's *Nacht mit Kompromissen* (1976; Night with compromises), depicting the revolutionary engagement of a German journalist in response to events in Chile, and Heiner Müller's dramatic poem *Verkommenes Ufer Medeamaterial Landschaft mit Argonauten* (1982; *Despoiled Shore Medeamaterial Landscape with Argonauts*), on the revenge of the barbarian Medea against the mythical "colonialist" Jason, the question of the Third World and the history of European involvement in it constitutes a major theme of GDR drama in the 1970s.[8] The list of relevant works on Latin America alone, for example, includes Volker Braun's *Guevara oder Der Sonnenstaat* (Guevara: Or, the sun state) and Peter Hacks's *Die Fische* (The fish), both from 1975, and Claus Hammel's *Humboldt und Bolívar oder Der Neue Continent* (Humboldt and Bolívar: Or, the new continent) and Heiner Müller's *Der Auftrag*, from 1979.

Here I am concerned with the specific status of the "Third World," in this case Latin America, in East German literary works written in the spirit of political solidarity. Hermann Kant closed his address at the Seventh Writers Congress in 1973 with an appeal that all future literary endeavors speak "always a word for Chile as well" (47); Volker Braun ended his presentation with an affirmation of the battle against counterrevolution "on all borders of our potential Chiles" ("Literatur" 134). In their speeches "Chile" extends beyond the legal and geographic boundaries of the country to denote the fight, as Kant says, "for humanity and culture, for peace and socialism" (47). A number of questions arise with regard to the literary representation of this struggle in the Third World—with regard to the poetics and the unspoken politics of East German solidarity.

The GDR, following Moscow, rejected Third World attempts to construct a "third way" that would be neither capitalist nor socialist (Sodaro 110). Given this official line, does the expression of solidarity on the part of GDR authors signify a process of ideological incorporation, such that Latin American developments become kindred, "European" socialist revolutions displaced into a foreign time and setting? Or are revolutions in Latin America seen to follow an inherent, indigenous logic? Do the European intellectuals, who play key roles in the texts, serve to define a vanguard role for Europe, to demonstrate implicitly the historical and continued dominance of European philosophies on a global scale? Or do they illustrate the limitations and dangers of a political engagement that would portray itself in ideological or intellectual terms while remaining silent on issues of economic and political self-interest?

To what extent do these texts prescribe an identity and a politics to the Third World that, intentionally or not, legitimizes a supportive role for the GDR in keeping with the proclamations of the SED? Do we find in them the construction of a position of solidarity that serves imperialistic aims of its own? Alternatively, does the issue of Third World revolution offer an opportunity for authors to reflect critically on the flaws and failures of the European tradition, socialist as well as bourgeois or capitalist? That is, to what extent do these texts reflect on the necessary limitations, rather than on the obligations or advantages, of socialist solidarity, presenting the role of the GDR (or of Europe) in the Third World as inherently problematic?

In this chapter I explore these questions in an extended treatment of Claus Hammel's *Humboldt und Bolívar oder Der Neue Continent* and Peter Hacks's *Die Fische*, which depict, more directly than other texts, the encounter of Europeans and the Spanish Americans and Indians of Latin America; in my concluding comments I expand the discussion to include Volker Braun's *Guevara oder Der Sonnenstaat* and Heiner Müller's *Der Auftrag*. The generally critical nature of this group of texts is surprising, given the usual Western categorization of Hammel and Hacks as politically affirmative and widely performed (thus as mediocre or uninteresting) authors, in contrast to the more critical, controversial, talented, and censored Braun and Müller (Emmerich 204–05).

Claus Hammel (b. 1932), one of the GDR's "career intellectuals" (Huettich 129), was theater critic for *Neues Deutschland* (1955–57), editor of *Neue Deutsche Literatur* (1957–58), and member of the editorial staff of *Sonntag* (1958–70), all leading cultural publications in the GDR, before joining the SED in 1967. His status as a playwright was established with the huge success of *Um neun an der Achterbahn* (1964; Nine o'clock at the roller coaster), which depicted a young woman who chooses the GDR as a moral and nurturing homeland after experiencing firsthand the coldness of human relationships in capitalist West Germany. Produced in thirty theaters and translated into Russian, Czech, and Hungarian, the play made Hammel an overnight sensation in the East. The key to his popularity lay in his talent for incorporating comic humor into the depiction of contemporary GDR society. Considered party-line and second-rate in the West (Emmerich 205), Hammel's entertaining comedies remained widely performed in the GDR through the 1980s. *Humboldt und Bolívar* was produced as soon as it was completed, at the Volkstheater in Rostock.

Peter Hacks (b. 1928) is generally seen as the affirmative counterpart to the critical and pessimistic Heiner Müller; they are the two literary giants of the generation of GDR playwrights born between 1924 and 1932, representing separate poles of aesthetic ideology and practice (Emmerich 363). The author of two plays in the early 1960s that explored problems in industrial and agricultural reform and that met with fierce criticism for their "bourgeois" and "vulgarized" viewpoints (*Die Sorgen und die Macht*, 1960, The cares and the power; *Moritz Tassow*, 1961) (Huettich 115–16, 136), Hacks turned soon afterward to an idealized program of socialist classicism (Emmerich 207–08). With his aesthetic change came an apparently political one: vilified in 1965 by Erich Honecker as an example of modernist, nihilistic, anarchic, and pornographic tendencies, Hacks was one of the few writers who supported the government's expatriation of the protest singer Wolf Biermann in 1976.[9] Prolific and talented, Hacks was the second most performed playwright in the GDR in 1980, surpassing Heiner Müller fourfold (Emmerich 361). *Die Fische*, interestingly enough, premiered in West Germany in 1978.

Conventionally placed at the opposite end of the aesthetic spectrum are Volker Braun (b. 1939) and Heiner Müller (1929–1995), for many Western scholars the most provocative and important playwrights of the GDR. Of the dramatists who remained in the East, Müller was probably the most embattled. From 1961, with a single performance of *Die Umsiedlerin* (The refugee) that led to his expulsion from the Writers Association, to 1973, with the production of *Zement* (*Cement*) at the Berliner Ensemble, Müller remained unperformed and largely unpublished in the GDR. Some of his most innovative work (e.g., *Der Bau*, 1965, The construction site; *Mauser*, 1970; *Die Hamletmaschine*, 1977, *Hamletmachine*) reached a GDR audience only by way of West German publication or in large-scale productions more than a decade after their completion. One notable exception was *Der Auftrag*, published in a special issue of *Sinn und Form* (where it was accessible to fellow intellectuals) and directed by Müller in the limited workshop space of the Volksbühne in East Berlin in 1980 — a cautious reception of a text whose content (solidarity and the failure of Western imperialism in the Third World) seemed praiseworthy enough. Braun, though never chastised through party channels as viciously as Müller had been, endured his share of production delays and de facto bans from the mid-1960s through the 1980s: *Guevara oder Der Sonnenstaat*, for example, was not produced in the GDR until 1984, nearly ten years after it was written. As different as these four authors are in their aesthetic philosophies and in their critical reception in the East and West, their works share a literary Third World discourse that raises profoundly troubling questions concerning the possibility of revolutionary solidarity.

In 1979, on the occasion of the thirtieth anniversary of the founding of the GDR, Claus Hammel wrote *Humboldt und Bolívar oder Der Neue Continent* to express his unconditional solidarity with the revolutionary struggles of the Latin American people.[10] At first glance, Hammel appears to offer a positive and unambiguous model for the stance of contemporary GDR solidarity: the meetings in Paris in 1804 and 1805 between the German naturalist Alexander von Humboldt, who had traveled and researched for five years in Spanish America, and the young Simón Bolívar, who would lead the fight for emancipation from Spanish colonialism in Venezuela, establish in the author's view a historical and moral bond between the GDR and the countries of Central and South America. Hammel explains: "When Humboldt and Bolívar met, Bolívar was still finding his way to himself and to his homeland, still far away from his later life's work as 'Libertador,' as liberator of South America. At this point he hardly knew his fatherland because he had spent most of his time in Europe. Humboldt meanwhile had just returned from his trip to America and was able to bring Bolívar's own country closer to him" ("Gespräch" 56). Just as Humboldt in Hammel's play instructs and inspires the future revolutionary Bolívar who will emancipate Latin America from colonialism, Hammel as playwright, in his imagined reconstruction of their historical encounter and in the parallel role of a modern Humboldt, offers his solidarity to the present-day Latin American liberators in their fight "for the second liberation—against North American imperialism" ("Gespräch" 56–57). Humboldt, whose "second discover[y]" of America is characterized, according to Hammel, "by peaceful, humanistic goals," in sharp contrast to the first discovery, which led to three centuries of Spanish colonial rule, thus becomes the model for the solidarity of contemporary intellectuals. Hammel states: "[I]n [Humboldt] I found for my play the vehicle for my own love" ("Gespräch" 56).

But both the figure of Humboldt and the play as a whole prove to be more complex than we might expect given Hammel's stated intentions. If in Hammel's fiction Humboldt provides Bolívar the knowledge of his country, the historical and political understanding that makes emancipation possible at all, we must ask whether the text does not project the continued domination of the Third World by Europe through a kind of imperialism of superior intellect. Furthermore, the positive and supportive nature of Humboldt's role is undermined by the scientist's tendentiously conciliatory politics. The play, for example, begins with a prologue that paints a tableau of colonial domination: the Spanish governor sits on his throne; a black child polishes his boots; a beautiful Indian maiden fans him with colorful feathers. Around the throne stand a Creole land baron with his wife, a white soldier, and a white foreman. Six Indians and black slaves offer gigantic horns of plenty filled with diamonds, fruits, gold, wood, silver, and tobacco, the riches of the native lands whose names are held high on banners: Venezuela, Cuba, Colombia, Ecuador, Peru, Mexico. Towering over the harmonious group is a gallows, from which hangs the corpse of a rebel. Entering the scene with notebook and magnifying glass, Humboldt investigates and categorizes the exotic bounty, "completely absorbed by science" (58,2). When the stage empties and five additional corpses at the foot of the gallows become visible, Humboldt turns away and proclaims, stubbornly, "During my sojourn in America I never came across any discontent" (58,2).[11] Pursuing scientific knowledge of the region while denying the devastating effects of colonialism on its human inhabitants, Humboldt would seem to offer a dubious intellectual or moral source both for Bolívar's revolutionary endeavors and for the GDR's promise of solidarity.

In his defense, Hammel takes care to demonstrate that the problematic Humboldt is constrained in his actions by specific historical conditions. On the eve of Napoleon's coronation, in a time of political restoration and European colonial aspirations, the scientist is wary of any political misuse of the vast knowledge of America that he alone possesses.[12] Accordingly, he explains his deliberate choice to withhold his research from the public and political arena:

> Picture for yourself . . . what would happen if politicians and researchers together seized hold of these countries, which for three hundred years have been the province of plunderers and policemen. Everything would be a thousand times worse. . . . Because then, you see, not only would despotism and the law of the stronger triumph, but scientific expertise would dispel their remaining moral qualms and, even further, provide the legitimation for their drive for higher returns. (63,2)[13]

Humboldt has not forgotten, he says, "what I owe the poor devils, whose circumstances I see all too clearly." It is not lack of concern for the people of Latin America, it turns out, but political pragmatism that has given rise to Humboldt's distanced attitude: "there are things under way that must come to an end before I make a decision" (63,2). Humboldt might display a Eurocentric bias in his belief that it is his (a European's) achievement to have seen through the oppressive conditions in Latin America, or that the fate of the revolution there depends on the political configuration in Europe or on his decision for or against it. Yet such views seem partially mitigated by Humboldt's key and precarious position in the society of Napoleonic France: the only European in the play with any sympathy for revolutionary struggle, Humboldt is vulnerable in the face of the nonrevolutionary European masses, who do not understand him, and an eager audience of the political and social ruling class, whose politics he abhors.[14]

No less problematic is Simón Bolívar, Humboldt's counterpart in the play. The young, not-yet-quite-revolutionary Latin American aristocrat appears as a Parisian flaneur who cultivates his most significant relationships with local prostitutes. Continually prodded by his mentors to desist from his amorous affairs, to educate himself, and to commit himself seriously to the cause of revolution, Bolívar offers—like Humboldt in his way—a dubious portrait of a revolutionary leader.

Not surprisingly, the encounter between the two is far from being the harmonious and joyful meeting of kindred spirits linked by a commitment to revolutionary ideals. From the first they clash. Although Bolívar is compelled to accept the returning European as the authoritative source of knowledge about his native land, he attacks the methodological and ideological blindness of the scientist who speaks of architectural ruins and earthquakes but not of political or social injustice: "[t]he incorruptibility of your judgment about rocks, plants, and insects is acclaimed. But I doubt that you have an eye for human beings. . . . No, you didn't come across any discontent. Because it doesn't lie out in the open like a shell cast up on the shore" (66,2). Humboldt is nothing but a tourist, Bolívar claims disdainfully (62,1), and he goes on to question point-blank the value of Humboldt's statements of empathy and support, which are not accompanied by concrete actions (66,2).

The European intellectual for his part provokes the young Bolívar, who knows neither himself nor his native country, with a barbed comment of his own: "[i]t would surely be strange if the people in those lands set their hopes on a hero from the Old World, of all places. Their liberator should definitely grow up out of their own ranks, if the situation requires it" (66,2). Humboldt refuses to play a direct role in the Latin American struggle against colonialism; indeed, explicitly rejecting the twentieth-century Orientalist model of the European expert who becomes a revolutionary prophet in an awakening new world (Said, *Orientalism* 226–54), Humboldt points instead to the necessity of a native hero of liberation. Made aware of the historical role waiting to be claimed, Bolívar then responds, promisingly, "The German is dodging. And he's lying. But he provokes me intensely" (66,2; omitted in the revised version).

Both figures are flawed, with each representing the potential corrective of the other. Bolívar's youthful naïveté and immaturity are complemented by Humboldt's expertise and political acumen; Humboldt's deliberate political passivity, grounded ultimately in ideals of bourgeois humanism, is counterbalanced by Bolívar's undisciplined revolutionary enthusiasm.[15] On the one hand, within the restorative and nonrevolutionary historical situation depicted in the play, the tension between the two figures remains necessarily unresolved: when Bolívar literally begs the European scientist for knowledge and enlightenment concerning his homeland—"[t]each me to know America as only you saw it. . . . [F]orce me to grasp what this is: my America" (68,3)—Humboldt clings resolutely to his ideal of a "world patriotism" (71,1) that isolates him from all specific, national issues.[16] The play's socialist readers, on the other hand, are meant to see that the resolution of the differences between Humboldt and Bolívar is reached, and the true nature of their bond revealed, in the politics embraced in a new time by the GDR toward Latin America. Humboldt's humanistic empathy is realized in its full potential, and its historical limitations are overcome, as Hammel would have it, in East Germany's active solidarity with the Latin American struggle against capitalist imperialism; in the time of the GDR, Humboldt's humanistic vision of world patriotism and Bolívar's revolutionary passion are finally united in an active commitment to socialist ideals on a global scale. It is in this sense that Hammel and his readers claim to find in the problematic Humboldt the affirmative precursor of the GDR's "committed and unsentimental solidarity" with the Third World.[17]

Hammel's text is intended to create a positive historical role for the GDR in Latin America, as elsewhere in the Third World, and to legitimize its commitment to active solidarity. Yet despite the unambiguous vision of GDR engagement it desires to project, the play leaves us with disturbing questions. The Eurocentric belief in Humboldt's authority regarding the land and people of Latin America goes unchallenged; further, his solidarity with their budding struggle against colonialism suffers serious limits. As we have seen, Humboldt's only recourse in a politically repressive European situation seems to lie in the fundamentally conservative stance of a universal humanism that dismisses the importance of local conflict. In Hammel's play, revolution in Latin America is never the straightforward matter—as Hammel initially described it—of Humboldt offering his expert knowledge to an uninformed, unformed Bolívar, who then emerges as the long-sought liberator of his people. In fact, the key to colonial emancipation lies in Bolívar's, and in the later GDR's, recognition of the limitations of Humboldt's position, as Bolívar formulates, finally, a revolutionary counterideology that signals the recognition of his cultural identity: "I will devote my wits to a region and to the preservation of its wretched egotistical trifles" (71,1).[18]

Paradoxically, the dominant image we are given is that of the European as principally nonrevolutionary. Restricted by reigning systems of power, the revolutionary-minded intellectuals of Europe are forced into political inactivity as a matter of sheer survival. And while Europe is seen as having abandoned its revolutionary ideals in favor of the restoration of a repressive order (symptomatic: Napoleon is crowned)—the contrast here is striking to Anna Seghers's narrative of European-led emancipation—we watch the promise of revolution displaced onto the Third World. Humboldt refuses to play a revolutionary role whether in Europe or in Latin America; Bolívar, however, goes off to liberate his people. Finally, we see not Europe helping the Third World but the Third World appropriating European traditions for its own ends. As Bolívar tells Humboldt, "I will have every book of yours that is of use to us translated into Spanish, and you will fight at my side without having to set foot outside the door of your self-imposed prison" (71,2).

If Hammel's project aims at the ideological legitimation of the GDR's active role in the Third World, it does so in a self-critical way. Not the supremacy of European knowledge is depicted but its limitation: European values are not imposed upon historical developments in the Third World, but instead the Third World liberators are seen to choose selectively from the European tradition—Bolívar will translate only those writings that are useful. Certainly the intellectual inspiration of the European tradition is never completely denied: in the play's epilogue the famous liberators of the Third World, from Toussaint L'Ouverture and Pancho Villa to Sandino, Guevara, and Allende, are joined by the French Inconnue (Unknown Woman), who enjoys the last, revolutionary, word in the play (71,3).[19] But if the spirit of the French Revolution goes abroad, it is translated and redefined according to local interests; Inconnue's Jacobin hat is worn above a black mask (69,2). Ultimately the superior knowledge of the European intellectual in Hammel's text is not used to justify or to enhance European political or economic supremacy in the Third World. Instead, Europe as a political force appears as supportive and secondary only, offering ambivalent intellectual goods to be used by Third World leaders for specific Third World purposes.

If *Humboldt und Bolívar* depicted a Europe that, equipped with its humanistic ideals and its budding natural science, was on the verge of literally worldwide colonial expansion, Peter Hacks chooses in his drama *Die Fische* a later historical period in which we see the emergence of forces that eventually bring the colonial era to an end.[20] The action of Hacks's play occurs in 1866, some sixty years after the fateful meeting of Bolívar and Humboldt, during the Mexican war of liberation from French rule. Once again, in the presentation of a European scientist's encounter with Latin America, the text explores the role of the European intellectual in the Third World.

Despite its historical setting, the immediate action of the play approaches the fantastic. A French natural scientist, Professor Simon, returns to a volcanic cave in Mexico, the site of an amazing discovery he made by accident seventeen years previously. There, in a deep lava basin, he had caught a member of a new species of fish, which, half-crazed with hunger, he devoured rather than categorized. To his shock, he later noticed a human breastbone in the fish's skeleton. The professor's scientific explanation ties the unusual finding to Aztec cult practices: young women who had become pregnant in violation of societal taboos were supposedly thrown into the water of the lava basin to drown. Simon surmises that some of the young mothers, in the throes of death, gave birth prematurely; some of the fetuses suffered from a gland abnormality that arrested their prenatal development, most crucially of their respiratory system; a small number were able to survive in the algae-rich water, eventually establishing a new species, the "*Homo pisciforme*" (194, 199–200). Simon explains:

> The human embryo is destined to become a human being. But before it reaches that point, it must undergo a series of transformations. It begins as an amoeba, changes into the lowest multicellular creature, and so forth. In a certain larval state it is something very similar to a fish. . . . [These fish] are nothing but the descendants of the larvae of those drowned pregnant women, which, as an exception, did not perish outside the womb, but instead reached sexual maturity. These fish are human embryos capable of reproducing. Fetal fathers or mothers. (199)

If nineteenth-century exploration writing constructed the discursive subjects (or, rather, the objects) that legitimized European colonial expansion, Simon's theory seems to provide a perfect example: in the Third World, the superior European discovers a prehuman species, creatures who are the product of an abnormal arrestment—itself the result of barbaric cultural practices!—in their development into fully human beings. The modern-day descendants of the Aztecs, as Simon would have it, are subhumans capable of reproducing.[21]

The French scientist plans to return with new specimens of the fish to Paris, where he will, scientifically, complete their evolution into human beings. (His project would appear to reverse the phenomenon of slavery, in that it brings hardy natives not to the New World to become slaves but to Europe to become human.) Simon has, in fact, living proof of the feasibility of his endeavor: his assistant Diego, we learn, is a former volcanic Aztec fish, spawned in the Mexican cave basin but "born" into the human world in Paris (208). Diego's evolution, Simon relates, was difficult. At first he tried to encourage the fish's development by gradually reducing the level of water in its container, but without result: "[t]he beast, instead of exercising its lungs, languished away in complete calm. It seemed like stubbornness. It was resisting becoming a human being" (209). To overcome the "beast's" (the native's) reluctance to become human (i.e., French), the professor was forced to resort to more aggressive tactics; with a series of injections and heat shocks, Simon turned Diego's watery, larval existence into a living hell, and the recalcitrant animal responded as desired. Simon concludes, "They don't want to become humans. They have to be forced, from within and from without. No ascension except through transformation. No transformation except through force and necessity" (211). One can easily translate Simon's reflection into another discourse: the natives are too lazy and too ignorant to change themselves; it is the humanitarian duty of the Europeans to force them to adopt civilized ways.

Simon's treatment of the humanized Diego, no less than his treatment of the New World fish, reveals the inhumanity of the European's civilizing mission. Not surprisingly, Diego, as a fully developed human being, speaks perfect French. Interestingly enough, this ability defines even for Diego a necessary aspect of his newly achieved humanity: "French," he explains (and one should hear through him the voice of his mentor, Simon), ". . . is the means of expression through which educated people are accustomed to communicate" (206). But the assimilated colonial Diego, despite his biological perfection and his French rebirth and manners, is still far from being considered the equal of a Frenchman. His first appearance in the play corrects any such mistaken assumptions. Diego arrives with Simon at the volcanic cave "loaded up with tools, sacks, tin containers" (173); he is not only Simon's well-trained assistant who competently performs all of the work involved in capturing new specimens in the cave basin, but he must function as Simon's pack animal as well. As Simon's coworker he is, Simon acknowledges, "invaluable" (literally "unpayable"), yet the word has an ironic double meaning: scientifically priceless as an assistant but still an Indian, Diego does not deserve to be, and is not, paid for his work (197). The New World native, it seems, has evolved under the professor's aggressive tutelage from cold-blooded animal to warm-blooded slave. When Diego dies, ironically at the hands of a French officer who takes the French-speaking Indian to be a spy, Simon regrets only that he is unable to preserve the corpse for further study and remarks coolly, "[H]e is really nothing more than a completely ordinary dead native" (213).[22]

While the remorselessly imperialistic attitude of the European intellectual toward the New World is revealed through the figure of Professor Simon, Hacks also explores the reciprocal vision, the views of the Mexicans toward the French, in his depiction of the wealthy landowners Ologa, Eraso, and Castillos, officers in the Mexican army of the emperor Maximilian. The play begins with their conversation over dinner. Eraso explains his decision to fight against the popularly elected president Juárez, whose politics he in fact supports: the Indian workers in his mines favor Juárez, and "[t]he war is aimed," Eraso points out, "as in Cortés's time, against the natives" (171). Ologa describes his difficulties at home: married to a woman who was brought up in a convent and who lacks erotic passion, he was forced to turn for satisfaction to their Indian maid, "a yellow-skinned rat with a flat nose" (172); upon discovering the affair, Ologa's wife insisted that he cleanse his honor by ridding the country of the Indian guerrilla bands (173). Castillos, all the while, speaks—with wonderful irony—of their good fortune to have caught fish for dinner from the volcanic basin; as good Catholics they would not have been able to eat their dried meat on a Friday. Two related points are noteworthy. First, the absence of a shared conversation among the three officers, who continually speak past one another, suggests the lack of a unified, common cultural discourse among the Mexicans. Second, to the extent that the officers are joined together, they are bound in solidarity not as Mexicans against the colonialist French but as Spanish Catholic landowners against the political and moral threat of the indigenous Indians. Indeed, the landowners identify themselves explicitly with the values and traditions of Europe rather than with those of their native country: Eraso states, for example, "Our entire military, our way of fighting, our concepts of honor come from Europe" (172).

The Mexicans, in short, lack an indigenous, independent cultural identity that might be reflected in a distinct dramatic discourse in the text. As nonspeakers of an unrecognized culture, they are also pointedly disqualified from participating in the dialogues of the Europeans. The French professor Simon and the French commander Goyon, discussing Simon's scientific project in Mexico, insist on absolute silence on the part of Ologa, Eraso, and Castillos, who are treated as though they were not present. Not only are they not allowed to speak, but Ologa is ordered not to "clang about" with his silver spurs (191). When Castillos breaks into the discussion about the human fish, his interruption is not even recognized as human speech, but rather his words represent for Simon nothing more than "clanging"—"You're clanging with your mouth," Simon says (198; cf. 200).

When they do attempt to speak with the French, the Mexicans prove incapable of appreciating the nonliteral use of language that defines the French sense of humor and social grace. As Ologa puts it, "pretty flattery" is "wonderfully European" (176). To give a seemingly banal illustration of this difference: the French count Pelletier sees the Mexicans rolling cigars and asks politely for a "little killer"; the Mexicans do not understand. Pelletier points out that cigars are dangerous to one's health, which confuses the Mexicans: if cigars are dangerous, Pelletier surely would not ask for one. The count responds that he does not consider them to be that dangerous; Eraso then insists, "So 'little killer' was an exaggerated expression." Ologa explains to his friends that such witty expressions are the mode in Paris, leaving Castillos to ask the pointed—and for him most perplexing—question, "Witticisms? Why witticisms?" (215–16). On another occasion, Pelletier describes the Mexican women, with their passion hidden beneath a cool, silent exterior, as "a volcano of alabaster," which leads Eraso to explain at length why alabaster volcanoes cannot exist (220). Mexicans, it appears, demand and understand only a literal, strictly referential use of language, while the French express themselves figuratively, with words that do not mean what they say. The French are, in a word, liars, as is amply proven when the French chiefs of staff vote secretly to withdraw their promised support of Maximilian's government (212), and Napoleon III issues his "imperial breach of promise" repealing his support of Simon (226). The Mexicans, in contrast, are profoundly incapable of "civilized," thus duplicitous, banter.[23]

The Mexicans' unqualified identification with and admiration for the aristocratic ideals of Europe that exclude them face a final, drastic challenge in the figure of Count Pelletier. The aristocratic Frenchman, bored with life in Paris, has traveled abroad to new territory not to serve loyally in the war against Juárez but to experience the passion of Mexican women (176). Indeed, his Mexican mistress, it turns out, is Ologa's allegedly dispassionate wife. While Ologa prefers his yellow-skinned, ratlike, smelly Indian maid to the "silent, wondering eyes" of his unwelcoming wife (172), Pelletier speaks of her "plum-sized eyes, deep brown, glazed with the luster of a secret moistness . . . that promise the connoisseur everything" (218). It is left to the true "connoisseur," the Frenchman, to discover and reveal the beauty of the Mexican women; the Mexican men, in contrast, are made to appear ignorant and unrefined.

But if the French count seems superior to the Mexican men in the art (or artifice) of love, his cultural refinement is shown to lack moral integrity and to reflect a tradition that is literally no longer vital. Ologa, who begins at last to suspect the identity of Pelletier's mistress, stakes his horses, his cash assets, then his hacienda in a card game against his rival. While Ologa plays for his masculine honor, Pelletier gambles away his entire fortune, including his mistress, to pass the time. When Ologa wins and Pelletier is forced to reveal the name of his lover, the injured husband challenges the Frenchman to a duel. In quick fashion Pelletier kills first Ologa, then Castillos and Eraso, who loyally defend the name of their friend. If the Mexicans die upholding their sense of patriarchal honor, the French count, lacking any ideals whatsoever, closes the absurd scene with his suicide, because he has literally nothing to live for: "I don't understand how I could go to the trouble of being victorious three times. It was in fact most senseless. . . . Funny. Writers meet their end at their desks, sergeants on the battlefield, and so I meet mine with a superfluous effort (*he shoots himself*)" (224). In this way the lifeless traditions of Europe embodied by Pelletier are contrasted with the confused self-image of the Mexicans, who, through the encounter, begin to gain a sense of their national and cultural identity: Ologa, Eraso, and Castillos are all brought to challenge the decadent Frenchman, who represents everything they had previously emulated. In doing so they actually move closer to the oppositional position of the Indians, whom they had initially seen as "completely different" (172), as now both groups contest the hegemony of the French in Mexico.

In such highly entertaining, ironic manner, Hacks's play offers a biting critique of French (European colonial) involvement in Latin America, of the adoption of European values on the part of the Mexicans, and of the French and Mexican treatment of the indigenous Indians as subhumans. Further, while the play depicts the impending demise of European military and cultural traditions in the Third World, it points also to the rise of new political forces that shape the contemporary world scene. While Hacks shows us in his play the French in Mexico and the Mexican officers and landowners of Maximilian's imperial army, pointedly not represented are the indigenous Indians who are organizing under Juárez. The absence of the guerrillas as figures in the drama, however, is as conspicuous as their victory over Maximilian and the French is obvious.[24] The forces of Maximilian and the French, as the encounter between Ologa and Pelletier demonstrates, are crumbling from within: the Mexican aristocracy dies ineffectually defending its outmoded code of honor, while the practical prowess of the French lacks any genuine political commitment or moral substance. The future, as Mexican history will prove, belongs to the dirty, yellow-skinned, uneducated guerrilla bands held in disdain by the "civilized" Mexicans and French and denied even a token appearance as dramatic characters in their play. Hacks's work signals in the victory of Juárez the end of the era of European domination in the Third World; again, as in Hammel's text, the fundamentally nonrevolutionary character of the European tradition is demonstrated alongside the emergence of a distinctly revolutionary Third World.[25]

Hammel's play, set at the end of the French Republic at the time of the crowning of Napoleon in 1804, presents the circumspect transference of European revolutionary ideals to colonized countries abroad. Hacks's play, set sixty years later during the Mexican civil war between the guerrilla forces of Juárez and the French-supported army of Maximilian, marks the impending end of European dominance in the area and the growing reflection of the Third World on its own culture and traditions. Hammel's text demonstrates his European's solidarity with Latin America in terms of a historical and moral bond between the intellectual traditions of Europe and the anticolonialist struggles of the Third World; in contrast, Hacks's gesture of solidarity valorizes the Third World by exposing the inhumanity and the decay of the European heritage.

Both texts focus on the central figure of the man of science whose work, despite or perhaps specifically because of its claims to be unconcerned with practical politics, can be used to legitimize or to inform European expansion in the New World. Both Humboldt and Simon, self-proclaimed humanists, are politically ambivalent if not potentially dangerous figures. The German explorer, by avoiding direct political engagement, appears to give tacit support to Napoleon; the French biologist subordinates political and moral concerns to the goals of his research and becomes, in the end, a murderer. Crucial to both plays is the connection between European science (or "civilization") and coercion: Bolívar begs Humboldt to "force" him to understand his country; Simon believes that the Aztec fish must be "forced" to evolve into civilized human beings. European science, potentially emancipatory, is simultaneously an instrument of domination; it is this dialectic that governs the actions of the Europeans in the two plays.

Furthermore, both Hacks and Hammel point to the developing insight on the part of New World revolutionaries regarding the limitations of the supposedly normative European tradition. Bolívar, though he needs the knowledge that only Humboldt can offer, must reject the German's idealist views of "world patriotism" before he can dedicate himself to the colonial conflict in his own country. Similarly, the key to victory in the Mexican civil war depicted in Hacks's play is the specifically non-European strategy of guerrilla warfare, pursued by the indigenous Indians, who are viewed as "rats" by the Europeanized Mexican aristocracy. The solidarity expressed in both plays lies in demonstrating not the wisdom but the cultural and political limitation of European ways.

Indeed, this self-reflection on the political ambiguities of European endeavors overseas seems to characterize East German representations of the Third World, specifically of Third World revolution, in the 1970s. Volker Braun's *Guevara oder Der Sonnenstaat*, for example, presents with unrelenting seriousness and apotheosizing overtones the revolutionary efforts of Che Guevara in Bolivia; interspersed in the chronicle of Guevara's struggle are grotesque scenes depicting Alexander von Humboldt (as the figure Bumholdt) and Regis Debray (as Bedray) as modern-day tourists in the Andes. While the figure of Guevara gains tragic proportions, the idealist Bedray from the invisible heights of his cliff-top lookout, his head literally in the clouds, sings Eichendorff's "Mondnacht" ("Night of Moon"), a famous poem of the Romantic period, and the "International," the song of the international labor movement; the crass materialist Bumholdt, who digs ever deeper at his archaeological site in a fruitless search for Incan artifacts, finally shoots and consumes Bedray to satisfy his growing hunger (88–90). In stark contrast to the moral demise of the Europeans in the penultimate scene, the final moments of the play portray Guevara in an elegant embrace of solidarity with a "friend" (Castro) in Cuba, the two Third World leaders disagreeing radically on revolutionary tactics but each respecting the choice made by the other. Thus while the serious revolution represented by Guevara survives in Latin America, the European revolutionary intellectuals are revealed to be nothing more than the romantic dreamers or the cannibals of history.[26] In another case, in Heiner Müller's *Der Auftrag*, which rewrites Seghers's *Das Licht auf dem Galgen*, the European revolutionary actually betrays the indigenous uprising of the slaves on Jamaica. Here, in an anti-*Maßnahme*, the orthodox European party abandons the genuine revolt in the Third World, while the Third World revolution is able to occur only when its leaders explicitly reject European ideals (Teraoka, "*Der Auftrag*").

As plays of solidarity, all of these texts assert not the universal authority or desirability of European science or European politics but rather the limits of their relevance for the experience of the Third World. All four texts raise the issue of European revolutionary avant-gardism in the Third World; all show that Europe cannot lead. This is a critique, furthermore, from which the socialist tradition is not excluded. Humboldt in Hammel's text is a flawed model for the GDR; Hacks's paradigmatic critique of the bankruptcy of European imperialism in the Third World, of the collapse of the "leading world power" ("Noten" 401; cf. note 25), applies potentially to the Soviet Union as well as to Western Europe and the United States (cf. Rohde); the model of the Brechtian learning play adopted by both Braun and Müller implicates the European socialist tradition in both form and didactic content. In sharp contrast to the universalizing visions of Anna Seghers and Peter Weiss, the four plays suggest the increasing emergence of a revolutionary Third World identity independent of that of Europe, from Bolívar's recognition that Europe cannot fulfill the promise of revolution in Latin America in Hammel's text, to the Mexicans' challenge against the values of the decadent European in Hacks, and finally to the proclamations of Müller's ex-slave Sasportas, who rejects the ideals of Europe altogether in order to formulate a new manner of revolution in the Third World.

Striking is the fact that the side of Europe in all the texts is represented by paradigmatic intellectuals, whether men of science or vanguard party elites. The definition of Europe in terms of the intellect suggests a number of possible opposing concepts, those of activity, corporeality, spontaneity, and will, all of which are present but not developed in the Third World figures of these works. As a whole the GDR plays of solidarity refrain from prescribing an identity or a role to the Latin Americans in their dramas but focus instead on exploring—and criticizing—the traditional attitudes of Europeans toward Third World peoples. Their common tendency is not to represent the other as an exotic object of friendly obser-vation, instruction, or sympathy but, in a self-critical way, their conflicted relationship to it. If anything, there is increased reti-cence about the Third World and an increasing obsession with European problems and attitudes: Hammel's text deals less with the emerging revolution in Latin America or the education and maturation of the revolutionary Bolívar than with the shortcom-ings and political ambiguities of Humboldt's "world patriotism." Hacks explores European attitudes toward the Mexicans and the Europeanized attitudes of the Mexicans toward the indigenous Indians, while the real "others," the Indian guerrillas, are in fact ab-sent in the play. Volker Braun's depiction of Guevara presents him as a revolutionary whose tragedy arises out of conflicts familiar to readers of plays such as Büchner's *Dantons Tod* (1835; *Danton's Death*) and, more importantly, Brecht's *Das Badener Lehrstück* (1929; The Baden learning play) and *Die Maßnahme* (1930; *The Measures Taken*); as a result, Braun's Guevara—despite his crucial difference from Bumholdt and Bedray—seems at times so conspic-uously European that the author appears to write not about Latin America at all but about the revolutionary tradition and heritage of Europe.[27] Finally, the overwhelming focus of Heiner Müller's *Der Auftrag* is the painful demise of the tradition of the "white" European revolution, while the "black" revolution of the Third World remains a promise deliberately unfulfilled in the text.

In sum, the plays of solidarity written by GDR playwrights in response to real events in Latin America have far less do with the Third World than with Europe. If international solidarity in the fight against imperialism is—so the official doctrine—"both state politics and a matter of the heart," then for these authors the matter of the heart offers an occasion for political soul searching. The revolutionary ideals, the science, the humanistic tradition of Europe, even specifically of a socialist Germany, cannot be shipped to the Third World as easily and unproblematically as, say, food, trucks, and medical supplies. As these plays illustrate, the intellectual traditions of Europe can be closely allied with hegemonic practice. And through their critique of this heritage, the texts question, however indirectly, uneasily, or even unwillingly, the party-line dichotomy between imperialist intervention and revolutionary solidarity.

4

"THE ROMAN
LEARNS THE ALPHABET
OF THE NEGRO"

*The "Third World" Voice
of Heiner Müller*

The Third World in the work of the GDR author Heiner Müller represents more than a thematic or political interest; it articulates both an oppositional aesthetic philosophy and an ideological critique of Western civilization. While *Der Auftrag* contributed to a broader discourse within East German drama on Western imperialism in the Third World, it is only one of a number of literary works, supported by numerous interviews and essays, in which Müller explored the political and philosophical import of the Third World for Europe.

Widely recognized by theater scholars and artists as the most important German playwright of the postwar period, Müller has led a career marked by irony and contradiction. Born in 1929, he grew up in fascist Germany and, at the age of sixteen, was drafted into Hitler's forces near the end of the war. From 1950 to 1956, while writing his first literary texts, he worked in East Berlin as a journalist for *Sonntag* and *Neue Deutsche Literatur*. In 1959 he and his wife, Inge Müller, were awarded the Heinrich Mann Prize for *Der Lohndrücker* (1957; *The Scab*), a "production play" that depicted the difficulties of improving industrial output in a socialist state with workers trained in fascist habits of thought and action. Two years later, Müller was expelled from the GDR Writers Association following the cancellation of a student production of *Die Umsiedlerin oder Das Leben auf dem Lande* (1961; The refugee: Or, life in the country) after a single performance. In 1965, his works were among those singled out by Erich Honecker at the Eleventh Plenary Conference of the Central Committee of the SED as examples of decadent, immoral, and bourgeois tendencies in GDR literature. As a result, the scheduled premiere of *Der Bau* (1965; The construction site) was cancelled. Müller became practically untouchable, and *Der Bau* was not seen in the GDR until 1980.

Only in 1973, twelve years after *Die Umsiedlerin*, was another major play by Heiner Müller produced in East Germany. This event, the Berliner Ensemble production of *Zement* (*Cement*), together with the publication of Müller's collected works by Rotbuch Press in West Berlin, secured his status on both sides of the Wall as a major German dramatist. Müller continued to face delays, restrictions, and criticisms of his work (certain of his plays were never published or produced in the GDR), but his growing international success provided an unusual degree of privilege and security. Committed to Communism even as he criticized its institutions, Müller became too important not to be tolerated by the East German state. His collaboration with the American theater artist Robert Wilson on productions in West Germany, Western Europe, and the United States in the mid-1980s brought him even greater renown among avant-garde artists and audiences in the West. Recipient of the most prestigious literary honors in both Germanies (Lessing Prize, 1973; Mühlheimer Dramatists Prize, 1979; Büchner Prize, 1985; National Prize of the GDR, 1986; Kleist Prize, 1990), he became president of the GDR Academy of Arts in 1990 and, in a reunified Germany, artistic director of the Berliner Ensemble. Like Christa Wolf and other prominent writers, Müller too was later accused of having collaborated with the East German Stasi (Ministry for State Security) (Detje et al.).

More than any other East German author, Müller transcends the political and literary boundaries of the GDR. A prolific writer and voracious reader, he draws from a vast array of traditions in the construction of his texts: Greek drama and mythology, Shakespeare, Artaud, Beckett, Mayakovski and Gladkov, Japanese Noh theater, the Brechtian *Lehrstück*, American popular culture, Fanon and Césaire, Deleuze and Baudrillard, in addition to authors and texts from the German literary canon reaching back to the *Ni-*

belungenlied — these are just a few of his sources and influences. There is a persistent interest in class struggle, in everyday forms of fascism, and in the history of German socialism in his works, but even here Müller's preoccupations extend beyond the GDR to encompass the Soviet Union, the Weimar Republic, and eighteenth-century Prussia. Given the historical and literary sweep of Müller's oeuvre, it would be misleading to interpret his interest in the Third World as a response to specific political events, or to read Müller's construction of it as an expression of uniquely East German sensibilities. Rather, I take Müller's Third World texts as an opportunity to explore an ideological and poetological critique of Europe envisioned in the broadest of terms.

Ever since the late 1970s, Heiner Müller has been "waiting for" and writing about the Third World.[1] In essays and interviews he has pointed to what he calls "islands of the Third World" in the metropolises of First World countries, pockets of disorder, resistance, and change that must be protected and nurtured by works of art and by political action.[2] Considerations of the Third World also provide the foundation for his attack against the peace movement: peace in Europe presupposes continued oppression in other parts of the world, he claims; "[p]eace along the East-West axis, war along the North-South axis—that's the situation" ("Gespräch mit Heiner Müller" 1200).[3]

The author's pervasive concern with the Third World ranges from the global to the mundane, as Müller states in his characteristically provocative tone that he would find it easier to relate to a Puerto Rican in New York than to a bank official in Bochum ("Deutschland" 207). The author projects a "Third World" that is deliberately eclectic, including within its bounds minority groups and their cultural forms (Turks in Berlin, subway graffiti in New York), and powerful beasts and overpowering natural landscapes of the non-European world (buffalo, elephants, panthers, deserts, volcanoes) (Teraoka, "Subway"). In Müller's dramatic texts the idea of the Third World is expressed also through images of madness or through laughter. Often it is connected with the body.

What binds these seemingly disparate phenomena in Müller's work is their resistance to the "European" principle of instrumental and authoritative reason. Not surprisingly, the critique of the European Enlightenment tradition in his writing is coupled with a meticulously executed, painful examination of the white male intellectual—the German author Lessing or Shakespeare's Hamlet, to name two—who represents it. Such thematic preoccupations are reflected, furthermore, in a formal poetological project that seeks, in Müller's terms, the "disappearance of the author" and the creation of a nonexclusive, nonprivileging "universal discourse" (Teraoka, *Silence* 17–50). The common concern of Müller's texts from the mid-1970s to the mid-1980s, in both form and content, has been to destroy the principle of privilege claimed by the European author by virtue of his language and his philosophical, cultural, and political heritage.[4]

The present chapter begins by following the "Third World" critique of Europe as it emerges and develops in *Leben Gundlings Friedrich von Preussen Lessings Schlaf Traum Schrei: Ein Greuelmärchen* (1976; *Gundling's Life Frederick of Prussia Lessing's Sleep Dream Scream: A Horror Story*), *Die Hamletmaschine* (1977; *Hamletmachine*), and *Der Auftrag: Erinnerung an eine Revolution* (1979; *The Task*). From the buffalo, alligators, and sharks of *Leben Gundlings* to the black slave Sasportas in *Der Auftrag*, the images and figures of the Third World in these plays express an alternative that seeks to resist the power of European authority. But what starts as often passive resistance in earlier works explodes in the violent revenge of the "barbarians" Medea and Aaron of *Verkommenes Ufer Medeamaterial Landschaft mit Argonauten* (1982; *Despoiled Shore Medeamaterial Landscape with Argonauts*) and *Anatomie Titus Fall of Rome Ein Shakespearekommentar* (1984; Anatomy Titus fall of Rome a Shakespeare commentary). The main body of this chapter focuses on these two texts to explore the dramatic construction of a Third World voice in Heiner Müller.[5]

The third scene of the "Horror Story" *Leben Gundlings*, entitled "OH HOW GOOD THAT NO ONE KNOWS RUMPELSTILTSKIN IS MY

NAME OF THE SCHOOL OF THE NATION: A patriotic puppet play,"
contains the first explicit reference in Heiner Müller's texts to
European imperialism (66).[6] The stage directions read:

> On the other side of the stage, larger-than-life figures of John
> Bull and Marianne divide the world by throwing knives at a
> globe, knives they are pulling from corpses of dead Indians
> and Negroes. After each hit, the winner cuts a slice off and
> ingests it. Having eaten their fill, they rub their (sometimes
> each other's) bellies, and burping and farting they watch little
> Frederick who is playing at war with his soldier-dolls. (66)

While the young Frederick II plays war with his people, the "adults"
England (personified as John Bull in the satire by John Arbuthnot)
and France (signified by the name of the secret society devoted
to republican government) have long since turned to the slaughter of Indians and blacks. The scene offers a visual allegory of the
Seven Years War (1756–63), in which Prussia emerged as a major
European military power while France and England engaged in
a struggle for control over North America and India. In Müller's
pantomime, political power is based on genocide, first of one's
peasant masses, then, as the massacre is wisely transferred overseas,
of the indigenous peoples of the Third World.

The scene fades into a film of a ghost ship whose dead sailors rise
up to nail their captain to the mast, an act of mutiny that is repeated
endlessly as the film runs backwards and forwards through time
(66). The suggestive image linking resurrection and revenge is developed further at the conclusion of Müller's play, where the author
Lessing meets the last president of the United States, a faceless
robot, in a scrap yard in the American Midwest. In the provocative scene, Emilia Galotti and Nathan the Wise, Lessing's famous
figures of Enlightenment self-determination and tolerance, stran-
gle one another; the robot president is executed in an electric chair,
a satirical image of the technocratic and technological rule that has
been (following Horkheimer and Adorno) the twisted legacy of
that Enlightenment vision. A voice and projections fill the black-
ened stage in the aftermath of this grotesque demise of humanism:
"HOUR OF WHITE HEAT DEAD BUFFALOS FROM THE CANYONS

SQUADS OF SHARKS TEETH OF BLACK LIGHT THE ALLIGATORS MY
FRIENDS GRAMMAR OF EARTHQUAKES WEDDING OF FIRE AND
WATER MEN OF A NEW FLESH LAUTREAMONTMALDOROR PRINCE
OF ATLANTIS SON OF THE DEAD" (78).

Images of buffalo, sharks, alligators, and earthquakes immediately evoke the natural Third World. Dead buffalo emerging from
the canyons suggest the resurrection of slaughtered nature; the
birth of humans of new flesh through the union of fire and water provides the image of an apocalyptic recreation of man. The
entire vision threatens us: the swarm of sharks appears with teeth
bared; the alligators are the allies of an unidentified post-European
voice that speaks only after the annihilation of Emilia, Nathan,
and the American president in a blast of white heat. The French
author Lautréamont (Isidore Ducasse), whose hallucinatory *Mal-
doror* (1868) is quoted in visions of black angels (74), represents in
Müller's larger oeuvre a tradition in European literature directly
opposed to the rationalistic ideals of the Enlightenment. Müller's
images, following his anti-Enlightenment models, are suggestive,
not descriptive, working viscerally, not conceptually: images evok-
ing the Third World are associated with a sense of resurrection
and apocalypse, strengthened by the play's concluding tableau of
the "APOTHEOSIS SPARTACUS" (78).

The juxtaposition of the European-American scrap yard and
Third World nature reappears in Müller's next play, *Die Hamletmaschine*; its last scene is set in the deep sea, whose natural life
makes its way among the junk and ruins of civilization: "[f]ish, de-
bris, dead bodies and limbs drift by" (58). The drowned Ophelia
also inhabits this undersea world, where she sits in a wheelchair
and speaks of revenge with the voice of the Third World: "[t]his
is Electra speaking. In the heart of darkness. Under the sun of tor-
ture. To the capitals of the world. In the name of the victims" (58).
Quoting Joseph Conrad's *Heart of Darkness* and Jean-Paul Sartre's
preface to Frantz Fanon's *The Wretched of the Earth*, Ophelia identifies herself with the colonized peoples of Africa who are engaged in
the fight for their liberation. And in the complex associative logic
of Müller's text that connects Hamlet with Gustav Noske, Ophelia also embodies the assassinated revolutionary Rosa Luxemburg,

calling for violent revolution from the depths of her watery grave: "[d]own with the happiness of submission. Long live hate and contempt, rebellion and death" (58). Semiotically the scene is intricate and dense, with the revolution of the German working class, the emancipation of the Third World from its colonial past, and the resistance of victimized women against an oppressive male world coexisting in the figure of an angry underwater Ophelia.

Already we can trace a kind of development in Müller's presentation of the Third World: what first appeared as images of nature in *Leben Gundlings* is embodied in a figure, Ophelia, in the subsequent *Hamletmaschine*. Both texts engage in an analysis and a critique of instrumental reason, which acts upon and against nature, women, sexuality, the body, the imagination. In their concluding scenes, both plays signal the revenge of what has previously been repressed or oppressed, rendered in visions of dead buffalo, sharks, and earthquakes, or in the figure of a woman speaking in the name of victims against the metropolises of the world. However, if we take drama even vaguely to represent the stage of history, the "Third World" has yet to emerge as an actor: there are only utopian images, visual projections, in *Leben Gundlings*, and a figure in a wheelchair slowly wrapped and muffled in bandages by men in white coats, immobilized and silenced, in *Hamletmaschine*.

In Müller's next text, *Der Auftrag*, a Third World actor appears full-fledged in the figure of the former slave Sasportas. Set in the Third World, the play rewrites both Seghers's *Das Licht auf dem Galgen* and Brecht's *Die Maßnahme* with a focus on issues of racial, cultural, and class difference.[7] Gone are the black slave women of Seghers's text: Müller's drama occurs among the three principal male revolutionaries, the color line drawn through their ranks, with Seghers's Sasportas, a European Jew, cast in Müller's text as a Caribbean black. Emancipated in the revolution led by Toussaint L'Ouverture in Haiti, Sasportas joins with two French revolutionaries in a mission to organize a slave revolt against British colonialism in Jamaica. From the start he is marked by his skin color as being different from the Europeans. Sasportas's role in the mission of revolt is, as his fellow revolutionary Galloudec remarks, "written all over [his] body" (89), and as Sasportas himself sets forth in his earliest speeches, the conflict on Jamaica is for him one of race, not of class: "[w]hen I leave here, others will be hanging in the cages, with white skin till the sun turns them black. Then many will be better off" (88). The point of race that separates the former slave from the European revolutionaries is further emphasized when Sasportas's body and skin come to symbolize, if not cause, his eventual break from the white revolutionary Debuisson, just as Debuisson's white skin foretells, if not determines, his betrayal of the slave revolt and his return to his parents' slave plantation. Proclaiming the theater of white revolution over (93), Sasportas carves a new banner into the skin of his black hand (100); in his last speech before leaving the stage, he announces the revolution of the Third World:

> When the living can no longer fight, the dead will. With every heartbeat of the revolution flesh grows back on their bones, blood in their veins, life in their death. The rebellion of the dead will be the war of the landscapes, our weapons the forests, the mountains, the oceans, the deserts of the world. I will be forest, mountain, ocean, desert. I—that is Africa. I—that is Asia. The two Americas—that is I. (100)

Where Ophelia spoke in the name of the world's victims only through the complex literary mediation of Conrad and Sartre, Sasportas's voice announces unambiguously its identity with Africa, Asia, and America. Certain themes are already familiar: again we find the notion of resurrection, as victims rise in revolt; again too we find the untamed landscapes of the Third World as threatening forces of vengeance. But for the first time in Müller's work, such images of revolt and revenge against European dominance are collected and centered in a single dramatic figure. Where Ophelia, wrapped in bandages in a wheelchair, literally bound and gagged, was unable to act out her role on a stage dominated by Hamlet, Sasportas is an equal player in the Caribbean drama of revolt.

There remain, however, important restrictions in the play that undermine the stature of Sasportas's voice. First, although Sasportas announces and carries the banner of Third World revolution, he must literally leave the drama to enact it. Sasportas will join the uprising of the Jamaican slaves and eventually lose his life in their struggle for freedom, but we witness none of that: his revolutionary revenge drama occurs only off-stage. Second, the action on Jamaica, involving the efforts of the three revolutionaries to organize the slave revolt and ending with Debuisson's betrayal and Sasportas's departure, takes place as the recreated memory of the French official Antoine. At the start of the play, Antoine, who was responsible for sending the three men on their mission, receives a letter from Galloudec that reports Debuisson's desertion and Sasportas's capture and execution. This begins a process of imaginative "remembering" in which Antoine (re)creates the events leading up to Debuisson's act of counterrevolution. As Antoine has distanced himself from his revolutionary past and now lives a secluded life in Napoleonic France, his own "betrayal" is reflected in that of Debuisson, and the drama on Jamaica that Antoine plays out in his mind is less a faithful reconstruction of fact than a painful, personal self-examination. The figure of Sasportas in the play, in short, is Antoine's dramatic creation, and the Third World revolution he proclaims against the European Debuisson represents the tortured, guilty conscience of a European intellectual in hiding.[8]

But here lies the problem. *Leben Gundlings*, *Hamletmaschine*, and *Der Auftrag* examine European traditions in history and drama; seen as discourse, all are dominated by the voice and perspective of the European male. The title figures of *Leben Gundlings* (Gundling, Frederick II, and Lessing) are completely absorbed in the examination of their relationship as individuals and intellectuals to the state. If anyone or anything in the text represents an alternative to the dominant order, it is destroyed (as is the homosexual Katte), imprisoned (the inmates of the Prussian asylum), or "projected" into a utopian time and space (the images of the Third World). The text of *Hamletmaschine* is dominated by Hamlet's monologues, the text literally a "Hamlet machine," while Ophelia as Hamlet's "other" ("I want to be a woman," he says [55]) is allowed only a fraction of the speaking time and printed space occupied by the male. *Der Auftrag*, finally, is structured as the memory of a French intellectual, such that the Third World revolution proclaimed by Sasportas is only the projection of an omnipresent European consciousness.

Can an alternative voice emerge within this discourse? The three texts discussed here seem to suggest, to the contrary, that any alternative is only a creation, another expression, of the literary and political structures already in place. If anything, Müller's plays seem to illustrate the inability of (white male European) drama to portray a true "other" except as a wishful projection, a pregnant silence, or an empty space.[9] Ultimately the three texts demonstrate the repeated failure of European intellectuals to offer a revolutionary alternative: Gundling, Frederick II, Lessing, Hamlet, Debuisson, and Antoine all end in resignation and compliance. The European bureaucrat in *Der Auftrag* sets off into the Peruvian landscape in search of his other but will find only his double with a face the color of snow (96). Is Heiner Müller's drama of an alternative to Europe, like the search of his hapless European, politically and ontologically condemned to fail?

This dilemma is the focus of Müller's *Verkommenes Ufer Medeamaterial Landschaft mit Argonauten*, which portrays Medea's emergence as a dramatic character with a distinct Third World identity.[10] The process is enacted and thematized in the middle section of the play, in "Medeamaterial Landschaft mit Argonauten" (hereafter as "Medeamaterial"), a drama of 190 lines dominated by Medea's monologue, which makes up three fourths of the text. From the beginning, the problem of the woman's identity is foregrounded: in the first lines of the text Medea defines herself solely in terms of the man Jason ("Jason My first one and my last one" [128]); by the closing lines, in contrast, she regains her self as "Medea" (133), while Jason is reduced to the anonymous state of his male gender ("Nurse Do you know this man" [133]). In Müller's text, the woman becomes Medea as Jason's identity is destroyed.

Three key passages record this transformation. In the first, Medea looks into a mirror and denies her identity; Jason enters and addresses her generically as "woman." In the second, accused of waning passion, Jason asks "woman" about her identity; she answers that she was "Medea." Finally, after Medea's monologue, which extends some 150 lines and accompanies her acts of revenge against Jason's bride and sons, the text concludes with the line quoted above: Jason returns to confront Medea, but she no longer recognizes him. The passages are the following; emphases are added:

MEDEA: ... This is not Medea
           Jason
JASON: *Woman* what voice is this (128)

JASON: What were you before I came *woman*
MEDEA: *Medea* (129)

JASON: *Medea*
MEDEA: Nurse Do you know this *man*. (133)

The symmetry of the appellations reflects a mirror reversal in the relationship between Jason and Medea: only after Medea has killed Jason's bride and her two sons does Jason call her by her name, while she sees him only as "man." The conqueror-hero "Jason" is stripped of his individuality and reduced to his sex ("man"), while the "woman" regains her identity to become once again the barbarian "Medea"; the relationship of dominance between "Jason" and "woman" becomes a drama of destruction between "Medea" and "man."[11]

Müller sees in Jason, notably, the first colonialist in Greek mythology and suggests that we might think of Medea as a Turkish woman in West Germany ("Deutschland" 196).[12] Within such a broadly conceived framework of political and economic colonialism, Medea's monologue of revenge expresses a stance of retaliatory violence on the part of an equally broad "Third World" against European power: it is here, in the long speech of Medea, that the European-centered discourse of a Hamlet, Lessing, or Antoine gives way to the self-centered actions of the barbarian.

Medea begins by stating her lack of property and identity, the foundations of European political history and philosophical thought. She possesses nothing, she says, not her body and not the products of that body; as "milkcow" and "footstool" (131), her self is defined explicitly as an object of Jason's possession and for Jason's use:

> . . . What can be mine being your slave
> All of me is your tool and all things from me
> For you I killed for you I did give birth
> I've been your bitch your whore is what I was
> I but a rung on your ladder of fame. (129)

Medea's self-estrangement is reflected further in terms of her inability to preserve her history—she has grown "blind" and "deaf" (130), she says, to the images of death and destruction in Colchis, the homeland and family she betrayed out of love for Jason.

Just as Ophelia and Sasportas expressed their revolt through images focused on the body, Medea experiences the body as the site of colonization, exploitation, and, ultimately, revenge. Ophelia promises to eject the sperm she has received, to transform her breastmilk into poison, to suffocate between her thighs the world she has given birth to (*Hamletmaschine* 58). Sasportas strips the white oppressor Debuisson of his skin, his flesh, his blood, his excrement, his semen, and his thoughts (*Auftrag* 93); he hears the drums of revolution through the pores of his black skin, cuts a new revolutionary banner into his black flesh (*Auftrag* 98, 100). For Medea as well it is the body that experiences betrayal,

> The ashes of your kisses on my lips
> Between my teeth the sand of our years
> On my skin only my own sweat
> Your breath a stench of alien bed, ("Medeamaterial" 130)

and the body that is the site of retaliation—"Oh could I bite her out of you your whore" (130).[13] Accordingly, Medea's return to her identity begins with the recovery of the eyes and ears of her bodily self and with them the history of events on Colchis:

> . . . Thanks for your treason
> That gives me back both of my eyes again
> To see what I saw once the images
> You've painted with the boots of your crew Jason

Unto my Colchis ears to hear again
The music you once played upon the corpses
The bones the graves of those who were my people. (130)

With the simultaneous regaining of her native history and her foreign body, Medea becomes for the first time barbarian: where previously she could speak of herself only as an object owned by Jason ("your slave," "your tool," "your bitch," "your whore" [129]), Medea now refers to herself repeatedly (seven times) as "the barbarian" (131–32). Significantly, she engages in her acts of revenge (131–32) as this barbarian self—that is, the vengeful Medea is Medea as barbarian, the self-proclaimed non-European who experiences herself fully as a body resisting the ideals of European civilization.

Always the target is the victor's flesh, revenge an act of reappropriating what is properly one's own. Medea's slaying of her sons takes back her body from theirs, an act of repossession that separates self from nonself:

I want to cut you right out of my heart
My heartflesh My remembrance My beloved
Give back to me my blood out of your veins
Back into my womb you who are my entrails. (132)

More complex is the attack on Jason's bride, to whom Medea sends a wedding gown that will engulf her in flames. The gown in Müller's text is the direct product of Medea's hands and history, "[e]mbroidered by the hand of her who has been robbed / With gold from Colchis and dyed with the blood from / The bridal feast of fathers brothers sons" (131), and it destroys the virgin body of the rival bride, who is as yet unspoiled by age and childbearing (131).[14] Notably, the fatal merging of the wedding dress with the bride's skin is described in explicitly erotic terms, so that Medea's revenge through the medium of the dress becomes a deceitful and violent rape, the "planting" of knives into virgin flesh. Medea as "bridegroom" repeats Jason's crime, against Jason's new bride:

The groom he enters now the bridal chamber
And now he places at the young bride's feet
The barbarian's bridal gown the bridal

Present soaked in my sweat of submission
Now see the whore she struts before the mirror
And now the gold of Colchis seals her pores
Planting a field of knives into her flesh
The barbarian's bridal gown it celebrates
Its wedding Jason of your virgin bride
The first night will be mine. (132)

Medea's act of revenge and Jason's actions of deceit, destruction, and betrayal then merge in Medea's explicit identification of the murdered bride with the ravaged city of Colchis, so that the statement "she burns" refers equally and simultaneously to both:

She screams now Have you ears to hear the scream
Like Colchis screamed when you were in my womb
And still screams Have you ears to hear the scream
She burns. (132)[15]

In these images, the woman who had once been robbed of her body, her history, and her identity regains everything by force. The sole act of violence that occurs on stage, the killing of the sons, rhetorically mirrors the murder of Jason's bride in Medea's imagination as it reenacts and avenges Jason's crimes in Colchis: Medea takes Jason's bride and Jason's sons, thus effectively destroying his patriarchal line, regains her self and her name, and avenges her family and city.[16] Everything occurs in a single, climactic act of violence that both crystallizes and shatters the history of European conquest. Jason's sons die; his bride ceases to scream; the screams of Colchis fade, now avenged; and Medea becomes Medea again, all in the apocalyptic moment that concludes her monologue. The now all-powerful Medea, for the first time fully herself, has destroyed the European Jason:

MEDEA: O I am wise I am Medea I
        Don't you have blood left Now it is all quiet
        The screams of Colchis silenced too And nothing left
JASON: Medea
MEDEA: Nurse Do you know this man. (133)

If alternative figures in *Leben Gundlings*, *Hamletmaschine*, and *Der Auftrag* were dominated—silenced, immobilized, exiled, or executed—by institutions and intellectual representatives of the European tradition, "Medeamaterial" demonstrates for the first time the newfound power and violence of the non-European, the barbarian, the Third World. This development continues with the figure of Aaron in Müller's *Anatomie Titus Fall of Rome Ein Shakespearekommentar*, a text in which the defeat of Europe—the "fall of Rome"—is made explicit, a matter of concrete politics rather than of poetic images.[17] Müller sets up just such an interpretation of the text with his comment that "[Shakespeare's] *Titus Andronicus* is a North-South play. Its theme is the clash between a European and a tropical politics, a politics that is concrete in the bloodiest sense of the word, that inscribes itself on bodies without translation through institutions or apparatuses. . . . *Titus Andronicus* is also a guest worker play" ("Deutschland" 207). Brought to the fore once again are the Third World and the importance of the body, in contrast to Europe and its institutions of control.

Ironically, the blind spot in the West German reception of the production of this play in 1985 identifies precisely what is at issue. Müller's text translates and comments on Shakespeare's *Titus Andronicus* of 1594, already an intriguing choice.[18] T. S. Eliot, expressing the judgment of many scholars before and after him, called the work "one of the stupidest and most uninspired plays ever written, a play in which it is incredible that Shakespeare had any hand at all" (qtd. in Barnet xxi).[19] For the most part, what is "stupid" and "uninspired" is the violence: scenes of murder, rape, mutilation, and cannibalism, unparalleled elsewhere in Shakespeare, seem a matter of sheer infatuation rather than high tragedy; the youthful Shakespeare runs amok, in rhetoric and in plot.

German theater critics, writing about the premiere of Müller's *Anatomie Titus* in Bochum, shared Eliot's abhorrence. Helmut Schödel in *Die Zeit*, Peter von Becker in *Theater Heute*, and Georg Hensel in the *Frankfurter Allgemeine Zeitung*—to name just three—joined in the familiar clichés of Müller scholarship: "a generalized slaughter," "universal senselessness," "the world as trap," "a bloody morass as the basis of existence," "bloody cul-de-sac," "the world is like a slaughterhouse," "human beings are animals." Hensel summarizes, "In [Müller's] *Titus* universal pessimism is a desolate mechanism: no human beings, no thoughts, no feelings; only monsters and murders." Heiner Müller, in turn: "Georg Hensel is my favorite critic. Naturally, he doesn't understand a thing" ("Ich scheiß" 120).[20]

What are Hensel and critics like him not seeing in Müller's play? The violent inventory of *Titus Andronicus* includes some dozen corpses, three amputated hands, two heads, a tongue, and two princes hacked to pieces and baked in a pie. The violence is overwhelming, but it is not the point. The most fascinating figure in the play is the black man Aaron, who, through his intrigues, is indirectly responsible for most of the murder and mutilation noble Romans and noble Goths inflict on one another, whites on whites. Interestingly enough, Hensel and Schödel are both compelled to mention Aaron, who provides the key to Müller's play, but only at the very end of their reviews and only to write him off: Hensel sees in Aaron the stereotypical Elizabethan figure of absolute evil and vice; Schödel interprets Aaron's laughter, which concludes Müller's text, as the laughter of the theater of the absurd. What these critics write out in such interpretations is the issue of Aaron's race.

We can gain a better sense of what Müller is doing by comparing his text with Shakespeare's. Shakespeare's play opens with the Roman general Titus Andronicus returning victorious from his campaign against the Goths, bringing with him the defeated queen Tamora and her three sons. Titus calls upon the Roman people to crown Saturnius, the elder son of the deceased emperor, as their new ruler and, following religious custom, offers the eldest son of the Goth queen as a sacrifice to his own dead sons. Tamora, who becomes Saturnius's bride, swears to take revenge against the Roman general. Her two remaining sons, encouraged by Tamora's lover, Aaron, trap Titus's daughter Lavinia in the woods and kill Lavinia's husband, Bassianus, the younger brother and rival of the newly crowned emperor. Lavinia is raped, and her hands and tongue are cut off. Aaron arranges that two of Titus's sons are accused of murdering Bassianus, then tricks Titus into chopping off his right hand in exchange for the lives of his sons. Instead Titus is rewarded with their heads. It is now Titus's turn to seek revenge, and he does so by butchering Tamora's sons and serving them to her in a pie. At the banquet Titus slays his shamed daughter Lavinia and kills Tamora for the rape her sons had committed. The emperor Saturnius, Tamora's husband, kills Titus. Titus's son Lucius, leading the Goth army against Rome, kills Saturnius and becomes the new emperor.

The gory plot is the same in Müller's version, but its significance is vastly changed. Müller's Rome is at the height of its political and economic power: it is "THE CAPITAL / OF THE WORLD" (126), "THE WHORE OF THE CORPORATIONS" (128), an empire that lives and thrives on exploitation and conquest.[21] As the defeated Goths are marched into Rome, the text highlights the foundation of oppression upon which the empire is built: "ROME IS WAITING FOR THE SPOILS SLAVES FOR / THE LABOR MARKET FOR THE BORDELLOS FRESH MEAT / GOLD FOR THE BANKS WEAPONS FOR THE ARMORY" (127).[22] Just as the glory of civilized Rome is revealed to be a matter of imperialist exploitation, so too are the virtues of its foremost citizens replaced by blatant considerations of political power. Titus Andronicus, rather than the pillar of Roman virtue and heroism he represents in Shakespeare's text, is defined strictly in terms of his military function: at the outset he is introduced as "TITUS ANDRONICUS WHO FOR TEN YEARS / HAS BEEN WAGING WAR AGAINST THE GOTHS," as "TITUS ANDRONICUS ROME'S FIRST SWORD" (126).[23] The rivalry between the elder Saturnius and the younger and more noble-minded Bassianus—in Shakespeare's text a conflict between the principles of primogeniture and virtue—becomes in Müller's adaptation a simple "STRUGGLE FOR POWER" between two infantile men who continually wave their swords in each other's faces (126, 131).

Even the implicit contrast between the barbarian Goths and the civilized Romans is eliminated in Müller's text; from the start, the Romans enjoy no advantage of civility, nobility, or virtue over their foreign enemies.[24] Rome's returning soldiers, for example, are referred to as her "WOLVES" (128); and Titus becomes in the very first scene the murderer of one of his thieving sons (132). With any distinction of virtue erased from Müller's text, Romans and Goths come to differ in name only. Or, as powerful nobles, Saturnius, Bassianus, Titus, and Tamora are essentially alike in that they all engage in the power struggle that defines for them life itself. The traditional conflict between civilized and barbaric peoples is thus replaced by a distinction of class in which, according to the view of the Roman masses in Müller's text, it doesn't matter who becomes emperor: rulers are all alike, "ROME IS ROME THE EMPEROR IS THE EMPEROR / . . . / AND A CROWN FITS ON ANY HEAD" (130).[25]

Seen from this subaltern perspective, life in Rome is permeated by death.[26] The commentator describes the march into Rome that opens the play:

> HAILED BY THE CHILDREN'S CHOIRS THE PARADE
> COFFINS IN FRONT THE CONTENTS DEAD SONS
> OF THE COMMANDER EVERY VICTORY HAS ITS PRICE
> INVITATION TO THE YOUTH TO RUSH AFTER
> THE DEAD INTO DEATH AND INTO FAME
> FOUR SONS ARE STILL ALIVE FOUR STANDARD
>   BEARERS
> THEY NUMBERED TWENTY AFTER THE FIRST VICTORY
> THE DEAD PLEBES ROT IN MASS GRAVES. (127)

Fame and heroism are revealed to be class-specific, reserved for the sons of Andronicus, who are carried home in coffins and honored by crowds, while the common people rot in anonymous mass graves. Such institutionalized rituals of death—and the power of the state to decide which corpses are deserving of them—signify for Müller an aspect of increasing state control over individuals; *Antigone*, as he explains, marks the beginning of the exercise of state authority over the dead (*"Jenseits"* 49–50; *"Zur Lage"* 56).[27] The two kinds of burial reflect also different attitudes toward history. When an Andronicus son dies, he reaffirms the continuity of (family and Roman) history as conquest: "A NEW PICTURE IS PASTED IN THE FAMILY ALBUM / A NEW COFFIN IS STUFFED IN THE FAMILY GRAVE / THE REST IS POLITICS" (133).[28] But the mass graves of the countless victims in that history create a huge reservoir for revolt that would bring an end to the tradition of exploitation perpetrated by the state.

The key figure is the black man Aaron, who suggests to Tamora's two sons that they rape Titus's daughter Lavinia. While Shakespeare's figure is taken to represent pure evil and cruelty, Müller's villain is motivated not by moral or metaphysical principles but by an explicit politics of revenge against European domination:

> . . . NIGHT BLACKENS ROME THE NIGHT
> OF THE NEGRO HIS SEX DREAMS AFRICA
> HIS SEMEN A STREAK OF LIGHTNING WHITE IN BLACK
> THE FLASH TRANSFORMS ROME INTO A FOREST
> INHABITED BY THE BEASTS OF HIS HOMELAND
> THERE HE WAITS FOR HIS OTHER HUNT
> WITH ROLES REVERSED THE HUNTER IS THE PREY
> WITH TOOTH AND CLAW INSTEAD OF HORN AND
>   HOUND. (139–40)[29]

In Aaron's vision Rome becomes a forest filled with African beasts, no longer the prey for Roman soldiers but now themselves the hunters: the black African seeks revenge against imperial Rome. If in Shakespeare's play the tragic chain of violence operates according to an ineluctable but mistaken logic of honor and justice, the bloody acts in Müller's text are the doing of the black man seeking to crumble Rome from within. The play's commentator thus presents Aaron's revenge in the context of the uprising of the Third World, of masses of victims, against European power;[30] the first scene ends with a powerful "EXCURSUS ON THE SLUMBER OF THE METROPOLISES," offering a summary vision of Müller's notion of Third World revolution:

> GRASS SPLITS THE STONE THE WALLS SPROUT
>   BLOSSOMS
> THE FOUNDATIONS SWEAT SLAVES' BLOOD
> BREATH OF PREDATORY CATS BLOWS THROUGH
>   PARLIAMENT
> WITH A HOT CLOUD WITH THE STINK OF CARRION
> HYENA SHADOWS PROWL AND VULTURES' FLIGHT

THROUGH THE ALLEYS AND SOILS THE VICTORY
    COLUMNS
THE PANTHERS LEAP SILENTLY THROUGH THE BANKS
EVERYTHING BECOMES THE SHORE WAITS FOR THE
    SEA
IN THE SLUDGE OF THE SEWERS HANNIBAL'S
DEAD ELEPHANTS TRUMPET
ATTILA'S SPIES WALK AS TOURISTS
THROUGH THE MUSEUMS AND BITE INTO THE
    MARBLE
MEASURE THE CHURCHES FOR HORSE STABLES
AND WANDER GREEDILY THROUGH THE
    SUPERMARKET
THE LOOT OF THE COLONIES WHICH THROUGH THE
    YEAR
THE HOOVES OF THEIR HORSES WILL KISS
BRINGING HOME THE FIRST WORLD INTO THE VOID.
    (140–41)

The dominant image in the excursus is that of nature (grass, cats, vultures), which begins to invade the civilized metropolis. It conveys the sense that civilization has been built upon widescale oppression and immense destruction: foundations sweat the blood of slaves; dead elephants, vehicles for Hannibal's conquest, lie buried in the mud of the sewers. Here too is the suggestion of resurrection, as they begin once again to trumpet. Such images prefigure revolt and retribution, the revenge against an imperial Rome that will be enacted by the barbarian Attila. Rome with its supermarkets offering the products of its colonies is the First World; Attila, and with him the elephants, panthers, vultures, is the unnamed "Third World," taking its revenge, "BRINGING HOME THE FIRST WORLD INTO THE VOID."[31]

Such is the promise of the play's opening scene. The black man Aaron, representing Africa and the historical victims of Rome, will seek his barbarian revenge against an imperialist state; in the view of the play's commentator,

THE NEGRO IS HIS OWN DIRECTOR

HE RAISES THE CURTAIN WRITES THE PLOT PROMPTS

. . . .

AND WITH MARKED CARDS PLAYS HIS GAME
IN THE THEATER OF HIS BLACK REVENGE. (142)

The minority figure in Müller's work has come a long way from the utopian images of natural revolt in *Leben Gundlings* and the immobilized and silenced Ophelia of *Hamletmaschine*. In the author's revision of Shakespeare, the Third World figure moves from the margins of a monolithic, European-centered discourse to the very center of the drama, rotting its core. Further, while Müller's earlier images and figures of the Third World were repressed, restricted, or destroyed, the figure of the African Aaron, in contrast, enjoys an ecstatic victory.

Müller takes greatest liberty with Shakespeare's plot in the final scene of his adaptation. The scene begins with the words of the commentator that announce again the uprising of nature and the resurrection of the dead:

GRASS GROWS OVER THE DATA BANKS RUST
GNAWS THE INDUSTRIAL PARK THE DUMPS
SEASON SUPPER WITH THEIR POISONS
THE DEAD RISE FROM THE SHIT OF ROME. (216)

In Shakespeare's play, vengeance is brought to an end and harmony restored: Titus's brother and last remaining son describe the sequence of violent and secret deeds that led to Titus's murderous rage; Titus's son Lucius is proclaimed emperor and promises "[t]o heal Rome's harms and wipe away her woe" (V.iii.148). In contrast, Müller's text, which begins with victory over the Goths and the burial of the dead in Rome, concludes not with the reestablishment but with the overturning of that initial order: the Goths destroy Rome, the masses applaud from their graves. In Shakespeare's text Lucius honors his oath to raise and protect Aaron's half-black infant son in a new Rome; Müller's Lucius instead throws the dead body of Aaron's and Tamora's son before Tamora's husband, Saturnius, demonstrating not the principles of a new Rome but the continuity of the old.[32]

Both Shakespeare and Müller have Aaron buried up to his chest in the ground to die slowly of starvation. But Müller's Aaron laughs wildly as the commentator tells of the final destruction of Rome by the Goths:

WHILE THE NEGRO GROWS INTO THE EARTH
TRANSFORMED SLOWLY BY THE WORMS OF THE DEEP
INTO DUST WHICH GATHERS INTO A DESERT AND
EXPANDS OVER ROME
THE GOTHS NAIL THE CAPITAL OF THE WORLD
WITH A STORM OF ARROWS ON THE CROSS OF THE
   SOUTH
APPLAUDED SILENTLY FROM MASS GRAVES
. . . .
IN CANNIBAL-LOOK THE BUTCHER OF THE GOTHS
DANCES WITH THE NEGRO ON THE ASHES OF ROME
THE FOXTROT IN RHYTHM TURNS THE SKY GREY
WHICH SHINES OUT BLACK AND BOTTOMLESS
   BELOW
UNTIL WHISTLING OVER THE LAST HAPPY END
THE TRAP WORLD CLOSES THE FIRMAMENT. (222–23)

Aaron, whose voice "COMES FROM FAR AWAY / WHERE THE DESERTS AND THE GLACIERS GATHER" (221), embodies in the end the long-awaited revenge against an oppressive Roman state, a revenge carried out in images of natural forces and in the name of the masses of victims rising from their graves. Shakespeare's Rome is reborn and restored in virtue; Müller's city is burned to ashes by barbarians in an apocalyptic end that signifies in the fall of Rome the fall of the monolith Europe. The catastrophic finale is not evidence of a pessimistic or nihilistic worldview on the part of the author; this is not the world as slaughterhouse, or history as perpetual, senseless destruction, but rather the natural violent demise of an imperialist state. Aaron laughs, Aaron wins; Africa defeats Europe.[33]

When we consider the four main figures and texts discussed in this chapter—Ophelia in *Hamletmaschine*, Sasportas in *Der Auftrag*, Medea in *Verkommenes Ufer*, and especially Aaron in *Anatomie Titus*—important patterns emerge. The women, Ophelia and Medea, are victims of noble European lovers; the two black men, historical victims of European imperialism. All four resist the structures and traditions of European domination: Ophelia and Sasportas reject the standard of the white European male, in different ways leaving the stage of his drama. The "barbarians" Medea and Aaron emerge full-blown as figures of violent revenge, leaving Europe in ruins. Unlike Ophelia and Sasportas, they offer not mere images of revolt, not rhetorical calls for mass uprising, but deliberate actions, self-consciously performed, that lead to the devastation of their enemy.

This raises once again the aesthetic and political problem of a text that is critical of traditional structures of domination yet is cast in a relentlessly, inescapably European discourse. The problem is one that preoccupies Müller at this time, as is evidenced by the painful reflections offered in his contemporaneous *Bildbeschreibung*: there the authorial "I" asks whether the emancipatory moments of his text are not merely aspects of his own obsessively violent self; seeking to expose the violence that underlies the deceptively calm surface of the picture he describes, he is led to questions about his complicity and culpability, and about the very possibility of change (Teraoka, "Writing").

Even the figures of Medea and Aaron, explosive as their actions of revenge may be, seem caught in the discursive trap. In the first case, my analysis focused on Medea's monologue to the exclusion of the two sections of text that frame it and complete the triptychal work. In the play as a whole, the middle "Medeamaterial" differs markedly from the other sections: it is written in distinct speaking parts, in the traditional form of drama, while "Verkommenes Ufer Medeamaterial Landschaft mit Argonauten" (hereafter as "Verkommenes Ufer") and "Landschaft mit Argonauten" offer the reflections of a single lyrical voice. More importantly, the speeches and theme of revenge given to the female voice of Medea contrast sharply with a lyrical "I" in the first and third sections that is unmistakably male. The Argonautic, misogynist voice of

"Verkommenes Ufer" speaks of a shore littered with used condoms and the menstrual pads of the women of Colchis, identifying them as the polluting agents of a once imperial, pristine culture: women, reduced to their sexual function, are seen as drainpipes for the removal of waste, "[g]utter that costs three weeks pay," "[w]aste pipes / Ejecting babies in batches against the advance of the maggots" (127). "Landschaft mit Argonauten" in turn presents a collage of images of—again, quintessentially male—exploration and voyage, ending in the shipwreck and destruction that represent, in this text, the inevitable fate of the European conqueror.[34]

Both texts are replete with images of sexual and political conquest and of death and decay. The placement of the Medea text between them on the one hand recognizes and reinforces the strength of her attack: "Verkommenes Ufer" ends with the male's fearful vision of "Medea . . . expert / In poisons" (128); Jason's family is then destroyed in "Medeamaterial," which follows. Further, the final triumphant question that ends Medea's monologue, "Nurse Do you know this man," is answered in the first lines of "Landschaft mit Argonauten," which record the loss of a stable, ruling male "I": "[s]hall I speak of me I who / Of whom are they speaking when / They do speak of me I Who is it" (133). On the other hand, however, the Medea text and the dramatic figure of Third World retaliation that develops within it are embedded—in terms of the structure of the text as a whole—within a larger discourse that, filled with allusions to works by Müller as well as Pound, Shakespeare, and other literary masters, is markedly male and European.[35] It is troubling, finally, that Medea's monologue is one speech of many divided among three speakers of the middle text: the form of Müller's text thus suggests the presence of a higher authorial consciousness (male again?) that composes a nightmarish internal "drama" of destruction directed against itself. Is Medea ultimately only the poetic creation of a male consciousness painfully aware of its crimes and its guilt?[36]

In *Anatomie Titus*, too, we must ask whether the vengeful voice of the other, the figure of the black African Aaron who dismantles Rome and all it represents, is not the hopeful projection of an overarching authorial consciousness that remains unshakably European, intact, and imperialist—whether it is even possible for the male European "author" of the text to escape his identity and to write from the perspective of the truly "other."[37] There is no question that a "Third World" voice exists in Müller's *Anatomie Titus*, but who is its speaker?

Broadly considered, Müller's text offers a powerful and accurate translation of the bulk of Shakespeare's play, interspersed with new passages unattributed to any speaking role and belonging presumably to the unidentified "commentator."[38] The added passages are unified, and can be identified, by their late-twentieth-century perspective (references are made to football stadiums, supermarkets, and Star Wars) and by their uppercase typeface throughout the play. Both the technique of anachronistic (suprahistorical) montage and the unusual orthography are so common in Müller's works that they constitute part of his discursive signature. The text's commentator, in other words, offers the "author's" voice, an interpretation that is strengthened by the fact that the passages of the commentator contain recognizable excerpts from texts by Heiner Müller.[39]

Significantly, the passages from Müller's text that I quote in my analysis consist almost exclusively of the uppercase speeches of the commentator. The geopolitical (colonial) context of the play that connects the Roman state with the enslavement of foreign peoples, the subaltern perspective of the masses in which moral distinctions of good and evil among rulers become irrelevant or sham, and the foregrounded issue of race that makes of Aaron a representative of the enslaved and now vengeful Africa—all are attributable only to the commentator, not to Shakespeare or to specific figures in the play. On closer examination, for example, it is not Aaron who speaks of the black man's revenge against Europe but the commentator who casts his intrigues in this particular light. Aaron plans—in his own words—"a rogue's play, unlike anything found in a book" (142); the commentator, in contrast, speaks of the African as the plotting director of a theater of black revenge (142) and envisions the Third World invading the First ("EXCURSUS ON THE SLUMBER OF THE METROPOLISES" [140–41]) and the Goths trampling down the Roman capital (222–23). Once again we seem to be confronted by a dominant, decidedly European and masculine authorial consciousness who orchestrates a drama of destruction among figures who do not (indeed, cannot) stand independently against him but who are his own creation.

At this point we might gain better access to Müller's project by moving beyond the discussion of the content, and even of the form or structure, of his Third World plays. For resistance is not only the topic or subject matter of these texts, which, as we have seen, is undermined by formal structures that uphold the dominance of an authorial consciousness. It is also the *strategy of writing* that they exhibit, the particular attitude they demonstrate toward literary and historical monuments of the past.[40]

In an essay on Shakespeare, Müller designates in coded fashion two principal points of view in aesthetic production. One is the perspective associated with privilege, reason, and the established rule of order represented by Hamlet and Prospero; the other, the subaltern perspective expressed in the curse spoken by Caliban in the language of the master: "[o]ur task . . . is to work on difference. Hamlet, the failure, did not do this; this is his crime. Prospero is the undead Hamlet: still, he destroys his staff, a reply to Caliban's (the new Shakespeare reader's) current indictment of all previous culture: YOU TAUGHT ME LANGUAGE AND MY PROFIT ON'T / IS I KNOW HOW TO CURSE" ("Shakespeare eine" 230). Prospero and Caliban—the practitioner of "white" magic seeking the restoration of a just political order and the alien being who desires to turn the tools of his oppressors against them—constitute two aspects, in dynamic tension, of Müller's authorial practice. In this chapter I have sought to uncover the principles of a Calibanic reading of a European master-piece, of the specific discursive, "cursing" practices that characterize and enact a critique of European culture in Müller's recent writings.[41]

In four texts that I have discussed, Müller takes institutions of European literature or European history (Hamlet, the story of Jason and the Argonauts, the ideals of the French Revolution, the history of the Roman Empire) to rework and rewrite them from the constructed point of view of their marginalized figures, in such a way that the relationship of oppression hidden in these European institutions is revealed. Thus *Hamlet* has to do with the preservation of male dominance and repressive rule handed down from father to son; the story of Jason and Medea is the myth of the European colonialist and the barbarian tribe he conquers by deceit; the attempt to export the ideals of the French Revolution to the Caribbean seeks to extend the authority of the European to other parts of the world. *Leben Gundlings*, as well, exposes the tradition of German Enlightenment and Idealism as one of philosophical and physical coercion.

Most importantly, Müller's *Anatomie Titus* becomes a play of revenge not of the Goths against Titus and of Titus against the Goths, as in the Shakespearean model, but of the black African against imperial Rome. The cultural opposition that structures the text is expressed in Lucius's statement at the play's end that "[t]he Goth is a Negro is a Jew" (222): Aaron as a black man stands for any and all ethnic and cultural minorities who differ from the normative whiteness of Rome. Through the added voice of its unidentified commentator, Müller's adaptation is able to attack the traditionally sanctioned mode of thought that would present Titus's demise as "tragic" and Aaron (or any member of a threatening minority) as "evil." Such a view, prevalent in literary and social history, deliberately ignores conflicts of race, class, and culture and thereby functions as ideological deception. In Müller's text, as its subversive commentary insists, the "tragic" noble figure stands upon the bodies of those he has enslaved; the "evil" figure is seen as such because he is powerful enough to comprehend, to expose, and to destroy the system of oppression that would enslave him. In the process, Shakespeare's title venerating *Titus Andronicus* as "The Most Lamentable Roman Tragedy" is abandoned in favor of Müller's anatomical dissection, the exposing of its structural "anatomy." The ideals of high tragedy are stripped literally to the bone; judgments of moral virtue are shown to be politically determined, with interpretations based upon them inevitably reaffirming the status quo.[42]

It is this ideological process that Müller's Third World plays seek to uncover. If Seghers's texts had celebrated emancipatory European values, the minority poetics and politics of Müller's works reveal that universal categories—the high ideals of European history—and the great political and aesthetic monuments that glorify them serve only to cloak relationships of power and domination. The motif of monuments in *Anatomie Titus*—Titus and his daughter are each described as a "MONUMENT" (155, 156) that Aaron manages literally to dismantle—is anything but coincidental.[43] A network of associations connects Müller's texts, in which the tenor of European history is presented as monumental and monumentalizing, from the attempt to cast Lessing in a bronze bust in *Leben Gundlings* (78), to the Stalin statue in *Hamletmaschine* (56), and the argument in *Der Auftrag*, based on a theme in Seghers's *Das Licht auf dem Galgen*, as to whose name will be immortalized in history books (93, 97). The motif permeates the text of *Anatomie Titus*: from its opening scene, in which the sons of Andronicus are entombed, to images of a prostrate Titus being turned into a "statue" by the bird droppings that cover him (155) or of Lavinia as an armless silent torso (156), finally to the "black monument" of Aaron planted into the ground with the names of dead Romans carved into his flesh (216–17), the text repeats again and again the idea of the monumentalization of Europe's victories and victims.[44] The practice of erecting monuments is seen as markedly European: in contrast, the Goths from the steppes belong to a landscape in which "[n]o stone can stand on top of another for even a year" (208); more importantly, they are unable to write (217).[45] In all these texts, the monuments signifying Europe are razed.

In a letter to the stage designer Erich Wonder, Müller calls for a theater of resurrection in contrast to the ideologically and artistically retrograde theater of restoration that has dominated and still dominates the stage. Müller writes: "When we have a theater, it will be a theater of resurrection (which naturally presupposes daily death); our work the conjuring up of the dead, the ensemble recruited from the spirits who must return to the grave after the performance, until the last performance" (Letter).[46] What follows is a wild collage of images of what such a theater would entail, including the path of panzers, modern-day versions of Hannibal's elephants, from the battlefields of World War I to the opera houses of Berlin; and the twentieth-century migration of (again, European) men, following a trail of chains and bombs, to the bordellos of Bangkok. Part of what Müller envisions is a drama of what has been destroyed or exploited — machines, animals, women, the Third World — in the making of European history.

Leben Gundlings, *Hamletmaschine*, *Der Auftrag*, "Medeamaterial," and *Anatomie Titus* begin slowly to reveal what such a theater might be like. From inchoate images of resistance in the earlier texts to the breathtaking figures of revenge in the later ones, Müller's tendency has been to seek out and to empower the traditional victims in European history and literature, with the result that the monuments commemorating Europe's dominance are left in literary ruins. In writing increasingly from the constructed standpoint of the victims of history (to the point that the black Aaron emerges, in the hopeful vision of the authorial commentator, as both playwright and director of his revenge drama), Müller engages in a strategy of resurrection in which dead victims "rise up" to avenge themselves and to rewrite the literary masterworks of Europe. The fall of Rome thus marks the end of traditional European drama and the beginning of a different, as yet undefined theater.[47]

Shakespeare's Prospero, weaving a tight intertextual web, quotes Medea's speech on the power of her magic from Ovid's *Metamorphoses* (*The Tempest* V.i.33–50; *Metamorphoses* VII.197–209). Both he and the barbarian queen claim the power to raise the dead. As such, the man of reason with the potential to call upon the powers of nonreason offers a helpful paradigm for Müller's notion of the author. The problem of Prospero is the problem of the white author engaged in a project to acknowledge difference within his writing: "[o]ur task . . . is to work on difference." This is to grant a place to a Caliban whose curses aim to destroy any privilege enjoyed by the author's language and culture — to work toward the "disappearance of the author," as Müller calls it in his essay on postmodernism ("Schrecken"; Teraoka, *Silence* 17–50). The result is a self-reflective dramatic enactment of artistic production as a violence directed against all oppressors, including, in particular, oneself. It is for this reason that the artist in *Anatomie*

Titus is depicted as violator, mutilator, murderer; art and the art-work represent and are created by mutilation, as exemplified by the sons of the Goth queen who, as "ARTISTS," rape and amputate hands and tongue from their "ART WORK," Lavinia (151). The critique of the artistic deed as bloody creation points to a new kind of writing, a new kind of authorship in Müller's work that is at once mindful of its complicity in the violence that maintains an imperial order, while participating in the vengeful project(ion) of its decimation.[48]

Müller's dismantling of Shakespeare's *Titus Andronicus* concludes with the commentator's vision of the destruction of Rome by the Goths, signifying, in his late-twentieth-century global perspective, the victory of the Third World over the First. Not only does the European commentator speak the point of view ascribed to the African Aaron. In what constitutes perhaps the most curious image of the play, the commentator casts the European nobleman Titus into the victory of the other. The Prosperean Titus, as a "NEW CHRIST" who calls forth the dead (216), joins the Calibanic Aaron in a dance upon the ruins of Rome: "IN CANNIBAL-LOOK THE BUTCHER OF THE GOTHS / DANCES WITH THE NEGRO ON THE ASHES OF ROME" (223). Perhaps through the injuries and injustices Titus has been forced to suffer upon his body and the bodies of his children, perhaps through the mediation of the madness that befalls him, the European conqueror has come to take on the "look" of the cannibal (of Caliban) and, awakening the empire's victims, to join with him in the destruction of Rome.[49] Not only does the commentator project the destructive vengeance of the Third World figure, he offers as well the mad and hopeful vision of the European who tramples upon his privileged traditions—a poetological projection of the First World author embracing, in a dance of ultimate suicide, a Third World voice. Historical roles are reversed, "THE ROMAN LEARNS THE ALPHABET OF THE NEGRO" (189).

5

TALKING "TURK"

On Narrative Strategies and Cultural Stereotypes

The latest chapter on Germany's construction of, and encounter with, a "Third World" concerns not imagined landscapes and peoples far away but resident foreign populations within its major cities. Today 5 million Turkish, Yugoslav, Italian, Greek, Spanish, and other non-German residents (of which 90,000 lived in the former GDR) constitute 6.5% of the nation's population. Their countries of origin, mostly in Southern Europe, are not usually considered Third World, yet the political discourse that defines (and limits) their presence in Germany marks them as categorically and essentially non-German, non-European, and nonwhite (cf. Goldberg 166).[1]

Numbering close to 2 million, Turks constitute by far the largest group of foreigners and, in the public imagination, stand *pars pro toto* for all undesired non-Germans.[2] Recruited beginning in 1961 to fill the labor shortage created by the building of the Berlin Wall, Turks became part of "one of the greatest migratory movements in human history" (Castles et al. 1).[3] Agreements for the recruitment of foreign labor were signed first with Italy in 1955, followed by Spain and Greece (1960), Turkey (1961), Morocco (1963), Portugal (1964), Tunisia (1965), and Yugoslavia (1968). In 1973, faced with a stagnating economy and a guest worker population of 4 million, the German government put a halt to recruitment with the expectation that the foreigners would steadily decrease in number. Although the size of the foreign work force declined, a secondary migration of dependents, a high birth rate, and, for the Turks, increasing political repression and economic disorder in Turkey, which made return impossible, resulted in an overall increase in the foreign population: in 1973, 4 million foreigners (with 65%

employed) comprised 6.4% of Germany's population; in 1985, 4.4 million, of whom 1.5 million or 35% were employed, made up 7% of the total. Turks represented the key group in these numbers: by 1971 they had become the largest minority group in Germany, numbering 653,000 and comprising 19% of the foreign population; in 1980, seven years after the recruitment halt, their total had swelled to 1.5 million (of whom only 600,000 were workers and nearly as many were children below the age of sixteen), a full third of Germany's foreigners. Their sheer number and the class, cultural, and religious differences that marked them made the Turks, more than any other ethnic group in Germany, the focus of fear, misrepresentation, and, especially in the years following reunification, murderous violence.[4]

A major factor in Germany's "foreigner problem" is its concept of a national identity defined by ethnic origin and rooted in language, culture, and history. This concept, codified in the Nuremberg Laws of 1934, which linked citizenship to blood, allowed ethnic Germans from the annexed eastern territories of the Third Reich relatively straightforward access to German citizenship, while denying similar rights to second- and third-generation Turkish residents born and schooled in Germany.[5] Naturalization, though possible in theory, is rare in practice: only 1% of foreigners (and 0.75% of Turks) are naturalized citizens, although the majority (60%) have resided in Germany for over a decade. German politicians of every party have held firm to the position that Germany is not a country of immigration; given this dominant view, naturalization, as Wilpert points out, signifies only an exception to, not a change in, the logic of a nonimmigrant country (73n).[6]

The GDR author Heiner Müller speaks of an invasion of the Third World into the metropolises of the First World. Indeed, the permanent presence of 5 million Turks and other foreigners in a nation that defines itself, and that distributes rights, according to a "sacred" ideology of ethnic origins (Wilpert 76) must seem just such an incursion to the German public imagination. This final chapter investigates three attempts to intervene in these political and imaginative constructions—to educate German citizens about the lives of Turks in Germany and, beyond that, to initiate change in the discriminatory and exploitive institutions that control their presence. Specifically, I explore the ways in which three authors—Max von der Grün, Günter Wallraff, and Paul Geiersbach—create a sympathetic Turk for German audiences, and the narrative strategies they employ that may unwittingly reinforce rather than undermine prejudicial stereotypes.

All three writers align themselves with liberal or leftist politics. Max von der Grün (b. 1926), the son of a shoemaker, was a member of the Social Democratic Party for fifteen years until its coalition with the conservative Christian party in 1966. The best-known and most important member of Group 61, an association of writers devoted to the literary and artistic exploration of the modern industrial work world, von der Grün had been a miner for thirteen years until he was fired after the publication of his second novel, *Irrlicht und Feuer* (1963; Will-o'-the-wisp and fire). The book, which depicted working conditions in the coal-mining industry, met the ire of both the miners union and a machinery manufacturer that launched an unsuccessful suit against the author. While deeply rooted in the working class, von der Grün read widely in world (Western) literature and educated himself in the classic "bourgeois" canon. His literary views proved to be too bourgeois, in fact, for Günter Wallraff (b. 1942), who split away from Group 61 in 1970 after long internal strife to found the praxis-oriented Workshop for Literature of the Working World (Werkkreis Literatur der Arbeitswelt) in the tradition of the Association of Proletarian-Revolutionary Writers (Bund Proletarisch-Revolutionärer Schriftsteller).

One of Germany's leading writers of documentary prose, Wallraff earned his reputation with a series of controversial exposés focusing on the illegal or immoral practices of political, military, industrial, religious, and cultural institutions in West Germany (see Wallraff, *Undesirable*). Wallraff's documentary evidence stemmed in most cases from undercover work; typically, the author gathered information under an assumed identity. His *Wir brauchen dich* (1966, We need you; republished as *Industriereportagen*, 1970, Industrial reports) and especially *Der Aufmacher* (1977; The front-page story), on the smear tactics and sensationalist journalism of *Bild-Zeitung*, led critics on the Right to denounce Wallraff as a terrorist sympathizer and underground Communist. The numerous lawsuits against him proved largely unsuccessful. *Ganz unten* (1985; *Lowest of the Low*), on the economic treatment of Turks, was Wallraff's most successful work and one of the biggest bestsellers in the postwar period, with translations into eighteen languages and close to three million German copies sold in its first two years.

Paul Geiersbach (b. 1941), in contrast, is largely unknown on the German market. The author of four ethnographic novels on the lives of Turks in Germany, he studied sociology, ethnology, and psychology before pursuing research and social work among foreign workers in Germany. Introductions to his works by Wallraff and by Bahman Nirumand, an antifundamentalist Iranian writer living in exile in Berlin, locate Geiersbach unambiguously on the Left. Innovative and self-reflective, his books stand among the best that Germany's writers have to offer on the complex situation of its largest minority population.

Before we read even a word of text, our image of and relationship to the "Turk" are subtly guided by title and book cover. Max von der Grün's *Leben im gelobten Land: Gastarbeiterporträts* (1975; Life in the promised land: Guest worker portraits) displays a photograph of a Turkish man sitting on a suitcase, holding a cigarette in his fingers and a jug in his hands. The man looks to be in his forties; he wears a white shirt and dark pants; he is thin, his face deeply lined; his thick curly hair, dark brows, deep-set eyes, and moustache offer the typical "portrait" of a Turk. Behind him two other Turkish men stand or sit next to their own pieces of luggage, with another jug of the unknown liquid. In the background is what might be the entrance to a modern subway station, in brick, chrome, and neon—the "promised land." Three dark, moustached men, with suitcases and without families, and clearly out of place. All are looking at the camera. Their expressions suggest that we have caught them by surprise; they do not know what we want, or what the photograph is for.

"Ali" stares again into the camera ten years later on the famous cover of Günter Wallraff's *Ganz unten*. In torn clothing and a construction hat, the figure of the Turk presents his familiar face—the hair, the eyes, that moustache. Over his shoulder in the not-too-distant background, the fumes from an industrial smokestack form a huge cloud that hangs in the air. This time the gaze into the camera lens is posed, deliberate, accusatory—we are confronted and challenged, perhaps threatened, by the stark image of life as the "lowest of the low" in the Federal Republic. We no longer stand safely behind our camera but are directly and actively confronted by what we see. But more than this: the Turk who stares at us in *Ganz unten* is—as we learned with a shock of recognition—Wallraff himself. It is a German staring back with the face of a Turk: paradoxically, the "other" we meet is created in our image.

While Wallraff and von der Grün deliver for our scrutiny a face that can be caught close-up, framed by telling details of suitcases and hardhats, the cover image of Paul Geiersbach's *Bruder, muß zusammen Zwiebel und Wasser essen! Eine türkische Familie in Deutschland* (1982; Brother, must together eat onion and water: A Turkish family in Germany) is one of distance and impenetrability. An unrecognizable figure (a Turk?) peers at us from a single window of an old brick building, high above the ground. The face is minuscule, framed by the blackness of the window that engulfs also his hair, eyes, and neck in shadow. The building may be a tall apartment house seen from its side alley, or perhaps a warehouse—it is impossible to tell from the cracking wall of brick that fills the photograph from edge to edge. Whatever the building, one thing is certain: the man (let us call him a Turk) is looking out at us. Again we are intruders, but unlike the subway scene of von der Grün's photograph, this is the Turk's world. We have trespassed onto unfamiliar turf, we find ourselves in a setting that we do not recognize. Instead of observing voyeuristically a group of Turkish men who stand out against an ultramodern city backdrop, it is we who are now being watched, we who are uncomfortably out of place.

Three texts—Max von der Grün's *Leben im gelobten Land*, Günter Wallraff's *Ganz unten*, and Paul Geiersbach's *Bruder, muß zusammen Zwiebel und Wasser essen!* — occupy a unique place in German literature on Turks. In these works of documentary reportage, an explicit and empathetic effort is made to present life in the Federal Republic of Germany from the perspective of the Turks themselves.[7] This fact alone makes them worthy of careful study. But while the authors share the goal of presenting things from the other's point of view, their project is fraught with political, epistemological, and ideological ambiguity. As our first impressions tell us, the relationship between ourselves (Germans) and Turks structured in these texts varies widely, reflecting differing politics of approach, understanding, and control. My particular interest concerns the rhetorical strategies that the authors employ in speaking "through" the Turk.[8] Von der Grün constructs portraits in which guest workers representing various national groups speak directly to us in the first person. Wallraff turns into a Turk so that we can experience, through him, life as the "lowest of the low." And Geiersbach's strategy is to give us the direct, unedited speeches of Turkish family members, just as they occurred in conversation with the author. What I would like to explore is the extent to which cultural stereotypes are embedded in and communicated through these narrative strategies themselves.[9]

Ostensibly the "guest worker portraits" promised by Max von der Grün's *Leben im gelobten Land* are self-portraits. The volume offers a gallery of such vignettes, labeled "Turk," "Greek," "Yugoslav," "Frenchwoman," "Italian," and "Spaniard," each representing an (imagined) real person with a name and a voice of his or her own. Introducing a narrative strategy that will characterize all the subsequent portraits, the text entitled "Turk" is composed of the first-person voice of "Osman Gürlük" and the voice of a narrator-commentator (figured as von der Grün), speaking in turn. The intended effect is to create the sense of the Turk who tells us directly about his life, supported by an informed German who acts as a kind of mediator.[10]

A telling disparity between the two voices emerges in the discourse generated in this way. The portrait begins:

This coldness here in Germany makes me sick; I am still home-sick today, sometimes even more strongly than five years ago; homesickness is an illness, and this illness can only be cured in Turkey; but in Anatolia there is no work for me, no earn-ings, no possibility of ever moving up in the world, of living like a human being, with a house and a steady income: I have to stay in Germany for now, I have to live with this illness; in this cold; the coldness here in Germany is its people.

Osman Gürlük lives today with his wife and three-year-old daughter Ipek in a two-and-a-half-room apartment in the northern part of Dortmund, in a district inhabited solely by Turks. (7)

The voice of the Turk sounds poetic and existential; the voice of the German commentator, in contrast, is dispassionate and dis-tanced, providing concrete information that serves to clarify and contextualize the Turk's feelings and emotions.

Already from the start von der Grün's text seems to fall into the familiar dichotomy of rational self and emotional other. This is indeed the difference that its narrative strageggies—intentionally or unintentionally—emphasize. Gürlük, for example, speaks as follows (the passage is chosen largely at random):

My father in the truest sense of the word got run down working for the patron; another worker ran over him with a tractor; my father was lying in a furrow and was sleeping; he who sleeps is guilty; but the man on the tractor must have been sleeping as well, otherwise he would have seen my fa-ther; so no money for the family, the patron paid only for the funeral; my uncle convinced me to go to Germany; he had already worked three years for Ford in Cologne by the time I arrived, one day he had come with his car, with his own car, to Sile; that was an event; I wanted to have a car like that too. (10)

Gürlük essentially recounts the events that led to his move to Cologne, yet his narrative, punctuated by semicolons, gives the impression of disjointedness and disorganization. His single sen-tence continues for two pages, moving from the uncle's visit to

Gürlük's part-time work as a mechanic, to the Turks' admiration for Germans, Gürlük's grandfather's experiences with the Germans in World War I, and Gürlük's uncle's accounts of life in Cologne, back again to the uncle's car and bundle of banknotes, and finally to Gürlük's impressions of Germany (the work ethic, the treatment of Turks in his factory, the restaurants and stores, the cars, the women), ending with what seems to us to be a nonsequitur: "even hot water comes out of the water faucets, but when you ask for a glass of water in a German restaurant, they bring mineral water" (12). The logic that structures the Turk's speech is made to seem purely associative: his marathon run-on sentence exhibits little in the way of logical transitions; the nonsequitur ending is telltale. The text creates the appearance that the Turk cannot speak in ordered sentences; rather, he simply opens his mouth for a gush of words that comes eventually and arbitrarily to an end.[11]

Compare the speech of the German that immediately follows: "Osman Gürlük earns 1,200 marks net in a heavy construction company in Dortmund, sometimes even more since he pushes for overtime. . . . If he were to earn the same money in Turkey, he would be a wealthy man. Whenever he was able to find work at all in Turkey, he earned at most 200–400 lira per month, approximately 30–60 marks according to the exchange rate at that time" (12). When the German commentator speaks, we hear numbers, statistics, hard facts that allow us to measure Gürlük's success in the FRG against the conditions of his former life in Turkey. The Turk offers disjointed memories and observations; the German presents documentary evidence that helps us to structure what we have heard. With his expansive body of information ranging from the most confidential (Gürlük's bank accounts) to the most "scientific" (public opinion polls from 1974), the German speaks with a distinctly authoritative voice in contrast to the personal and impressionistic statements of the Turk. In large part, the shifts from one voice to the other reflect a basic difference in knowledge and analytical rigor: without the German to order the text, we would have something like babble, a flood of words barely punctuated by logic.[12]

Such stereotyping of the Turk, mirrored in the rhetoric with which he is presented (or presented as presenting himself), is consistent with the general image we are given of his life in the FRG. For in many ways, the specific case of Osman Gürlük follows widely held stereotypes of the underclass Turks: the narrator's first speech tells us that Gürlük and his family live in a Turkish ghetto in Dortmund, a part of the city where German children come to play cops and cowboys to the Turkish children's robbers and Indians, in two rooms furnished with appliances and furniture from the garbage dump (7–8). Also noteworthy is the use of the present tense: "Osman Gürlük lives today" (7); "Osman Gürlük is thirty years old. . . . Gürlük lives [has been living] in the Federal Republic for five years" (8), and so forth. The effect is to set the Turk in a timeless realm untouched by historical and cultural change—in our minds Gürlük (who will stand for all Turks in Germany) is always thirty years old, with a three-year-old child and a wife, living in a tiny apartment with garbage dump decor.[13]

Yet certain details tend to call these clichés into question and bring to light the real agenda of von der Grün's portrait. For Gürlük, our typified Turk, is in striking ways atypical.[14] He speaks, the narrator tells us, "amazingly good German" (8); he reads a newspaper "for openminded Turks" (15); and he is an enthusiastic member of the union. Most significantly, his wife has given up wearing her headscarf, a move that meets with disapproval on the part of Gürlük's friends: "my wife is twenty-five years old, she is beginning to dress German now, she is becoming more and more beautiful in her German clothes . . . my friends grumble because my wife dresses so modern, they want her, if she's going to wear German clothes, to wear at least a headscarf and long skirts; why; does everyone have to see from far away that my wife is a Turk" (13). Gürlük's goal is to shed all conspicuous signs of his Turkishness and to "pass" as German—why should our clothes give us away as Turks, he goes on to ask. The wives of his Turkish compatriots dress "impossibly" (i.e., in their native style); if they are laughed at (i.e., conspicuously different), he warns, they will not be taken seriously (13). Von der Grün's Turk urges a program of cultural assimilation; what we see in this portrait is a typical Turk, reminiscent of Seghers's Caribbean blacks, on his way to becoming acceptably "German."[15]

This is in fact the implicit subtext of *Leben im gelobten Land* as a whole. Many of the themes that emerge in the portrait of Osman Gürlük recur in depictions of other "typical" guest workers and shape a strong narrative undercurrent of assimilation and prosperity in Germany. It is striking, for example, that several of the guest workers come from rural villages that seem extraordinarily similar.[16] Von der Grün describes Gürlük's natal village: "their houses are huts, the street unpaved, everywhere dust and more dust. There are goats, sheep, and chickens, and fields of corn, wheat, and melons" (10). One has the sense that the scene has remained unchanged for generations. The same holds true for the descriptions of the villages in Greece, Yugoslavia, Italy, and Spain, with the detail of dust (to which the German observer seems acutely sensitive) as a recurrent motif signaling a backward, rural existence untouched by modern technology (26, 49, 101). The description of the Italian village is paradigmatic; we see and hear through the German visitor:

> About twenty houses, one pub; two massive pine trees offer shade; old men sit in the pub telling stories. . . . Old women sitting under the pines knit or sew and watch their grandchildren, they tell of their sons who work in cold but rich Germany. . . . The landscape is bleak and yet somehow grand, the village is bleak. . . . [T]he bleakness is the hopelessness that speaks in the faces of the people. . . . Home for Ricardo: twenty houses, one pub, two massive pine trees, desolate mountains, and poor mountain peasants. (94–95)

The scene is virtually timeless (note again the use of the present tense). The men tell stories of German and American soldiers, but the war has had little effect on the village except to leave it even poorer. The only significant change that has occurred is the migration of young men to the Federal Republic of Germany, a move that has redefined the rhythm of village life in a permanent way: "the old women say that the hot months July and August used to be dead months and that they are now the months of continual celebrations, because their sons are back" (94). It is as though the migration of workers from rural areas in the Mediterranean to the urban centers of West Germany has shattered the eternal hopelessness of the dusty village and catapulted its young men into a new life of opportunity and progress. Ricardo: "I have built up something for myself here that I could never have done in Italy, not even in twenty lifetimes; . . . what is there for me in Calabria, there is the sun and hunger and parched land and no hope that things will ever get better; but they continue to hope there, they've been hoping for three thousand years" (98).[17]

This places Gürlük's newly acquired progressive views and practices into world-historical perspective. Like him, the other guest workers in von der Grün's portraits express their sense of cultural and personal liberation in their new northern home: the Greek contrasts the economic oppression of his native country with the favorable working conditions in West Germany (33–34); the Spaniard, beaten and scorned in his natal village because of his homosexuality, finds a tolerant environment in the FRG and cannot imagine returning to Spain (102, 112–13). Reflecting von der Grün's views, several seem drawn to the Social Democratic Party (SPD) and to its leading politician, Willy Brandt (35, 50, 56).[18] All have taken great care to learn German well; they inform themselves by reading newspapers; they become dedicated union members. In what constitutes a reverse stereotype, all praise the German values of cleanliness, diligence, and order (15, 27, 56, 79, 92, 95, 96) they find lacking in their own countries. This is taken even to ridiculous extremes, as Gürlük reports that he now changes his underwear daily, something that would never have occurred to him in Turkey (15)![19]

After three thousand years, guest workers are experiencing for the first time what modern civilization and a supposedly enlightened society have to offer—so the metanarrative of von der Grün's text. Its title, "Life in the Promised Land," is meant completely without irony. Yet the themes of prosperity and increased liberality, the vision of social harmony and cultural progress that the guest worker portraits display and that their author intends, are belied, undermined, subverted by the very narrative strategies employed in their transmission: a Turk can "pass" for a German, but the magnitude of this achievement is measured against the prevailing image of Turks living in ghetto apartments furnished from the garbage dump, of Turks who cannot think or speak in orderly fashion. Von der Grün's message of liberal humanism is flawed by the very stereotypes it presupposes.[20]

Unlike a traditional ethnography, which attempts to present a unified picture of a life or a culture, Günter Wallraff's *Ganz unten* is episodic in form and fragmentary in content. Wallraff's central figure, Ali, moves from job to job—from playing a hand organ, to cooking at McDonald's, to sacrificing his body for pharmaceutical research, to cleaning toxic waste. The sequence of jobs seems to have little internal order; they neither represent a spectrum of the West German economy nor compose an integrated picture of the work world of guest workers. The sole element that holds the episodes together is the figure of Ali (ironically composite, as we know from the scandals that ensued regarding research and authorship),[21] yet the unity he provides is again only illusionary. It is telling that in two hundred and fifty pages we never learn how Ali really lives. Wallraff gives us an address—Diesel Street—but we never learn whether or how Ali is able to survive on the money he makes, who his friends are, how he spends his time, or how he is treated in the grocery store or the bank. "Ali" has no genuine identity, no individual history, no integrated "life" as such.[22] *Ganz unten* is not an attempt, as was von der Grün's text, to create a portrait of the Turk in West German society. It is not about a real, or even fictive, "Ali."[23]

From the first, Wallraff strives to establish his voice and person as authoritative. The uniqueness and power of the work were never a matter of its discovery of previously unknown facts but rather its claim to be based on the direct, personal experience of the author. "Wallraff was there again," we are told on the German book's back cover, and we are made to see in its photographs that Wallraff was the "Ali" of his text. When the acknowledgments list Wallraff's physician, Armin Klümper, who strengthened Wallraff during the undercover activities, increased credibility is lent to the claim of authenticity. But it is not only Wallraff's authority—his having indisputably "been there"—that must be documented. The author is also compelled to indicate his political loyalties. An announcement is made that proceeds from the book's sale will go to the foundation Solidarity with Foreigners (Ausländersolidarität) (viii); Wallraff states his expectation (omitted from the English translation) that the work will become the object of legal action. A dedication is offered to Cemal Kemal Altun, a Turkish refugee who jumped to his death from the offices of the administrative court in West Berlin in 1983. In this way alliances are announced, enemies (those unnamed persons who will set lawsuits in motion) are already sensed—we are promised not an unbiased account but one firmly in solidarity with the cause of the guest workers of the Federal Republic.

The question then arises whether Wallraff's reportage does not in fact reflect the author's biases or self-image—whether the game is not thrown, as is its presentation in *Ganz unten*, before it is begun. On the one hand, Wallraff claims to have direct access to the truth about West German society: "[m]y disguise meant that people told me directly and honestly what they thought of me. . . . I was the fool to whom the truth is told" (2). On the other hand, this "truth" turns out to be something carefully, sometimes brutally, manipulated. Wallraff has only the most clichéd view of the role that he plays: it is life "on the outside" or as "the *lowest of the low*" (1; emphasis in original); Ali is "an outsider, *down in the shit*" (2; emphasis in original). It is not surprising, although Wallraff expresses shock, that "Ali" receives exactly the kind of work that Wallraff asks for in his newspaper ad: "work of any kind, including heavy and dirty jobs, even for little money" (1). Wallraff seems attracted to situations certain to elicit displays of animosity—the Turkey-FRG soccer match, or a political rally in honor of the archconservative politician Franz Josef Strauß (where Wallraff compares "Ali's" presence to that of a gypsy at a Nazi meeting in a Munich beer hall [11]). Indeed, Wallraff knows even before taking on the role of the Turk exactly what he will find (this then becomes exactly what he seeks out) in West German society: already in his opening remarks he speaks vehemently of "the narrow-mindedness and coldness of a society which believes itself to be so clever, confident, perfect and fair," and of conditions comparable to life a hundred years ago or to apartheid in South Africa (2).[24]

The climactic scenes of *Ganz unten* reveal nicely the paradigmatic aggressiveness with which Wallraff pursues his object ("truth") and the paradoxical nature of his project. He stages a scenario for the entrepreneur Adler in which Adler is asked to provide Turks for top-secret repair work in a nuclear reactor, a job that will expose them to extreme doses of radiation. Wallraff calls the endeavor an oxymoronic "staging of reality."[25] The reality in question has apparently already been established; Wallraff's task is only to demonstrate (to "stage") for us what he already knows—that Adler, as he puts it, is selling "Turks to burn" (*Ganz unten* German original 217; omitted in English).

Wallraff engages in continual editorializing, so that at every turn a damning image of Adler is reinforced:[26] "Adler sells us the trip like a promotion man putting on a bus trip with free coffee and cream cakes" (192); "Adler makes himself comfortable, lets his new chauffeur give him a light, and settles down to present himself as a benefactor of [those] humiliated and oppressed [by him and others like him]" (193; *Ganz unten* 235); "phrases like 'working with' and 'working together' are supposed to sound like music to the ears of those crushed by sweated labor" (193); "[t]hat must sound a bit rich [monstrous] even to him, so he expands his statement [concealing even further his crooked plot to burn human beings]" (195; *Ganz unten* 237); "[like all clever deceivers above a certain income level,] Adler assures us of his reliability for the umpteenth time" (196; *Ganz unten* 238). Moreover, "stage directions" stipulate what tone of voice we are to read into Adler's lines, whether it is loathing, greed, paternalism, or unconcern (193–98).

Not only does Wallraff direct his scenario, and our reception of it, with a heavy hand, he also casts himself in one of the starring roles, as Adler's interlocutor in the confrontation between Adler and the Turks. This key scene of the book reveals most clearly the implicit cultural and political assumptions that structure the work. Wallraff has at this point gathered six Turkish "friends" whom he has initiated into his scheme (191). They meet at Wallraff's ("Ali's") room, where Adler will explain the task they have been selected to perform. Especially noteworthy is Wallraff's treatment of his Turkish coconspirators. In particular, he does not offer complete disclosure of his project: "[t]hey are less surprised than I am by the nature and purpose of the job, and by Adler's brazen lack of conscience. This has been their experience and their reality for a long time. However, I haven't told them that I'm German, so as to avoid any distance developing between us. Adler might notice and become suspicious" (191).

Wallraff credits these six Turkish men with a profound understanding of the conditions of their life. But while he can recognize their superior experience and insight, he cannot treat them as equal partners in his plan to expose Adler. He does not and cannot tell them that he is German, he says, for this would generate a rift between them that would threaten the entire project. And yet this project is aimed at bringing to light the very reality in which these men live and that they in some sense—by Wallraff's admission—know better than he. The devastating irony here is that Wallraff cannot reveal his identity so that the Turks will continue to trust him; their trust in him is conditioned upon his inability to trust them. Further, while the Turks are excluded from this circle of confidence, we as readers are privileged to share Wallraff's secret. We "Germans," in short, are the real coconspirators here, while the Turks constitute the means by which we will gain the information necessary to help them. Implicated in "our" benevolence toward them is an ugly paternalism that says that they are not worthy partners in a project to illuminate and to change their lives. Ironically, Wallraff's scene enacts what it sets out to expose—it is an example of abuse based on the assumption of inequality between Germans and Turks.

Nowhere is the role of the six Turks more apparent than in the speech situation depicted in this scene. Wallraff explains the peculiar nature of the interaction that will ensue between himself and Adler: "[i]n order to draw him out even further, I have arranged with my Turkish friends for them to put questions in Turkish. I, with next to no knowledge of Turkish, translate 'freely,' that is to say, I ask Adler those questions which seem to me to be important" (192). In this way, the Turks are explicitly excluded from any communication—with Adler, with Wallraff, and with the reader. Since neither Wallraff nor (presumably) his German readers have any competence in Turkish, the language and its speakers are disqualified from any reciprocity in communication. With the confrontation between Adler and his Turks structured in this way, it does not matter what the Turkish men have to say—indeed, they could speak nonsense and would serve Wallraff equally well. Only Wallraff's concerns and questions are expressed; the Turks are there only to provide him the opportunity to confront his adversary.

I would argue that this scenario, considered as a communicative situation, is paradigmatic for Wallraff's book as a whole: Turks in *Ganz unten* merely help Wallraff set the stage, enabling him to place Germans in a situation in which they must respond to his probing questions. This suggests that Wallraff's work is not really about Turks at all but rather about creating a vehicle through which Wallraff can present his views of the Federal Republic. As in von der Grün's portrait of Osman Gürlük, the clichéd and stereotyped image of Turks in *Ganz unten* is used not intentionally to reinforce prejudice but to promote a particular political subtext—the presence of the Turks enables Wallraff to promote his own broad narrative of the way "reality" is.

The exact nature of the subtext surfaces when we examine the stereotypes that support it. If we look again at the type of editorializing in which Wallraff indulges, we find that the implied collective noun "Turks" is often replaced by reified abstractions such as "the oppressed," "the exploited," "the insulted," "the tortured." Or, if we consider the kinds of situations in which Wallraff's "Ali" finds himself, we see that they are not restricted to Turks. Wallraff explores the inhumane practices of the pharmaceutical industry or the unsanitary conditions at McDonald's restaurants, yet it is difficult to identify these venues with the specific situation of the Turks. Even in the case of the FRG's illegal labor market, Wallraff lets us know that there are Germans among the exploited workers.[27] The "guinea pigs" of pharmaceutical research include punks, unemployed youth, and alcoholics; the participants in these experiments are referred to as "one," "another," "some," or "test persons" (126–28). Wallraff's exposé of mortuary practices documents the "macabre, soulless and inhuman death cult of our time, in which someone still alive is disposed of as if no longer human, like a dead object" (59). Wallraff's "Ali" is not simply the prototypical "Turk" in the Federal Republic; in Wallraff's language Ali stands in the various episodes for any and all mistreated persons—the categories "one" and "someone still alive," unmarked by national origin, culture, or language, are meant to include anyone treated in less than human terms.[28]

This in effect redefines the two sides portrayed in Wallraff's work. To the extent that we experience through Wallraff what "Ali" experiences in Germany, the society of *Ganz unten* is divided between "us" as victims (aligned with "Ali") and the evil "them" as oppressors (incarnated in the figure of Adler). That is, Wallraff's exposé is not about the treatment of Turks at the hands of Germans but about prejudice and oppression in general. Thus Ali can stand for the homeless, the unemployed, and Jews, for oppressed groups in earlier historical periods (the nineteenth century) and in other parts of the world (South Africa) (2).[29] Similarly, Adler becomes the cipher for all oppressors—whites in South Africa, industrial corporations under National Socialism in Germany, or capitalists everywhere.[30] In sum, the situation of Turks in the FRG, ostensibly the subject of Wallraff's reportage, is (only) paradigmatic. The minidrama of Ali and Adler encapsulates the struggle throughout history between slaves and masters, the powerless and the powerful. With global generalizations reminiscent of Peter Weiss, the "Turk" is made to represent oppressed groups everywhere. As a result, specific issues of race and culture become erased within the now universalized fight against injustice in whatever form it may take.

Bruder, muß zusammen Zwiebel und Wasser essen! by the sociologist Paul Geiersbach offers a strong contrast to the manipulative tactics of Wallraff's *Ganz unten*.[31] The titles of the two books reveal much

about their differences: Wallraff's "lowest of the low" tells us immediately the nature of the experience that he will relate; the German
who is in the know gives us his label—in idiomatic German—for
life as a Turk in the FRG. In contrast, Geiersbach's title is not an authoritative statement or designation but an enigmatic quotation
from direct conversation. It is not idiomatic German but rather a
Turkish saying rendered in broken "guest worker" speech. Further,
it is a quotation of direct address: a Turkish voice is speaking to us;
we understand the words, but, ignorant of Turkish culture and its
unique expressions, we do not comprehend their meaning. All of
this signals a widely different stance toward the Turkish population
of the Federal Republic. While Wallraff speaks to his reader about
the Turks, giving us a handy label for their experience, Geiersbach
is present only as a kind of mediator, passing on to us what the
Turks have to say, whether we understand them initially or not.

In a foreword Geiersbach explains and defines the limits of his
role as author. *Bruder, muß zusammen Zwiebel und Wasser essen!* follows between May and October of an unspecified year the crises
that arise within one Turkish family and the ways in which family
members cope with these problems in the FRG: the father is sus-
pected of carrying on an affair and is being watched by his wife and
daughters; the eldest daughter, estranged from her husband, has
taken up with a Turk who is unemployed and also married. Geiersbach takes pains to state that the subject of his work (which he
characterizes as something like a reportage, something like a case
study, and something like a novel [11–12]) is not "the" Turkish family but "a" Turkish family. Stereotyping is thus explicitly denied
and replaced by an insistence on individuality and diversity within
the Turkish population:

> The Yorulmaz family, the name I will use for the family in
> question, is explicitly not meant to stand for *the* Turkish or
> for *the* foreign worker family here in the Federal Republic.
> *The* Turkish and especially *the* foreign worker family do not
> exist. The foreign population and also the group of Turks
> display . . . a much too heterogeneous picture for that, het-
> erogeneous with respect to their social origin, the cultural

norms and values they brought with them, their length of residence in the FRG, their achieved level of assimilation to the conditions of life here, and much more. We must not lose sight of this multiplicity. (7; emphasis in original)[32]

Geiersbach's commitment to avoid typifying the experiences depicted in his work influences also his specific choices regarding the manner of presentation. His unorthodox study is the result of a tension between the standard procedures of data collection Geiersbach was taught and the personal nature of his experiences with his subjects: "I had originally approached these [foreign families working in the FRG] with a 'strict' scientific research model (representative research sample, questionnaire, collection of 'hard data,' etc.) but then abandoned this when a relationship of trust began to develop with the 'research subjects'" (9). Geiersbach, increasingly in the role of "confidant" for all family members, is drawn into their conflict; thereby, he claims, he achieves an "intimate look" into their hopes, fears, and psychological problems (9). Following in part a famous model in American anthropology, Oscar Lewis's *The Children of Sánchez*, Geiersbach's book lets the family members speak in their voices about what is happening, accompanied by the author's observations. Geiersbach claims to record these speeches exactly as they occurred: "I do not 'enhance' or pare down their speech. I duplicate it word for word, just as it unfolded in conversation with me" (10). "The individuals' language was not corrected either stylistically or grammatically. Here and there words and syllables were added, but only in places where the reader would otherwise have difficulty understanding" (12).[33] Further, the sections that claim to offer long, uninterrupted, direct speeches of the main family members involved in the crisis—the father, Param, the daughter Alda, and her lover, Hoppa—are set in a different type from that of the rest of the book, where Geiersbach's mediating activity is more evident. Always the effort is made to maintain the voices of the Turks intact.[34]

Where both von der Grün and, even more so, Wallraff take an explicitly active part in shaping the thoughts and experiences of Osman Gürlük or Ali, Geiersbach describes his role toward the

Yorulmaz family and his readers as that of "witness and chronicler" (11) or of "mere reporter" (12). Authorial intervention is restricted to a few, explicitly stipulated tasks—to relate important incidents in the past, to describe the broader context within which events are occurring, to sketch transitions, or to provide necessary factual information (regarding laws, regulations, and the like) (11). Much of this is accomplished in footnotes set apart from the body of the text. The goal is to allow the Turkish individuals to speak and act on their terms and to allow us the freedom to observe and interpret for ourselves:

> I provide little if any commentary or interpretation of the events in my work. The "story" of the conflict, the many events on the margins and in the background, the persons in their different characters, all this unfolds essentially through the spoken word and through the actions of those involved in the conflict. . . . Whenever in the process of "data collecting" I intervened in the events and influenced their course in an essential way, this is clearly indicated in the requisite manner. Otherwise I have removed myself as an active, thinking, feeling, and sympathetic person completely from the course of events. Essentially the author appears only as witness and chronicler for the reader. (11)[35]

From all appearances, Geiersbach promises an unusually honest, conscientious attempt to grant "real" Turks the opportunity to speak for themselves. But we would be right to question the possibility of an author's writing himself out of his text. Indeed, Geiersbach's claim to present the "real thing" just as it occurred, without exercising authorial control, proves deeply problematic. The very first speeches, for example, are given largely in indirect discourse, which by necessity normalizes the German spoken by the Turks. Compare the direct speech of the father, Param—"I don't want forget my children, I don't want forget my wife, but my opinion so: if starting no luck [any more], if starting problems up to nose, better return Turkey!"—and the continuation of his speech, rendered in indirect discourse—"Param insists that his decision is unshakable. With or without his family, he will return to Turkey.

He is only waiting for his German social security contributions to be paid back to him. He has already contacted a lawyer with regard to this matter" (19–20).[36] The level of German spoken directly by Param indicates that the sentences in indirect discourse do much more than relate what he said. (Param, for example, would never have spoken the sentence "I have already contacted a lawyer with regard to this matter.") The strategy of indirect discourse creates only the fiction of transmitting the actual speech of the Turk, where in fact the contrast between Param's words and Geiersbach's rendition of them is enormous: the two passages, meant as a single speech, actually bring to light the great difference between "Turkish" German and the standard German of the native speaker.

Other narrative and editorial strategies include the pervasive use of "etc." to indicate ellipses in the Turks' speeches. Param at one point tells Geiersbach about his most recent trip to Turkey, during which he was to accomplish, among other things, important family business relating to his daughter's divorce. Geiersbach's editorializing indicates impatience with Param's "circuitous detail": "[b]ack home in Yurtsehri everything is in order. His father was still enjoying the best of health. Even his mother . . . (etc.) He himself suffered for a week with a very painful nerve inflammation in his right upper thigh. Probably he had . . . (etc.)" (186; ellipses in original). Geiersbach cuts off Param's report of the road trip, of the performance of his new car, of recent changes in the political and economic situation in Turkey, only to give us Param's speech in full when he turns to the topic of his daughter. Only certain aspects of Param's life are of relevance to Geiersbach: there is an authorial project according to which he selects the material that is to be recorded for the reader. What Geiersbach wants to hear and what Param wants to tell him are at least in this instance vastly distant.

Geiersbach's biases reveal themselves again when he promotes a typically Western pattern of relating to the other, that of a universalizing humanism. He insists that there is nothing typically "Turkish" about the behavior of the Yorulmazes but that they exhibit the "overreactions" of human beings under severe social and psychological stress (9). The implication is that others in a similar situation

would behave in similar sorts of ways; we need only to understand reigning social conditions in order to explain what appears
to be aberrant behavior. The Yorulmazes, like all guest workers,
are *"human beings"* (emphasis in original), "sympathetic and un-
sympathetic, ambitious and complacent, frail and strong, active
and lethargic, open-minded and narrow-minded, etc." (11). Turks,
Greeks, Italians, and Spaniards are seen as essentially no different from Germans. Cultural, social, and economic differences are
placed in the background, while the operative distinctions become
open- versus close-mindedness or ambition versus complacency.
In his admirable effort to present a nonjudgmental, nonprejudicial
view of his Turkish family, we must wonder whether Geiersbach
does not in fact lose sight of important differences that do exist.[37]

If there is considerably more editorializing and more authorial
intervention in Geiersbach's text than he seemed to allow in his
prefatory remarks, Geiersbach's programmatically passive role as
"witness and chronicler" is similarly open to question. What is striking here is not that Geiersbach must add to or embellish what the
Turks say to him but that they seem willing to say so much to an outsider, especially one who sees himself as trying to stay out of things
as much as possible. For the Turks in the Yorulmaz family seem to
tell Geiersbach everything and insist vehemently as they do that
they are telling him the way things really are. In encounter after
encounter they rush to his side, grab his arm, pull him into a quiet
corner or into their room, and relate in great detail the catastrophic
events that have most recently transpired. Over and over again
we hear their appeals to their sympathetic listener: Param's first
long narrative begins "Honestly, Paul" (21) and repeats its promise
of candor and confidential disclosure: "But honestly, Paul"; "But,
Paul, I say to you honestly"; "Paul, I tell you whole truth"; "Honestly. . . . Honestly. . . . Paul, I tell completely honestly" (22, 24, 28,
29). Such constant admonitions of trust create for us the figure of
the author Geiersbach ("Paul") who is above all else a sympathetic
confidant, a listener. This role is carried through also in the form
of the text: in the section "Param speaks" (21–33), for example, we
hear only Param's voice; Geiersbach is present as listener but—at
least in the transcription we are given—never as speaker himself.[38]

Param and other members of the Yorulmaz family confide their deepest secrets to their silent friend. Param will tell Geiersbach of his adulterous relationship and of his sexual dysfunction—things that are not spoken of among, or not known by, the members of his immediate family. At times Geiersbach is sworn to secrecy: "[i]t has to do with a matter that I am sworn absolutely not to speak about to other Turks and even to Param's best friend, Boga Öztürk" (77). He speaks with Hoppa "just between [him] and me" (89, 197). Param's daughter Alda confides in Geiersbach, telling him things that he is not allowed to tell her parents—we hear again and again, "But Paul, not a word to my parents!" (121; cf. 123, 183). And toward the end of the work even the younger daughter Uslu begins to tell him about her love life, swearing him to secrecy once more (264).

Two things are disturbing about these encounters. First, it is difficult to believe that the Yorulmazes would demonstrate such confidence in Geiersbach, entrusting him with the most intimate details of their lives, if they knew that their speeches would be transcribed in a book. At least the question must be considered whether Geiersbach was as candid with the Turks about his intentions as they were with him about their thoughts and feelings—whether the conversations displayed in Geiersbach's text took place on the basis of mutual respect and parity. Second, Geiersbach is strangely silent about the process through which the speeches of the Turks were finally transcribed. Param's long discourse, for example, extends some fourteen pages in length. Was it recorded on tape, then transcribed? If so, it becomes even more implausible that he would reveal the fact of his sexual impotence in front of a running tape recorder. If Geiersbach was taping in secret, this would also raise difficult questions about the fairness with which he acted toward his Turkish friends. Or, finally, if Geiersbach reconstructed conversations from memory, then his claim to be presenting the real speech of the Yorulmaz family cannot hold up to scrutiny (Schöning-Kalender).

Such nagging questions, however, legitimate and important as they are, should not obscure the unique achievement of Geiersbach's reportage. For I would argue that this work, more than that of von der Grün or Wallraff, can offer a promising model for presenting the voice of the Turk while preserving his or her individuality and integrity.

In a memorable scene in the text, Geiersbach visits the Yorulmaz family at a particularly difficult moment of crisis. Param has thrown Hoppa, his daughter Alda's lover, out of the house. When Geiersbach arrives, Alda pushes her way over to him and leads him into the children's room. In the pages that follow, Alda tells Geiersbach what has happened while her mother, Rosa, constantly interrupts in Turkish. The nine-year-old Kemal translates Rosa's interjections into German. Alda is crying, Kemal also interrupts with information of his own, the seven-year-old Murat is in the room doing his arithmetic homework and asks each person the product of seven times fourteen; later Uslu will arrive to help him read aloud. A wild, loud scene is the result, in which we hear a multitude of individual voices, each reflecting its set of immediate and urgent concerns.

Both Alda and Rosa strive to present their versions of what has happened. They argue about whether Hoppa has really stolen family money and whether Param was right to throw him out of the apartment. Rosa vilifies Hoppa; Alda defends him; and each seeks to gain Geiersbach's support, Rosa in the more demanding tone ("Isn't that right, brother?!"; "Right, brother?"; "No, brother! No, no!"; "Listen, brother!" [205]), Alda more pleadingly ("Paul, and if he loves me, he'll come! He isn't bad! Really, Paul, he's not!" [206]). At one point the competing viewpoints of the two women, both intent on convincing Geiersbach, are reflected in the graphic organization of the text: Alda's and Rosa's simultaneous speeches are presented on two sides of the page, divided diagonally (206).

Geiersbach, to be sure, remains the focus of the scene, and as such he is much more than just a witness to the family crisis. In a footnote he describes how, by providing assistance in dealing with various officials and bureaucrats, he has become the Yorulmazes' revered "guardian angel" (28n). Geiersbach is appealed to continually as a source of information and confirmation; in this particular scene, Param will speak with Geiersbach, promising not to undertake further action without first discussing it with him: "Paul, you are my brother. I do what you say" (207). Not only does Geiersbach listen to the Turks' speeches; they also seek out, listen to, and heed his advice.[39]

Nonetheless, the crowded scene in the bedroom and the attempts of the Yorulmaz family to express their concerns and to demand Geiersbach's attention suggest a notion of reality that had been absent in the texts by von der Grün and Wallraff. *Social reality in Geiersbach's work—what is really going on and why—is at every point urgently contested and argued.* Different people present different concerns and differing versions of the same events (we see this most graphically in the contest between Alda and Rosa). Here we have no German expert with privileged access to the Turks who speaks authoritatively to us, claiming to know the truth about their lives. Rather, we hear discordant *Turkish* voices, each representing individual concerns, who compete for our consideration. Much like Geiersbach, we are forced to listen as they argue about the significance and meaning of what is happening. Unlike Osman Gürlük and Wallraff's Ali, Rosa, Alda, and Param Yorulmaz are granted the authority to speak for and about themselves while the German listens carefully and confusedly, not quite in command of the multilingual situation. While the German still occupies the center of events, he does so largely as a formality, without an authority grounded in special knowledge.[40]

In this chapter I have examined three attempts in West German reportage to bring us closer to the lives and experiences of the Turkish guest workers of the Federal Republic. Max von der Grün's *Leben im gelobten Land*, Günter Wallraff's *Ganz unten*, and Paul Geiersbach's *Bruder, muß zusammen Zwiebel und Wasser essen!*, all written with the claim of confidential access to the Turkish experience, illustrate different models of encounter with the Turkish other.

Von der Grün's strategy is to help the Turk introduce himself to us. We hear the voice of Osman Gürlük telling us about his life, paired with commentary by the author, who amplifies and clarifies Gürlük's testimony. But in this turn taking between Gürlük and von der Grün, it is the author's voice that is always sovereign. The

Turk speaks without logical coherence, expressing his feelings and emotions in a confused manner, while the German, the expert, delivers hard facts, statistics, and historical background. In this way, ethnic and cultural stereotypes are enacted and reinforced. Von der Grün endeavors to demonstrate prosperity and increased liberality among guest workers and to offer a vision of social harmony and cultural progress in the Federal Republic—following three thousand years of backward rural life in their home countries, guest workers, we see, are beginning to take on civilized (read: German) ways. But despite von der Grün's liberal intentions, the implicit message of his portrait of the Turk conveys a sense of his own superiority: we are introduced to a Turk who wants to become like us.

Wallraff is blatantly manipulative. Here, the author ostensibly puts himself and us in the situation of the other, but this other is completely of Wallraff's making. "Ali" does not reveal to us the life of a Turk or of Turks in the Federal Republic but rather is made to represent all victims of capitalism—whether families in mourning who must deal with funeral parlors, the youth who work at McDonald's, alcoholics and the homeless who sell their bodies for pharmaceutical research, or Jews who provided labor for the Nazi war efforts. Issues specific to the treatment of Turks in Germany are thereby obscured, as the real concern of *Ganz unten* becomes a kind of universal fight against injustice, with Wallraff carrying the banner.[41] We are to be incensed, aroused, moved to action; the specific experiences, questions, and concerns of Wallraff's Turkish colleagues are swallowed up by a presumably larger concern—that of fighting against dehumanizing practices everywhere. There are no real Turks in *Ganz unten*, except as symbols of victims and oppressed groups everywhere.

Finally, Paul Geiersbach's strategy is to let the other speak and as much as possible to remain silent himself. Geiersbach strives explicitly to avoid typifying his Turkish friends; indeed, his reportage does not rely on stereotyped views of Turks but rather presents Geiersbach (and places us) in the difficult process of trying to understand them. We share his moments of confusion as he is made to listen to a plurivocal reality, to contested accounts representing conflicting concerns. Where von der Grün and Wallraff claim to give us the direct voice or experience of the Turk, their strategies prove to be only guises through which they tell us their own views of things. (Both, we saw, argue a kind of Social Democratic liberalism.) Interestingly enough, their stance toward the Turk is captured in the cover photographs of their works: in both, we stare at and are stared back at by the Turk. There is no communication, no participation between viewer and viewed—the stare, in a very real sense, is a silent one. Their titles, too, promise little in the way of a participatory venture, as both present essentially the Germans' authoritative labels for the Turkish experience. The cover of Geiersbach's text in contrast gives us a blurry view of a distant Turk who looks at us from a window high above. There is no claim made for direct and immediate perception of the other's reality, only a kind of tentative approach. It is, above all, Geiersbach's title that is suggestive of a new stance toward the other. Not our label for the other but the other's voice, speaking to us directly in an idiom that we do not yet understand: the model is no longer a visual one, promising direct access yet denying the possibility of two-way communication, but a dialogic one.[42] They speak while we learn to listen. We are no longer sovereign or manipulative toward their reality but unsure and ignorant. And it is only when the self can suspend the imposition of its beliefs that it can hope to listen carefully to what the other is saying.[43]

Conclusion

By 1914 Europe and America controlled 85% of the world's surface and an "unrelenting Eurocentrism" ruled Western culture (Said, *Culture* 8, 221–22). The identification of Europe with rationality and the superiority and universal validity of its institutions went unquestioned, even by the workers, women's, and avant-garde arts movements (Said, *Culture* 222). Europe's centrality was political fact: notably, until the end of World War II, the continent fought largely within itself, with nations having other European nations as their enemies (Amin xiii). In such times, Anna Seghers and her fellow Communists in Mexico took little notice of the culture of their exile homeland: for them, the European war against fascism defined and determined political relationships throughout the rest of the world. But the establishment of almost a hundred decolonized states after 1945 dramatically restructured global politics and political thought: with anticolonial struggles waging in the Third World (the term was coined in 1952), Europeans confronted themselves for the first time "not simply as the Raj but as representatives of a culture and even of races accused of crimes" (Said, *Culture* 194–95). In the postwar period, the view of Europe as the locus of political progress and enlightenment was replaced by the image of the West as colonialist oppressor. For Germans, this general European crisis of identity was compounded by the trauma of fascism and the defeat and subsequent division of the German nation.

The texts I have investigated take up, with considerable differences and similarities, the challenge of reconfiguring Europe discursively in the postwar era. Works by Anna Seghers, Peter Weiss, Max von der Grün, and Günter Wallraff continue to reaffirm principles of universality, unity, and sameness as fundamental components of European identity. For these authors, there still exists a basic (European) humanity, anchored in reason, that transcends differences of class, race, or nationality. The white author, in his or her unique calling, reveals and analyzes traditions of prejudice and oppression, a classical task of enlightenment that would define political emancipation. At the root of this discourse lie the historical and philosophical traditions of the European Enlightenment, the French Revolution, and German Idealism, which claim their ongoing vitality in the historical settings, political rhetoric, aesthetic structure, and specific motifs of these writers' works. White ideals are asserted as emancipatory and superior; their adoption by other cultures demonstrates civilization and progress. Subordinating sensual, personal, private aspects of life to the liberative rule of reason (the revolutionary cause), the European presents himself as a self-sacrificing hero who takes on the battles of others. In the process, his Europeanness goes unchallenged.

As I have shown, Anna Seghers's texts project a strong narrative of emancipation and enlightenment, associated with Europe, in contrast to the oppression and "unreason" of the Third World. Following a developmental or evolutionary model, the blacks of the Caribbean are elevated to the level of the whites, who represent universal reason and normative, civilized culture. The Caribbean is associated accordingly with stereotypical images of sensuality and nature, with animals and bodies, with a materiality that lacks form, direction, order, or insight. It signifies cognitive oblivion, a forgetting of political realities, a falling back into timelessness and brute corporeality, while the emancipatory European revolution orders and preserves itself in memory and monuments for the future. Thus in the telltale subplots of Seghers's trilogy, the childlike, sensual black slave woman develops physically and politically after her impregnation with white ideals of freedom and progress. In this reproductive scenario, Europe remains (if only) intellectually vital—and this, we must remember, as it fails to realize its goals in the subordinate, material realm of nature and practical politics. Even decades later, Max von der Grün's *Leben im gelobten Land* continues to construct the backward, irrational, incoherent, emotional other who traverses thousands of miles and years to become a liberal-minded European. Neither author indicates an awareness of the Eurocentrism of his or her liberative views or of the imperialist projects carried out in the name of the humanism they espouse.

Works by Peter Weiss and Günter Wallraff depict an oppressive

Europe that redeems itself by joining the revolutionary battles of the Third World. For Weiss in particular, who was haunted by his family's escape from Nazi Germany, European (here: German) identity is marked, even in a reconstructed postwar German state, by its failure to combat the crimes of fascism, by an absence of resistance, by flight. But in the "Third World" the formerly unengaged white European is able to rewrite his past and to distance himself from the present by assuming the role of freedom fighter; in doing so, he claims an emancipated position that overcomes all differences and failures of race, class, and nationality, an unassailable moral stance that would allow for the revolutionary action of a heroic (white) self on behalf of vast numbers of undifferentiated victims. Yet despite the now positive, even utopian evaluation of the Third World as the arena of revolution and humanity and the vilification of Europe and North America as colonialist and imperialist aggressors, Weiss's discourse remains firmly within the framework of a Eurocentric universalism. Western aggression in the Third World only reenacts the paradigmatic situation of Auschwitz; once again, rational analysis is presented as the quintessential strategy for political emancipation. Thus we witness not the recognition and valorization of Third World struggles in themselves but their reduction to European categories.

Like Weiss, Wallraff pursues a Manichaean model of the world that pits the forces of good against the powers of evil. While Wallraff belongs to the West German economic and social system that exploits its minority populations, national guilt is shed when he dons the mask of the oppressed to do battle against society. Notably, for both Weiss and Wallraff, the other, equated with "the oppressed," possesses no specific culture, history, class, or race; he is the generic victim—simultaneously the black in South Africa, the Jew in Nazi Germany—in a global conflict of oppressors and oppressed. In like fashion, the bourgeois liberal German escapes the burden of his cultural and historical identity through a purifying process of education that leads to an informed choice to side with the oppressed. Differences of race, class, culture, or nation, in other words, can be nullified as right-minded human beings join forces in the fight of reason and freedom against unreason and oppression. For all four authors, Seghers and von der Grün, Weiss and Wallraff, universal values—reason, freedom, humanism, equality—are upheld in a struggle in which, once we learn to see, the fronts are clearly drawn.

An alternative discourse, exemplified by texts by Claus Hammel, Peter Hacks, Paul Geiersbach, Hans Magnus Enzensberger, and Heiner Müller, focuses not on universality but on difference and doubt. If Seghers and Weiss projected a transparent world in which the European could act with moral clarity, the discourse constituted by these other writers foregrounds his complicity, the boundedness of the author and his protagonist in their national and European history, the tension between hegemonic cultural heritage and liberative intention. Reason, no longer offering direct access to universal truth and political freedom, is now seen as a potentially coercive force, a colonizing mentality. Texts belonging to this discourse no longer display the unproblematic Enlightenment belief in the rational unity of humanity but explore an encounter with others who are recognized as radically different, with an otherness that approaches incomprehensibility. Faced with the fact of irrefutable difference, the European self no longer offers a stable point of departure: encountering differences of race, culture, or class that cannot be sublated, it becomes vulnerable and confused, falling into silence and merciless self-examination.

With European intellectual traditions brought into question, we increasingly find the depiction of the Third World as essentially unrepresentable, as categorically other: its representation becomes a conscious discursive problem. Associations with the unconscious, with utopian fantasies, or with emptiness and absence illustrate these authors' attempts to delineate what for them remains unincorporatable within an inescapably European discourse. The author emerges not as revolutionary prophet, as was the distinct tendency for Seghers, Weiss, and Wallraff, but as liar, as murderer, as untrustworthy and guilty. And the texts begin to reflect in formal terms the discontinuity of representational systems, the rivalry of competing discourses, the heterogeneity of the world's cultures. Their fragmented, ruptured structure signals the demise of European rationality, as the seamless narratives and monolithic visions of Seghers and Weiss give way to poetic expressions of incoherence, paralysis, and suicidal meditation. Painfully aware of their privileged status, the second group of writers shifts the focus of their Third World discourse from the other to the self, to reflect on the flaws and failures of European traditions.

Texts by Claus Hammel and Peter Hacks construct a narrative of European oppression set against the resistance movements of the Third World. Both humanistic ideals and party doctrines are brought into question; the European intellectual no longer offers unambiguously positive leadership but becomes an ambivalent, even complicitous figure. Europe is represented not as the bastion of revolutionary energy, as was the case in Seghers's texts, but as a political system weakened by the resignation of its intellectuals or marred by selfish interest thinly disguised as humanism. Reversing the earlier logic that equated European intellectual traditions with emancipation, European men of science in the plays by Hacks and Hammel demonstrate the limitation, failure, and blindness of this heritage. Offering solidarity, these authors announce their political loyalties while eschewing any leading role in emancipatory battles abroad; needed instead, as the character of Humboldt admits, are heroes from the Third World.

Similar self-reflection is evident in Paul Geiersbach's novels, which attempt to curtail the European's scientific authority in order to allow a space for the competing voices of Turkish others. That Geiersbach falls short in important ways reveals the conflicted nature of the European self that his texts project: the leftist intellectual cannot shed his privileged identity as he offers aid to the disprivileged. The works by Hammel, Hacks, and Geiersbach are the most difficult to subsume in interpretive categories. Are they Eurocentric and universalist like the texts of Seghers and Weiss? Fragmented and self-flagellatory like the works of Enzensberger and Müller? Texts between discourses of universality and difference, they recognize the distinct otherness of figures like Simón Bolívar or Param Yorulmaz who challenge, both politically and discursively, the views of their European interlocutors while still holding dear European traditions of humanism and emancipation in their attempts to construct narratives of political solidarity.

European values, limited and coercive as they may be when prac-
ticed in bad faith or without self-reflection, are still seen in a
fundamentally positive light.

Enzensberger and Müller, in contrast, point to the utter bankruptcy of European traditions, while the Third World is imagined
as a utopian realm representing authenticity and vigor. Each
launches an incisive critique against European civilization: for
them Europe is marked fundamentally by failure and decay; it exhibits nothing in the way of progressive enlightenment. If Europe
was defined for Seghers, Weiss, Hammel, and others in terms of
the liberative program of the Enlightenment and the French Revolution, it is here epitomized by the Roman Empire that builds on
the bodies of its slaves—not freedom, equality, and brotherhood
but colonialism, oppression, and mass murder—or by the frozen,
sunken, and irretrievable *Titanic*. While other authors wrote with
the conviction of themselves as prophets or as explorers of truth,
Müller and Enzensberger replace this Dantesque role with the image of the (European) writer as murderer and forger, as an illicit,
parasitic figure who appropriates rather than creates. Accordingly,
their texts offer self-incriminating meditations on the imminent
death of the author on a sinking ship or in a waning empire.

In these texts the Third World becomes the place of heterogeneity, fantasy, and the unconscious, equated with women, nature,
unreason, sexuality, and the dead—discordant images reflecting
realms of experience that Enlightenment reason had attempted to
tame. That this diverse list of analogic others expresses sexist, racist,
and Eurocentric stereotypes is precisely the point: at issue is the apparent inescapability of a tyrannical European discourse that must
isolate and conquer all phenomena of difference. Representations
of a "Third World" thus appear as the products of a European consciousness that has become aware of its oppressive history—the
return of the repressed in obsessive fantasies of strange bodies in
the hold of a luxury liner, of barbarians penetrating the walls of
Rome.

What visions of a German or European subject are reflected in
such dreams of sensual black women, dirty Indian rebels, incoherent Turks, or victims rising from the grave? Whether hero, political

ally, or tortured accomplice obsessed with the necessity of his own demise; whether taking sides against fascism, acknowledging coercive potentials within the self, or fantasizing one's destruction at the hands of the other, such roles reflect a continuing and common need, in the East and in the West, to construct a good European, a nonfascist German. The postwar German literary interest in a "Third World," whether represented as historical reality, poetic image, or poetological praxis—by Toussaint, volcanoes and underwater Ophelias, or principles of rupture and contradiction—is shaped by the war against fascism, by the demise of the student movement of the 1960s, by East and West Germany's positions within an increasingly decolonized world. What takes shape in the leftist German dream of a non-European otherness is the dream of the German liberated from his fascist past. But it is a dream, as we have seen, deeply marked by the conflicts, contradictions, and clichés of an oppressive heritage.

I began some pages ago with reflections on the complexities of white European selves representing others without bias. That unintended, even unconscious hegemonic habits can infect the most self-critical and liberative of projects has been amply illustrated in the chapters of this book. But the power of Eurocentrism, which accompanies us in our routines of thought and action, is not the whole or sole issue. The examples of postwar German writers should serve to impress upon us the political and philosophical complexity inherent in any self and any other that precludes easy categorizations or labels. Neither our selves nor others are ever pure, coherent, or consistent. Rather, it is in the blurred, smudged, continually reforged space between enlightenment and prejudice, universality and difference, solidarity and helplessness that we must read our authors and negotiate our lives.

Notes

1. I use the term "Third World" not to refer to peoples, countries, or regions of the world but to designate a political and cultural idea, a broad image, in the literary texts of certain postwar German writers. My aim is to explore a discursive problem, not a political reality per se. On the origins and uses of the term, see the debate among Love; McCall; Mountjoy; Muni; Wolf-Phillips; Worsley, "How"; also Goldberg 163–68; Stavrianos; Worsley, *Three*.

2. For such a survey, see Sareika, *Dritte*. Streese picks up where he leaves off with a study of selected works from the 1970s and 1980s. Surprisingly little has been written on the Third World in German literature; see also Köpf 327. Gugelberger ("Rethinking") discusses the significance of Third World literature for German studies.

3. The model of the self that constructs a self-confirming other does not easily allow for nonhegemonic, nonrepressive modes of representation. This constitutes a major criticism of Said's analysis of Western constructions of the Near East (*Orientalism*): see Clifford, *Predicament* 255–76; Porter; Young 119–40; Said responds in "Orientalism" and "Representing."

4. JanMohamed and Lloyd warn minority critics against the danger of reproducing dominant ideology ("Introduction: Toward" 10); Baker asks how one can explode the simplistic duality of the Prospero/Caliban iconography to make possible "the *sound* of Caliban" (190). The dilemma is cited as well by critics who seem less willing to sacrifice the values of dominant ideology: see Fromm 197–98; Todorov 175. Haraway argues for partiality as an alternative to relativism and totalization; S. P. Mohanty specifies a "minimal rationality" that negotiates between the claims of relativism and Reason.

5. Consider the appeal of hooks's "Choosing the Margin as a Space of Radical Openness" (*Yearning* 145–53). Haraway warns us, however, of the "serious danger of romanticizing and/or appropriating the vision of the less powerful" (584).

6. As Alcoff puts it, "The problem is a social one, the options available to us are socially constructed, and the practices we engage in cannot be under-

stood as simply the results of autonomous individual choice" (11). Cf. Peck, who urges our "consciously taking a position on the periphery" ("Methodological" 207). "Marginalize yourself!"—Hortense Spillers's challenge to a white, male, tenured professor (Schmidt 304–05)—is impossible or heuristic only, as is Deleuze and Guattari's exhortation that we "become woman" (Jardine). The call can be taken to mean that we, whatever our locations along the shifting spectrum of margin and center, can endeavor to be oppositional. But oppositionality and marginality are not equivalent.

7. Cf. Gates on the relationship of margin and center ("'Ethnic'" 297–98).

8. For this reason I find Gökberk's suggestion, that exile and displacement are productive paradigms for decentering the self, to be potentially misleading (167–68). It is not a matter of replacing the stability of home with the disorientation of exile (although the experience of exile can alienate, sensitize, and politicize the self in productive ways); rather, we need to recognize how the self in any location is both "at home" and "in exile," inside and outside, central and marginal. The concept of positionality developed by feminist critics acknowledges the self as multifaceted, not unified, not self-consistent, not stable, and therefore not containable within the frozen terms of any binary opposition: see Adelson, *Making* and "Racism"; De Lauretis; Kaplan; Martin and Mohanty; Trinh, *When* 229. For various exhortations that we confront our privilege and interrogate our whiteness, see Frye; hooks, *Yearning* 54, 124; Pratt, "Reply"; Trinh, *When* 19, 114; cf. Alcoff 31n. Peck's essays discuss the significance of our identities and positions for a reconceptualization of German studies.

9. I see parallels between, on the one hand, my critiques of these writers and, on the other, arguments, posed largely by women of color, that combat the white, middle-class, heterosexual bias of mainstream feminist criticism. See, for example, Adelson, "Racism"; Alarcón; De Lauretis; hooks, *Feminist*; Lanser; Lugones and Spelman; Chandra Mohanty; Moraga and Anzaldúa; Ong; "Panel"; Smith; Spelman; Trinh, "Difference: 'A Special Third World Women Issue'" (*Woman* 79–116). For parallel arguments in the German context, see Hügel et al. Gates reminds us that racism need not be aggressive or malicious but can be benevolent or "well-intentioned" ("Talkin'" 204–05). That the "reinscription . . . of a specifically white masculine authority and privilege" can infect the work of left-leaning scholars is demonstrated again by Newton and Stacey 74; see also Spivak's discussion of Deleuze and Foucault. My own interpretations go strongly against scholarly opinion on these postwar German authors. Literary treatments of the Third World have been subject to se-

rious (and revealing) misreading as scholars attempt to deflect potential critique from their authors and the progressive German tradition they represent. hooks, in contrast, offers an instructive essay on Wim Wenders's *Wings of Desire* in which she demonstrates "the role whiteness plays" in its construction and reception (*Yearning* 165–71).

I. RACE, REVOLUTION, AND WRITING

1. The Heinrich Heine Club, the major cultural center for German exiles in Mexico with a membership of 150, was dedicated to "the promotion of freedom-oriented German and Austrian art, literature, and science"—its programs included Mozart, Beethoven, Liszt, Schönberg, Goethe, Schiller, and Brecht—and to the "strengthening of bonds with Mexican culture past and present" (qtd. in Kießling 275). Of its sixty-eight evening programs, Kießling notes only five "in honor of the host country or of peoples oppressed or threatened by fascism" (277, cf. 283). *Freies Deutschland*, according to its editor Alexander Abusch, reached a readership of over 20,000 in North America, Latin America, England, the Soviet Union, Palestine, India, New Zealand, Australia, and China (qtd. in Kießling 306). Abusch saw as one of the journal's most important tasks the preservation of "true," that is, humanistic and antifascist, German literature and culture (Abusch 559).

2. De Bopp documents that the German exile community was oriented toward Europe and had little to do with Latin America or with the Latin American German colony; on this point, see also Köpke. One exception seems to have been Egon Erwin Kisch (Kießling 471–86). Kießling's is the best general work on German exile in Latin America; see also Abusch; LaBahn; Moeller. The concentration of German Communist Party members in Mexico made it, LaBahn notes, "the center of communist political and cultural activity in Western exile" (5). For information on Seghers's work in Mexico and on the country's impact on her writing, see Batt, "Jahre."

3. See Gutzmann, "Eurozentristisches" 192–93. Seghers's reminiscences are given in her "[Ein Brief]," in *Aufsätze 1954–1979* 252–58; see also her interview with Wilhelm Girnus in that volume (441). Seghers lists Schoelcher's *Esclavage et colonisation* as a source for her works (*Aufsätze 1954–1979* 256); Streller cites also R. C. Dallas, *Geschichte der Maronen-Neger auf Jamaika* (1805), ed. T. F. Ehrmann ("Geschichte" 746n).

4. All three texts are published in Seghers, *Hochzeit*. References are given

to work and page numbers in this volume. See James for an impassioned account of revolt in the Caribbean.

5. There are numerous examples of such interpretations particularly, but not exclusively, from the GDR. See Batt, *Anna Seghers* 217–23; Herting 17–39; Neugebauer 117–26; the essays by Streller; Wagner. Western critics discuss the same themes; see, for example, Behn-Liebherz; Tulasiewicz. Greiner, in contrast, begins to question the interpretive clichés of Seghers scholarship: " '[r]emaining true,' 'becoming alive,' 'finding one's identity under the sign of loyalty' — such literary formulations are mixed with the dubious, the vacuous, the transitory; they contain meaninglessness within themselves" ("Bann" 153).

6. For other discussions of blacks in Seghers's texts, see Grimm, "Germans"; Hodges; Kassé; Milfull. Gutzmann was first to tackle the problems of racism and Eurocentrism in Seghers. See also Romero, *Anna Seghers* 109–11; Weigel, "Neues."

7. Touristic and nostalgic clichés persist in Seghers's essays on Latin American culture and history; see "Die gemalte Zeit: Mexikanische Fresken" (1947), "Brief nach Brasilien" (1962), and "Brief über ein Buch" (1969), in Seghers, *Aufsätze 1927–1953* 214–20; and *Aufsätze 1954–1979* 196–200, 341–44.

8. Beauvais's decision to remain in the Caribbean presents a revolutionary lesson:

> The choice was a cursed one between what one called happiness: a young, snow-white thing who was like pure glass with a spring in every movement, even in the sound of her voice, who by chance was called Claudine! And what had nothing in the least to do with happiness: an island in the Caribbean sea that by chance was called Guadeloupe, inhabited by less than ten thousand Negroes, who had won their freedom six years before with his assistance and who were supposed to be slaves again this year. . . . The island could no more fade away than some star. Much more easily Claudine. That is probably the lot of all earthly happiness, to fade away like vapor. (*Wiedereinführung* 91–92)

The European chooses the revolution above any private desire; personal happiness is fleeting, while the fight for freedom is a universal imperative. Angress argues that in Heinrich von Kleist's antiimperialist works the individual's claim to love is incompatible with a commitment to social change — "[e]rotic love is the antithesis of political engagement" (27). For the white revolutionaries in Seghers's texts, the same holds true. Seghers, who drew from Kleist's "Die Verlobung in St. Domingo" while criticizing his understanding of the black revolution, is close to him at least in her presentation of the existential dilemma of the white revolutionary. See her remarks on Kleist in *Aufsätze 1954–1979* 255–56.

9. As one critic put it, Ann is won over to the revolution in bed (Hölzel 127).

10. The trait is shared by Michael's unmarried sister Mali (*Hochzeit* 13). Note also the sexual impotence of the revolutionary in Seghers's "Aufstand der Fischer von St. Barbara" (*Aufstand* 30, 60–61, 130–31, 156).

11. Cf. Lorisika's discussion of Seghers's female types (93–98). The physical stature of the women illustrates what appears to be the case for their race in general: blacks are not fully developed. In this way Seghers's narratives are heir to the view in nineteenth-century natural science that placed non-European, nonwhite peoples at a lower stage of human development (Gould, esp. 113–19). Milfull explains the "virtues" of Seghers's black women (speechlessness, loyalty, self-sacrifice, etc.) as a model for "genuine" revolutionaries (53–55). This levels any problems raised by her depiction of women and blacks.

12. The narrative makes an explicit point of this: "[w]hen the memory of Margot left him in Toussaint's quarters, then it was only proper that she should vanish completely like sweet, sometimes stinging, generally painful dreams" (*Hochzeit* 57). Not only forgotten, Michael's family has actually been dead for weeks.

13. Tulasiewicz takes this as evidence of the blacks being "unaware of historical processes" (65).

14. See also the remarks about Bedford (*Licht* 173). The lack of sharp definition characterizes not only time but any sense of order in the black world. Michael Nathan's father sees in Haiti a "tangled, inexplicable, senselessly motley world" (*Hochzeit* 11); for the blacks Christophe and Ismael, the world is "too confused" (*Wiedereinführung* 113).

15. N.B. The timeless black world represents a positive alternative to the European model of history in Heiner Müller's *Der Auftrag*; see Teraoka, "*Der Auftrag*," esp. 77. Müller's text reworks Seghers's *Das Licht auf dem Galgen*; for comparisons, see Chiarloni; Romero, "*Seghersmaterial*"; Vodoz.

16. The GDR writer Christa Wolf, an astute reader of Seghers, points out the "exemplary Enlightenment impulse" in her writing and thought (141). See also Wolf's comments on the importance of Lessing for Seghers (132).

17. See Seghers, *Aufsätze 1954–1979* 254. Seghers writes about Toussaint

in the essay "Große Unbekannte" (Great unknowns) in *Aufsätze 1927–1953* 221–57.

18. Gutzmann writes that "in Seghers's portrayal, equality of the races seems to mean rather the elevation of blacks to the cultural and educational niveau of whites" ("Eurozentristisches" 195).

19. White history and white culture provide the standard for Seghers's view of Latin American history in general. She writes in her essay honoring the "great unknowns" in Latin America: "[t]he struggle for freedom, which causes astonishing capabilities to flare up in remote peoples all over the world . . . has brought forth here and there, on an unknown island or in a jungle village on the Pacific, a Thomas Müntzer or a Liebknecht or a Dimitroff" (*Aufsätze 1927–1953* 222). Later in the same essay, Seghers speaks of Toussaint as "the only one who, on the basis of his intellectual and moral qualities . . . could have overcome the gap between his people and those who had been free for thousands of years" (255–56). Toussaint's greatness, in short, was his ability to catch up to the whites; cf. *Hochzeit* 46, 56.

20. See Gutzmann on "the white man assisting the black in the articulation . . . of his own revolutionary goals" ("Eurozentristisches" 199). Other examples of blacks educated in white ways are the house manager who tells how she became "reasonable" (*Hochzeit* 7–8) and Bedford, whom Galloudec teaches to think (*Licht* 173–74).

21. The political and emotional affinity between Michael and Toussaint at this point is underscored by a sudden physical similarity: Toussaint's chin hangs down like Michael's when he is deep in thought (*Hochzeit* 53).

22. My reading of Seghers, like Gutzmann's, disputes Grimm, who sees an "utterly clear, sober, straightforward, and unequivocally progressive" depiction of blacks in Seghers's writing ("Germans" 158). Decisive for him is "the simple fact that blacks, Jews, and mulattoes are depicted together, and that their joint portrayal is meant to bespeak and symbolize the unity of all the wretched of the earth, regardless of race or color" ("Germans" 160). Kassé 57, Milfull 52, and Streller, "Zauber" 189 also defend Seghers against any charge of Eurocentrism.

23. Equally, Europeans should feel themselves in solidarity with the struggle for freedom in all parts of the world. See Seghers's remarks in "Aufgaben der Kunst" and "Abschied vom Heinrich-Heine-Klub," in *Aufsätze 1927–1953* 172–73, 205. In Heiner Müller's treatment of the same material, revolutionaries are bound by their class and race, thus undercutting the purported universal validity of the French ideals (Teraoka, "*Der Auftrag*"). Milfull dismisses Müller's text as a "desperate postscript" to Seghers (52).

24. Michael Nathan, returning to Europe after Toussaint's capture, marries and becomes the father of two sons (*Hochzeit* 59–60). In a conventional, nonrevolutionary life, he is capable of producing progeny, yet the matter is of no consequence to him (59).

25. The written document is meant to save those "who would otherwise have disappeared without a trace in deep waters or in a jungle; their names are not in any book nor on any monument; perhaps they didn't even have real names" (*Licht* 245). Writing in books or on monuments is the mark of white history.

26. Müller again provides the contrast. In *Der Auftrag* the betrayal of the revolution is depicted as the symbolic shredding of the written mission. For Müller the sexual and political bond between white revolutionary and black slave does not find its transposition into a mission of solidarity and revolt for future generations. Rather, the revolution is abandoned, while the European loses consciousness and his political conscience in the experience of physical ecstasy (*Auftrag* 100–01). Seghers, for whom the task of the author is to function as the "memory of the revolution" (Batt, *Anna Seghers* 223), writes in order to preserve the memory of something still very much alive: the revolution lives on, in and through the activity of its writers and readers. For Müller there is only the fading recollection of something past. His text ends not with remembering but with Debuisson, the white European, forgetting the storming of the Bastille (*Auftrag* 100–01).

27. JanMohamed and Lloyd make a similar critique of universalist humanism; see their introductions to two special issues of *Cultural Critique* on minority discourse. Delacampagne traces a connection between racism and Western rationalism from antiquity to the present; Gates notes that the Enlightenment offers also a "conceptual grammar of antiracism" ("Critical" 323). For investigations of ways in which Enlightenment discourse constructed and controlled its others, see Hofer; Pickerodt; Weigel, "Nahe"; as well as Horkheimer and Adorno; Mayer.

2. "WORLD THEATER" VS. "EUROPEAN PERIPHERY"

1. On developments in West Germany in the 1960s and 1970s, see Demetz 57–87; Krueger; Parkes; Wasmund 193–96.

2. Krueger and Parkes each offer comprehensive discussions of West German writers and the state.

3. Cohen provides an excellent account of Weiss's life.

4. On *Kursbuch*'s importance in the 1960s, see the comments by Karl Markus Michel and Peter Hamm quoted in Lennox 185.

5. On Enzensberger's notorious reluctance to pin himself down, see his "Gespräch" 116–19 and "Ende."

6. For other discussions of Weiss's engagement with Dante, see especially Heidelberger-Leonard; also Blumer 121–30; Bohrer, "Tortur" 202–06; Cohen 76–82; Haiduk, *Dramatiker* 119–24; Kehn, esp. 68–85; Krause 30–101, 134–46; Salloch; Sareika, *Dritte* 188–90; Scherpe; Schmitt 26–38, 148–64; Vormweg 83–93; Vormweg, qtd. in Kaiser 341–42.

7. Further details on this project are given in Gerlach and Richter 59, 60n, 80, 115, 292, 326. Much of Weiss's reception of Dante is worked out in his *Notizbücher*, especially Books 5–9, which accompany the Auschwitz trials and the writing of the two Dante works (*Notizbücher 1960–1971* 211–386). Book 10 contains fragments from a *Divine Comedy* adaptation (*Notizbücher 1960–1971* 398–99, 475–81). Regular notes on Dante, the *Divine Comedy*, and Weiss's *Divine Comedy* project continue from Book 10 (in *Notizbücher 1960–1971*) to Book 27 (in *Notizbücher 1971–1980*), stretching from the mid-1960s to the early 1970s, from work on *Die Ermittlung* through the early stages of *Die Ästhetik des Widerstands*; substantial discussions are offered in *Notizbücher 1960–1971* 592–601 (Book 16). Cf. the narrator's reflections on his first encounter with the *Divine Comedy* in Weiss, *Ästhetik* 1: 79–83; and Weiss's remarks in Gerlach and Richter 292. For discussions and surveys of Dante reception in Germany, see Hempel; Naumann; Rüdiger; Wais. To my knowledge there has been no general examination of the reception of Dante by postwar writers.

8. On Weiss's "Beatrice," see Cohen 10–11, 81; Heidelberger-Leonard 258; Krause 476n. The identification with Dante continues through Weiss's career; cf. *Notizbücher 1960–1971* 474–76, 551, 601; *Notizbücher 1971–1980* 81, 84–85.

9. Scherpe writes that the Inferno-Purgatorio-Paradiso schema provides the "symbolic order . . . according to which Weiss . . . schematizes and structures all of his experiences, from personal ill health to world-historical crisis" (92).

10. Cf. Weiss's "10 Arbeitspunkte" on the necessity of choosing sides and the nonviability of a "third position" (18).

11. The connection between emancipated thought and political action is made also in Weiss, "Ständiges" 48, 54–55.

12. Cf. Weiss, "Antwort," "Luftangriffe," and "Vietnam!"

13. Cf. Schlunk 27–30 and Demetz 47–56. For Baumgart the Princeton speech "seems to follow the model of Christian confessions and conver-

sion stories" (11). In an interview from 1981, Weiss states that his effort to rewrite his past is "a construction but also at the same time not a construction" ("Ständiges" 44). Cf. Weiss on his depiction of Max Hodann and on the connection between aesthetics and resistance ("Ständiges" 50–53). Bohrer writes of the therapeutic function of politically engaged literature; as he puts it, Weiss "is looking for a surrogate realm controlled by individuals, where there are destinies instead of balance sheets, where personal volition still exists" ("Revolution" 94) — in short, where heroism is possible.

14. Rischbieter connects the text's structure to the *Divine Comedy* (101). On the topic of the Third World in Weiss, see Bathrick; Sareika, *Dritte* 182–234 and "Peter Weiss' Engagement." Of postwar German works on Africa, Gugelberger cites Weiss's *Lusitanischer Popanz* as "[p]erhaps the best known and most enthusiastically received play (particularly in Third World countries)" ("Them" 97). For discussions of Third World revolution in postwar German drama, see Ismayr 236–37; Mittenzwei; Sareika, "Von der Systemkritik."

15. Weiss writes in "Notizen zum dokumentarischen Theater" that the definitive aim of documentary literature is the "critique of concealment ... of distortion ... of lies" promulgated by the media and supported by reigning groups and institutions (ii; references given to sections). Directed against "obscurantism and opacity," the task is to produce "explanations" [to illuminate] (iv), to formulate an analytical "model" (viii), to attain a broad overview or a "synthesis" (xii) of what appears to be fragmented, chaotic, and impenetrable. Enlightenment is thus connected to the process of political emancipation.

16. The English translation combines scenes 6 and 7 of the German, resulting in a total of ten scenes.

17. Khamis emphasizes this effect. Krause, however, criticizes Weiss's assumption that facts are sufficient to change political consciousness (87–88; cf. 511n); Bohrer argues that Weiss's methods and moral judgments accomplish nothing in the way of political analysis ("Tortur" 205); Mennemeier too finds moralizations and oversimplifications that lack explanatory power (2: 228). For further expressions of doubt regarding the efficacy of the play, see Schmitz 108–09; Thurm. Blumer provides a review of its reception (159–73). The juxtaposition of conflicting testimony, calling for critical analysis whose final judgment falls always against the colonialists, is an organizing strategy of the play. Cf. Blumer 182–83; Haiduk, *Dramatiker* 160–61; Fred Müller 87–88; Schmitz 98.

18. Here I part company with scholars who emphasize nonverbal aspects of the play: for example, Bathrick 145; Baumgart 12–13; Cohen 101; Haiduk, *Dramatiker* 159; Haiduk, "Peter Weiss' *Gesang*" 82; Fred Müller 93; Schumacher, "*Gesang*" 83.

19. Bathrick 140–41; Gugelberger, "Them" 99; Haiduk, *Dramatiker* 161. According to Gugelberger, Weiss's text demonstrates "how close Africa, the Third World, and all oppressed people in the First and Second worlds really are, once one has learned to approach things from the point of view of class" ("Them" 100).

20. See also Weiss's comments in "10 Arbeitspunkte" 23; and in Polacco 92. As Schlunk sees it, Weiss is searching for an identity not "given from the beginning" and "based on something other than race, religion, or place" (12).

21. On this responsibility, see Weiss, "I Come Out" 655. Bathrick makes the point that Weiss does not acknowledge the "reality of contradiction inherent in black-white solidarity" (145) but projects the "unequivocating submersion" of his European persona in the collective black African voice of his play (142). For Weiss any locational bias can be neutralized by a methodological or political decision.

22. Cf. Gerlach and Richter 122; Weiss, "Ständiges" 41. Weiss's "Che Guevara!" concludes: "[t]he day when we have acquired enough knowledge to understand that the struggle concerns us, too, that the struggle is not conducted in distant places but in our own society . . . that day will be the beginning of the defeat of imperialism" (561). Education overcomes barriers or limitations of class, race, or nation; note that in this passage the European's knowledge is already equivalent to the demise of imperialism.

23. On the title, see Gerlach and Richter 137; Haiduk, *Dramatiker* 175; Sareika, *Dritte* 218–19 and "Peter Weiss' Engagement" 258.

24. Cf. Weiss's comments in Gerlach and Richter 125–26, 143. Bohrer argues that Weiss does not recognize that Vietnam and South America (for example) are not comparable ("Revolution" 94). For critiques of the political and aesthetic tenets of Weiss's play, see Blumer 186–210; Ismayr 317–30; Warneken.

25. On the voluntaristic tendency in Weiss's work, see Baumgart, esp. 14; Ismayr 348, 350–54.

26. See Baumgart 14; Blumer 190–91, 203, 208–09; Cohen 112; Ismayr 323; Mennemeier 2: 229–30; Schmitt 41–42; Schmitz 113–14, 116; Warneken 116.

27. Accordingly, political enlightenment is depicted as the primary task of the Vietnamese Communist Party during World War I (129–32). Ed-

ucation seems to constitute the sole strategy—revolutionary work *par excellence*—of the party cadre, as the connection is asserted again between political learning and revolutionary action.

28. Schmitz's description of part 1 provides a good account of the development of the Vietnamese people as a unified historical subject in the play (113–21).

29. Weiss states in "Notizen zum dokumentarischen Theater" that documentary theater "takes sides" (x). There should be no nuance or ambivalence in the depiction of political struggle: "[i]n the description of rapine and genocide, black and white strokes are justified; no conciliatory traits need be indicated in the aggressor, while full solidarity must be shown for the underdog" (x).

30. On the play's monotony, see Baumgart 13; Haiduk, *Dramatiker* 190–91; Ismayr 322–23; Sareika, "Peter Weiss' Engagement" 260; Schmitz 112, 145; Schumacher, *"Vietnam-Diskurs"* 107; Warneken 116.

31. See Weiss's comments in Gerlach and Richter 125; Polacco 88; Weiss, "Peter Weiss" 6. The pleasure of the reader or viewer lies in the intellectual activities of "recognition," "learning," "contemplation," and "doubt" (Gerlach and Richter 151–52).

32. Weiss, qtd. in Gerlach and Richter 147; Weiss, "Amerika" 158. The "Notizen zum dokumentarischen Theater" explains: "[a]ll non-essentials, all digressions, can be eliminated to lay bare the basic problem. Lost are the moments of surprise, local colour, sensation; gained are universal truths" (xi).

33. Excerpts from the *Bericht* were published in *Der Spiegel* (Weiss and Palmstierna-Weiss, "Büffel"); the issue also includes the interview recorded in July 1968 (Weiss, "Amerika"). A German translation of the Swedish interview is published as "Weiss in Nordvietnam." See also Weiss, "Ständiges" 36–37, 41.

34. On the Weiss-Enzensberger debate, see Bathrick 135–36, 147–48; Claas and Götze 380–81; Große and Thurm 151–52; Sareika, *Dritte* 68–71 and "Peter Weiss' Engagement" 252–54; and especially Sadji.

35. Cf. Enzensberger, "Unsere" 183. Enzensberger shares Heiner Müller's view that détente in Europe does not establish world peace but perpetuates a coalition of aggression against the poor ("Europäische" 167–68); see also Enzensberger, "Berliner" 146. He claims in "Zum *Hessischen Landboten*" that the tension between rich and poor constitutes the only revolutionary factor in the world today (122). Sadji criticizes the *Kursbuch* essay as Eurocentric and paternalistic (262) but acknowledges that Enzensberger comes closer to reality than does Peter Weiss (264). In

Sadji's view, Enzensberger fails, however, to recognize the antagonistic differences that exist among Third World countries themselves (262). Mader in turn disputes Enzensberger's claims regarding the nonviability of resistance movements within rich societies; cf. Sareika's discussion of Mader in *Dritte* 72–73. Lennox traces a Eurocentric thread through Enzensberger's Third World writings.

36. Enzensberger notes a "trace of private spiritual cleansing" in statements of solidarity (172). This is certainly true of Weiss. Cf. Enzensberger on the revolutionary commitment of European intellectuals, in "Berliner" 144–45, 146–47.

37. Enzensberger sees "a lot of self-deception, a lot of legend-building, many facile myths" in Europeans' attitudes toward the Third World; their solidarity is "abstract and rhetorical," their attitude toward Third World revolution marked by consumerism ("Entrevista" 115). Elsewhere he asks whether revolution in the Third World is not a wishful projection on the part of Europeans who, engaged in a critique of their society, seek an exotic, alternative utopia ("Eurozentrismus" 27–28, cf. 30–31). Enzensberger even raises the issue of racism on the part of European sympathizers ("Eurozentrismus" 29). Blumer asks whether Enzensberger's critique of the "doctrinaires" does not apply to Enzensberger as well (337). The author did attempt to put words into action when he resigned his fellowship at Wesleyan University in 1968 to travel to Cuba (cf. Enzensberger, "On Leaving"; Berghahn 283). But see his image of the superfluous "foreigners who were posing for photographs / in the canefields" (*Untergang* 28); his statement in "Revolutions-Tourismus" that the outsider's role of the European intellectual cannot be shed by walking through sugarcane fields (159); and the remarks reported in Grimm, "Enzensberger" 98. On the tension between socialist countries and European leftists who desire to demonstrate their solidarity, see Enzensberger, "Revolutions-Tourismus," esp. 164–66. Enzensberger speaks primarily of European socialist countries, but his remarks are applicable to the socialist countries of the Third World (cf. 178). For summary remarks on the solidarity of literary intellectuals in West Germany, see Sareika, *Dritte* 295–306.

38. Enzensberger defines his enlightenment ideal in the following terms: "I have in mind centers of ongoing critical debate, where the general problem of culture is taken on ruthlessly and with revolutionary élan, and every form of censorship, self-distortion, and administrative coercion is rejected" ("Entrevista" 113).

39. In contrast, Enzensberger argues against "treating crime, business, and politics as equivalent" and for maintaining distinctions in order to pre-

serve "what is specific and particular" (Arendt and Enzensberger 172–73, cf. 179). Throughout his essay on Las Casas, however, he too draws parallels between the Holocaust, the bombing of Dresden and Nagasaki, colonialist efforts to exterminate peoples in Africa, Asia, and Latin America, and U.S. involvement in Vietnam. His "On Leaving" also links an imperialistic United States and Germany in the 1930s (32). Cf. "Entrevista" 112; *Freisprüche* 453–54.

40. See Kant's prefaces and introduction to his *Critique of Pure Reason*; also his introduction to the *Prolegomena*.

41. See Enzensberger on the imperative of "self-critique and demystification" ("Entrevista" 116). This fundamental difference between the two writers is illustrated by their stances toward Cuba and Vietnam. While Enzensberger's vigilantly critical attitude leads him to severe attacks against Castro ("Bildnis"), Weiss remains loyal to North Vietnam in the face of mounting criticism in the late 1970s. On Enzensberger's disillusionment with Cuba, see Melin and Zorach 487–91; Grimm, "Bildnis" 159; and especially Grimm, "Enzensberger." Weiss's remarks on Vietnam are found in his *Notizbücher 1971–1980* 738–39, 764–74; and in "Vietnam bleibt." See also Schmitt 48–49; Weiss, "Ständiges" 24–25.

42. As Enzensberger puts it, "[Our hands] are completely empty, and remarkably white" ("Unsere" 189). Or, as he states in "Berliner Gemeinplätze," any identification with Third World revolution remains premature and unproductive if it forgoes an examination of one's historical position (146). Enzensberger analyzes the century-long failure and the continued futility of revolutionary movements in Germany in "Zum *Hessischen Landboten*." Cf. Enzensberger, "Berliner," esp. 138–47. On the nonrevolutionary character of German postwar literature, see Enzensberger's "Entrevista" 113–14, "Gemeinplätze," "Gespräch" 123–28, "Interview" 80–89, 92–93, "Klare."

43. On the literary-historical context of the play, see Melin and Zorach. On the Third World in Enzensberger's work, see Sareika, *Dritte* 131–81.

44. N.B. Enzensberger attacks the Cuban Communist Party in "Bildnis einer Partei," published that same year. The denunciation of both sides suggests that he locates himself on neither front; cf. Berghahn 290–91. Enzensberger offers further comments on *Verhör von Habana* in "Interview."

45. This contrasts sharply with his "Bildnis einer Partei," which focuses on unique circumstances rather than generalizable principles.

46. Reinhold makes the point, however, that Enzensberger is interested in the psychology of the ruling class, while Weiss focuses on the reconstruc-

tion of historical processes ("Literatur" 109–10). See also Enzensberger, "Interview" 74–75.

47. Grimm argues that Weiss exhibits the "commonplace Manichaeism" that separates good and evil, while Enzensberger does not ("Bildnis" 147, 187). Cf. Mader 146; Sareika, *Dritte* 145–46, 169, 174, 176.

48. Grimm describes Enzensberger's gesture as "invitation" rather than "persuasion"; his aim is to motivate viewers and readers to examine the facts ("Bildnis" 154–56). Berghahn argues too that Enzensberger's goal is a "process of knowledge" involving self-critique on the part of the audience (288–89).

49. Sadji notes a shift in the 1970s, evident in "Zur Kritik der politischen Ökologie" and "Bildnis einer Partei," in which Enzensberger's earlier enthusiasm for the Third World is subjected to critical examination (272–73). See also Lennox on the political and ideological shifts in Enzensberger's Third World texts between the late 1960s and the early 1980s.

50. As Enzensberger puts it, "We are in the same boat, all of us. / But he who is poor is the first to drown" (*Untergang* 59). It is not just that divisions (of class, culture, or First, Second, and Third Worlds) must be recognized. Enzensberger suggests that heterogeneity protects a society from ultimate catastrophe: a multitude of cultures strengthens the possibility of survival ("Eurozentrismus" 30). Cf. "Ende," in which Enzensberger argues that consistency leads to disaster.

51. Cf. Enzensberger on the epistemological aporia of the ethnographic project that seeks to capture difference in a scientific discourse ("Eurozentrismus" 18–19), and on historical writing in "Erste Glosse." According to Götz Müller, the insights of the latter essay are recast in poetic form in *Der Untergang der Titanic* (256–58).

52. In "Erste Glosse" Enzensberger suggests that truth lies in the "seams" of a text (14)—at those always visible edges where discrete pieces have been made to join.

53. This description matches in every detail but one Eduard Ender's *Humboldt und Bonpland am Orinoko*, in the holdings of the German Academy of Sciences in East Berlin. In Ender's mid-nineteenth-century portrait based on Humboldt's sketches, the assistant Aimé Bonpland sits illuminated in the center while Humboldt occupies the darker background, studying a flower under a microscope. The painting emphasizes Bonpland's role as secretary—he sits surrounded by paper—while the domain of research remains reserved for Humboldt. Gnüg identifies Enzensberger's model as a portrait by Friedrich Georg Weitsch (297). For discussions of *Mausoleum*, see Franz; Schuhmacher 57–61.

54. Bürger remarks that Enzensberger ends where Weiss began, with a "suffering from the failure of a revolution" and a subsequent "escape into an inflated individualism" (21). Bürger contrasts the views of history in Enzensberger's *Der Untergang der Titanic* (as a text of fatalistic aestheticism) and Weiss's *Ästhetik des Widerstands* (a text on the viability of resistance); see also Claas and Götze. On Dante in Enzensberger's work, see Schuhmacher 54–55 and especially Wiedemann-Wolf.

55. As Lehmann puts it, the text on the sinking of a technological miracle reflects a "rejection of the presumptuous theoretical faith that one was sitting with dead certainty on the right boat"—a critique of the faith of the Left in a historical telos (322–24). Seeba argues against seeing the text as an expression of conservative politics or a renewed focus on the private sphere (293, cf. 286–88). Bohrer urges that the work enacts an "anarchic mobility" that is anathema to the conservatives ("Getarnte" 1276).

56. N.B. In "Europäische Peripherie" Enzensberger characterizes the fear of impending catastrophe, perceived as a private end (the death of the bourgeois individual), as a colonialist syndrome arising from the division of the world between "us" and "them" (153–54).

57. For more on the parallel between Berlin and the *Titanic*, see the line "Imperceptibly Berlin was buried [sank] in snow, in isolation" (60) and esp. cantos 31 and 33, in which the author's room becomes a sinking boat. Discussions of the significance of the *Titanic* in Western culture and in the postwar German context are offered by Grimm, "Eiszeit"; Koebner 227–29; Lehmann 328–30; Schuhmacher 45; Seeba 281–89.

58. In its allusion to the closing image of Edgar Allan Poe's *The Narrative of Arthur Gordon Pym of Nantucket* (Pym is one of the ghostlike passengers aboard Enzensberger's *Titanic*), the approaching iceberg spells both final disaster and the moment of absolute self-knowledge. The connection to Poe is discussed by Grimm, "Messer" 159–62; Holthusen 63–66; Lehmann 330; Götz Müller 260–61; Schuhmacher 55–56.

59. In fact, the passengers belonging to the working or lower classes died in disproportionate numbers. The text notes that those in steerage and the ship's black-faced stokers—in contrast to their poetic refiguration as the indomitable Shine—remained, constrained by force, intimidation, or resignation, on board the sinking ship (16–17, 63). Canto 22 cites data on the survivors: roughly 60% of the first-class passengers and 40% of the second-class and steerage passengers were saved, while three-fourths of the crew perished (59). Cf. the hordes of "Wogs, Jews, camel drivers and Polacks" who are forced at gunpoint into the engine room, while a millionaire disguised as a woman (wearing, ironically, a turban) saves himself

in the last lifeboat (63). The text makes continual reference to the class structure of the ship's passengers. Cf. Enzensberger's comments on the political significance of diverse populations in the First World in "Berliner" 150–51, "Eurozentrismus" 31–33.

60. Götz Müller sees the view of the poet as simulator and as liar—the insight into the impossibility of accurate, documentary representation—as central to Enzensberger's text (258–59). In contrast, Sorg argues that the poet in *Der Untergang der Titanic* maintains himself as a visionary who, like Dante, sings of what is yet unseen (49). See also Reinhold, "Geschichtliche" 125–26.

61. Enzensberger's "Erste Glosse" also presents the author as reconstructor. Künzel shows that Enzensberger does not describe actual paintings in his text but invents or mixes motifs from a number of artworks.

62. For other discussions of the secret turtle, see Lehmann 331; Melin 15; Schuhmacher 64. On other paintings described in the text, see Grimm, "Messer" 157–58; Holthusen 77–80; Künzel; Lehmann 326–27; Schuhmacher 63–64; Wiedemann-Wolf 260.

63. Not the sovereign perspective of the elected prophet but a collective polyphony in which no single position is authoritative—this is Enzensberger's aesthetic aim at this time; see his "Gespräch" 131–32. For Holthusen, Enzensberger's attempt to render the incommensurable in his text is articulated through "an aesthetics of the absurd and the grotesque," resulting in a "genuine piece of nonsense poetry" (92, 95). On Salomon Pollock, see Claas and Götze 375; Holthusen 73–76; Götz Müller 263. Holthusen; Melin 15; and Wiedemann-Wolf 257n identify Pollock with Enzensberger.

64. Lehmann describes the play's structure as "less a progressive narrative organization than a circular one" centered on the sinking of the *Titanic* in cantos 13–20 (316). See also his thematic ordering of the play (314–16); cf. Dietschreit and Heinze-Dietschreit 120–24.

65. I thus differ with Lehmann, who argues that the text remains too rational, too lucid, and too clever. In his reading, the authorial voice maintains its ability to represent everything in the literary work of art (332–33), thereby upholding the poetic ideal symbolized by Dante.

66. Cf. Lamping, who sees neither apocalyptic despair nor revolutionary optimism but rather the "grotesque comedy of survival, which is a survival without grandeur" (231). On the play's end, see also Brady 26; Holthusen 96.

3. SOLIDARITY AND ITS DISCONTENTS

1. See Streese for an investigation of Third World themes in West German literature after the 1960s.

2. The Solidarity Committee, established in 1960 as the GDR Committee for Solidarity with the Peoples of Africa, was expanded in 1964 to become the Afro-Asian Solidarity Committee and again in 1973 to encompass solidarity actions for the peoples of Latin America, especially Chile (Krüger 54–55).

3. The solidarity actions in the case of Vietnam indicate the breadth of the GDR's commitment. In response to the Chinese invasion in 1979, ships and planes rushed medical supplies, food, trucks, paper, media equipment, and other goods worth 172 million marks to the Socialist Republic of Vietnam. Over a fifteen-year period, members of the Free German Trade Union League (Freier Deutscher Gewerkschaftsbund) contributed over 525 million marks. Over six thousand Vietnamese received technical training in East German schools and factories. Assistance was given in constructing Vietnamese schools and hospitals, and the Free German Youth (Freie Deutsche Jugend) helped to provide 3 million marks' worth of educational materials. The Writers Association organized solidarity actions between 1966 and 1973 aimed at supplying bicycles, electricity, health care, and aid for children; the last of these campaigns ended in 1973 with close to 500,000 marks collected from its membership. See Krüger 56–58; Stern 65. For purposes of evaluation: the average monthly net income for a family of four in the GDR was 1,440 marks in 1974, 1,670 marks in 1978 (Staatliche 115). Sodaro presents a useful overview of GDR involvement in the Third World.

4. In East German scholarship the Federal Republic of Germany is consistently labeled the second greatest imperialist power in the world. See Liebscher 47, 49, 58; throughout her analysis the adjective "neocolonial" seems obligatory in referring to West German activity in the Third World.

5. On German literary interest in Latin America, see Melin and Zorach. The sudden, pervasive concern with the Third World at this time in the GDR is all the more striking in light of the dearth of relevant East German works written in the period of the Vietnam War. Posharskaja's play provides the proverbial exception that proves the rule.

6. The proceedings of the Congress are published in *Neue Deutsche Literatur* February 1974. In that issue, see especially 3–4, 5–6, 13; the speeches by Seghers (15–22) and Kant (23–47); and the contributions by Stern (63–65), Neutsch (80–83), Heiduczek (96–98). Cf. Haase et al. 780–83.

7. Further sections on Latin America are contained in *Sinn und Form* 27.1 (1975); 28.2 (1976); 29.2 (1977).

8. Hörnigk makes the same observation (148). Kaufmann discusses Heiner Müller's *Der Auftrag*, in the context of the importance of Latin American literature and revolutionary history for the GDR, as "indicative of broader tendencies" in East German literature of the 1970s (8–10).

9. The incident is usually cited as a litmus test for oppositionality among GDR writers. Twelve authors, including Braun and Müller, responded to the government's action with an immediate letter of protest; eventually it was endorsed by over seventy others. Hacks, Anna Seghers, and Hermann Kant, who succeeded Seghers as president of the Writers Association, issued statements in support of the SED. The party and the Writers Association retaliated against the original signers with a variety of measures, including imprisonment, publication bans, suspension or expulsion from the association, and deportation. The incident initiated an exodus of over three hundred artists and intellectuals to the West over the next five years (Demetz 140–42; Emmerich 249–53).

10. The play appeared in *Theater der Zeit* in 1979 and in a revised version in 1980. References will be given by page and column number to the earlier text. Apart from changes in scene divisions to reduce the play's complexity, Hammel revised the work mainly to make Humboldt more of a revolutionary, with the "ideas of 1789 in his heart" ("Zu diesem Stück," *Humboldt* 141). Very little has been written about Hammel and virtually nothing about this play. See Rödel for an introduction to the author; also Fischborn 19–42; Maczewski. An informative interview with Hammel appeared in *Weimarer Beiträge* ("Interview"), followed in the same issue by a discussion of Hammel's plays from the 1960s (Böhme).

11. Both the description of Humboldt given in the stage direction and Humboldt's denial of the rebellion are eliminated from the revised version. Hammel in his commentary to the first version attests to the historical accuracy of the excised statement ("Zu diesem Stück," *Theater*). The commentary to the second version, in contrast, emphasizes Humboldt's critique of slavery and claims that "[Humboldt's] regret for the conditions he finds, which he neither can nor wants to change, quietly develops into an indictment of a social system that is ripe for change" ("Zu diesem Stück," *Humboldt* 141). Humboldt repeats in the closing moments of the first version that he has not seen the people of Latin America "in a state of unrest" (71,2); again the remark is omitted in the later version from 1980 (135).

12. "The circumstances . . . are shaped essentially by the Napoleonic realm: it is the year of Bonaparte's public seizure of power and of the

definitive burial of revolution and republic in France" (Hammel, "Zu diesem Stück," *Theater*). Both the repressive atmosphere and the political significance of Humboldt's science are foregrounded when we see that Humboldt is spied upon throughout his stay in Paris.

13. A similar understanding of the value of Humboldt's research for the colonialist project is expressed by peripheral figures in the play. The one-legged French soldier, for example, states matter-of-factly, "He scouted out America for the emperor. That's the way it is. . . . Never again will we be uninformed about the area where we land" (61,1). In an article on the discourses of nineteenth-century European exploration, Pratt demonstrates how the historical Alexander von Humboldt, writing in the name of science, reduced America to landscape, marginalized its inhabitants, and recorded its culture as archaeological ruins and mythologies of a distant past. His discourse thereby prepared the way for European expansion into a region seen to be rich in natural resources and native labor and whose diminished indigenous culture appeared ready for capitalist transformation ("Scratches" 128–30). Hammel's Humboldt seeks explicitly to avoid the role performed by his historical namesake.

14. Humboldt describes the "arrogant simplemindedness" of his audience "who occupies the parquets and steals the seats from those struggling to see. I shudder at the thought that I am supposed to report about the culture of executed Indian tribes in front of these cannibals" (70,2). In some respects, Hammel's Humboldt approaches the German literary type of the disillusioned revolutionary (Georg Büchner's Danton, Tankred Dorst's Toller, to name two) whose emancipatory message goes unheard. Humboldt complains of the masses: "[i]n spite of all my ambition to make myself understandable to the people, they stare at me with open mouths. They may well have the feeling that they are hearing something astonishing but nothing they can use" (70,2).

15. Hammel seeks in the later version to soften the flaws of his characters, emphasizing that each learns from the other. See his "Zu diesem Stück," *Humboldt* 142–43; cf. "Zu diesem Stück," *Theater*.

16. "It is fatal to cling to a fatherland. . . . A free spirit loses its free perspective. . . . I'm planning a description of the cosmos—should I fritter myself away in regions that, after all, will use the freedom they may have achieved only to preserve their wretched egotistical trifles?" (71,1). Both Bolívar's request for instruction and Humboldt's warning against provincial interests are retained in the revised text. Bolívar notes the closeness of Humboldt's position to that of the classical German playwright Friedrich Schiller (71,2). In almost stereotypical fashion, the bourgeois intellectual

withdraws from a revolutionary situation into the ethereal sphere of universal idealism. Hammel points in his comments on the first version to the ultimate contradiction and inadequacy of Humboldt's views: "[t]he problem of the idealistic world citizen emerges: the desire to embody a third force, to side with no one, to be if not the judge then the standard, to let humanism take effect on its own, by being a humanist and nothing more than that" ("Zu diesem Stück," *Theater*). Again the critique is softened in the later version, in which Hammel presents Humboldt as a man "who doesn't expressly resist the fact that his more accurate knowledge . . . encourages, and in a certain sense even authorizes, the national revolutionary forces to pursue the liberation of South America from the Spanish" ("Zu diesem Stück," *Humboldt* 141).

17. Hammel writes, "We are dealing . . . with one of the first examples of committed and unsentimental solidarity toward peoples who are reflecting on themselves; with the first stirrings of a tradition that is preserved and continued in the first socialist state of the German nation, through internationalist practice, free from capitalist-imperialist goals" ("Zu diesem Stück," *Theater*).

18. Bolívar's pointed remark is omitted in the 1980 publication (120–21).

19. In Hammel's words, "Inconnue's ultimate defection from the European to the Latin American scene is an allegory for the spread of revolutionary ideals overseas" ("Zu diesem Stück," *Theater*).

20. Said points out that "from 1815 to 1914 European direct colonial dominion expanded from about 35 percent of the earth's surface to about 85 percent of it" (*Orientalism* 41). Hacks's *Die Fische* is seen to mark a turning point in his work, moving away from classicistic projections of an emancipated society toward a critical, more directly political exploration of contemporary socialist reality (Hörnigk 167–73; Jehser; Mitchell 143–48).

21. Simon's hypothesis reflects the nineteenth-century scientific view that "ontogeny recapitulates phylogeny." Primitive (i.e., non-European, nonwhite) peoples were seen as "children," reaching adulthood prematurely, at a stage of inferior, incomplete development. The theory of evolutionary recapitulation provided a useful justification for imperialism (Gould 113–19). Cf. chap. 1, note 11.

22. My interpretation of Simon differs markedly from other accounts. Both Jehser (1739–40) and Mitchell (144–45) criticize Simon's inhumanity and intellectual rigidity but ignore or dismiss the colonial context of the play. Leistner moves beyond his critique of Simon's fanaticism to glorify him as a tragic figure who remains "'sublimely' true" to his beliefs (387). Trilse also vindicates Simon, who rises above his limitations to perform

the "liberating deed" of resistance against the "ss-type" Goyon (255–56); in fact, it is in order not to give up his project that Simon kills Goyon, unshakable in his belief that progress must be forced upon humankind. Hörnigk, missing Hacks's critique of the authoritarian claims of European science, reads the play as an argument against the "undialectical" idea that progress is possible without the exercise of force (171–72). Similarly, both Rohde and Ziermann take Simon's statement "They have to be forced, all of them" as the view of the author Hacks.

23. My reading of the Mexicans' speech challenges the evaluation by Heitz, who points out their "individual incompetence," their "unfitness for community life," and their "lack of communication" when measured against the norm of rational dialogue, understood to be the sign of political and intellectual maturity (576–77). Heitz's interpretation does not allow for cultural differences between Mexico and France.

24. From the outset, the outcome of the civil war is clear to its participants; see the statement by Goyon (*Fische* 189).

25. Although Simon claims that science will bring the final conquest of the New World (189), the opposite holds true: the Third World proves victorious over European science. Hacks writes on the historical situation:

> News reaches the ears of the leading world power that, far across the ocean, a nation of yellow-skins has fought and secured for itself a type of state that is too innovative to be entirely approved of. A spread of the contagion to its neighbors, who are similarly rich in natural resources and thus in need of developmental aid, is to be feared. In addition, the indisputable interests of Big Money, with which the said world power is most intimately intertwined, demand action. It is necessary to take seriously the responsibility for law and order all over the earth, a burden that was initially adopted as a matter of civilized behavior. ("Noten" 401)

After a long campaign against guerrilla forces, the superpower is forced to withdraw, with wide-reaching consequences: "[t]he retreat of the world power, although affecting only a portion of its military forces and in no way disorderly, nevertheless severely unsettles its role as leader. From this time on its foreign and military policies are unsuccessful, and internal collapse is impending" ("Noten" 403). These comments allow the play to be read as a parable of the rise of Third World independence and the demise of European and American imperialism. Cf. Mitchell, who downplays the colonial background and argues that the play maintains an "unrelievedly negative tone" (147–48).

26. Critics have focused on the Guevara chronicle while refraining from a discussion of the Bumholdt and Bedray scenes. Symptomatic in this regard is Ullrich's review of the GDR premiere of Braun's play: Ullrich addresses the Bumholdt-Bedray interludes in a postscript, then only to claim that the production found no way to convince the audience of the necessity of these scenes. For brief treatments of the Bumholdt-Bedray material, see Cosentino 44; Hörnigk 177–78; Rosellini 100–03; Schuhmann, "Anmerkungen" 32–33 and "Nachwort" 368; Heinz-Dieter Weber 97. In general their discussions ignore the gravity of the difference, upheld in the structure and tone of the play, between the Latin American revolutionaries and the Europeans Bumholdt and Bedray.

27. Scholars treat the play as a text regarding social, political, or historical issues in the GDR and not as a reflection on Latin America or on the relationship between the GDR (or Europe) and the Third World. See, for example, Profitlich, "Dialektische" and *Volker Braun* 12–13, 15–17, 22–23; Timm 1512–13; Wallace. Cosentino 45; Rosellini 102; and Schuhmann, "Anmerkungen" 30 relate Braun's work to the Brechtian learning play (*Lehrstück*). Actually Braun's text asserts Guevara's difference from Brecht's model, in that the Latin American revolutionary rejects the dictates of the party represented by the secretary, Monje, and the "friend" in Cuba. It is the party secretary who, in place of the individualistic pilot in Brecht's *Badener Lehrstück*, is exiled "into nothingness" (Braun, *Guevara* 88). Likewise, Guevara's "exit into the abyss" (96) is not the fulfillment of the Brechtian model of the young comrade disappearing into the anonymity of the lime pit in *Maßnahme* but its opposite: not the affirmation of party discipline and doctrine but an inchoate expression of an alternative. In Braun's reversal of Brecht, the young comrade is allowed to live, to attempt "the new beginning" (95) as a revolutionary unaffiliated with the party.

4. "THE ROMAN LEARNS THE ALPHABET OF THE NEGRO"

1. "The West is waiting for the crisis of the Soviet empire and the East is waiting for the final crisis of capitalism. . . . I'm waiting for the Third World" ("Walls" 25). "It's like a big waiting-room, waiting for history. And history now is history of the Third World with all the problems of hunger and population" ("Walls" 11).

2. "Walls" 22, 26; "Mich" 50. Müller offers the example of the large Turkish population of West Berlin. For further comments on the political and cultural importance of guest workers and other minorities in Western

countries, see Müller's "Ich scheiß" 124; *"Jenseits"* 40, 54, 76–81, 93–94; *"Zur Lage"* 27, 36.

3. Müller continues: "[m]ere prevention of war becomes a prevention of history, a prevention of progress—that's the danger I see. The status quo as the entrenchment of hunger, underdevelopment, environmental problems, and developmental aid against the populations of three continents" (1201). Cf. Heiner Müller, "Diskussionsbeitrag"; *"Ich bin"* 20–21. Müller put the point succinctly in "Walls": "[t]he Western paradise is based on hell for the Third World" (13); cf. "Ich scheiß" 124.

4. Emmerich places Müller's texts within a "paradigm shift" in GDR literature from an orthodox Marxist belief in historical progress to a critique of the totalitarian and self-destructive effects of Enlightenment reason (271–78). In this period, Emmerich writes, literature becomes a "critique of civilization" (273). Carl Weber connects the shift in Müller's writing to his visit to the United States and Mexico in 1975–76 (9).

5. Only Fiebach attempts a similar analysis; see esp. chap. 4, 160–206. On the Third World in Müller, see also Bathrick; Vaßen, "Entfremdete"; in part, Domdey and Herzinger. By "Europe" I mean a set of values (the Enlightenment) and a historical tradition (imperialism), not a geographic entity.

6. My discussions of this work, and of *Die Hamletmaschine* and *Der Auftrag* that follow, are based on earlier arguments (Teraoka, *Silence*). On these same plays, see Raddatz.

7. For an examination of Müller's rewriting of his Brechtian model, see Teraoka, *"Der Auftrag."* Vaßen ("Entfremdete") discusses the cultural and literary significance of the Third World for this text.

8. This suggests a response to critics' dismissal of Müller's Third World images as mere poetic utopianism. Here the structure of the play demonstrates that the "Third World" is not a depiction of "reality" but the deliberate construction of a European subject. The mythical, mythological character of Müller's Third World reflects in a self-conscious way one dominant mode of conceiving the non-European realm from a European perspective: the European intellectual presents the Third World (whose experience he categorically cannot share) as irrational, quasi-mystical, wholly "other"—and thereby utopian.

9. See Fehervary for explorations of this problem with regard to Müller's portrayal of women.

10. Schulz suggests why Medea offers a paradigm for the emergence of the woman as a dramatic figure: men are traditionally the makers of history; the woman must defy the social order if she is to assert herself as a

historical agent ("Abschied" 60–62; "Medea" 245–46). Detailed analyses of Müller's text are offered by Eke, *Heiner Müller* 190–225; Teichmann 157–71.

11. See also Eke's discussion of these passages (*Heiner Müller* 208–09, 216). Others have focused on gender in their treatment of Müller's women figures, including earlier versions of his Medea. See Fehervary, "Erzählerische"; Fischer; Maltzan; Schulz, "Abschied," "Bier" (esp. 26–28), "Medea." But gender in the Medea text is the vehicle through which a larger issue—that of colonialist and colonized—is played out. In my view, Medea would be closer to the men Sasportas (in *Der Auftrag*) and Aaron (in *Anatomie Titus Fall of Rome*) than to the women ErsteLiebe (FirstLove), the Goth queen Tamora, and Titus's daughter Lavinia in those same plays.

12. Cf. Müller, "Brief an den Regisseur" 104. The program volume accompanying the premiere of Müller's play in Bochum contains a passage from Oskar Negt and Alexander Kluge's *Geschichte und Eigensinn* that supports (perhaps inspired) Müller's reading of the Jason-Medea myth. Negt and Kluge describe the Argonauts as elite heroes, hungry for adventure and profit, who turn their superior technology upon a nonindustrial culture abroad (162–63). See also Heiner Müller, *Krieg* 320, on the "guest worker issue" in *Verkommenes Ufer*.

13. On the body in Müller's work, see Vaßen, "Tod." Müller says the following: "[a] critic saw in my last plays an attack on history, the linear concept of history. He read in them the rebellion of the body against ideas, or more precisely: the impact of ideas, and of the idea of history, on human bodies. This is indeed my theatrical point: the thrusting on stage of bodies and their conflict with ideas" ("Walls" 38). In my analysis of Müller, ideas are often European, white, and male, while the body is aligned with the non-European, nonwhite, nonmale.

14. Medea's line "It's on her body that I write my play" (131) reinforces the connection to Sasportas, who speaks of the mistreatment of blacks "[w]ith the same whips our hands will use to write a new alphabet on other bodies" (*Auftrag* 89), and points forward to the black Aaron, who writes "A DIFFERENT ALPHABET" (*Anatomie* 156).

15. Here Medea embodies aspects of Ophelia and Sasportas while moving beyond them in key ways. For both Ophelia and Medea, exploitation is a bodily phenomenon (Medea's question, "Jason / Do you want to drink my blood," echoes Ophelia's challenge, "Do you want to eat my heart, Hamlet?" ["Medeamaterial" 129; *Hamletmaschine* 55]); and as Sasportas wanted, Medea directs a drama written in blood upon the other's body. But the drama of rape she describes, punctuated by directorial commands

("now . . . now . . . now . . ."), actually reenacts Hamlet's symbolic rape of his mother, also accompanied by a series of "nows," through which he preserved an oppressive patriarchal role (*Hamletmaschine* 54). In other words, Medea incorporates oppressive aspects of the men Jason and Hamlet in her act of vengeance against Jason's bride. Her actions, however, result not in the perpetuation of the rule of the white male conqueror but in its irrevocable demise.

16. See Schulz on Medea's nonreproductive, antipatriarchal, "anti-Oedipal" sexuality in which her primary bond is to her brother, not to her husband or her sons ("Medea" 252–53). My interpretation of Medea contests that of Bogumil ("Poesie"), who argues that Medea fails in her attempt to reestablish the identity of her former life. Eke takes issue with Bogumil as well (*Heiner Müller* 200, 215–16).

17. For other discussions, see Bogumil, "Theoretische"; Eke, "Neger"; Lehmann and Schulz; Weimann; and especially Fiebach, who discusses the play in the context of the author's Third World concerns (160–206). References to the play will be given to the version in *Shakespeare Factory 2*.

18. Müller has commented that the work, considered to be Shakespeare's first, contains everything developed in later dramas; see "Form" 146 and "Für ein Theater" 134. In his view, first plays—he cites among others Shakespeare's *Titus Andronicus*, Goethe's *Götz von Berlichingen*, Schiller's *Die Räuber*, Büchner's *Dantons Tod*, Grabbe's *Herzog Theodor von Gothland*, and Brecht's *Baal*—contain conflicts that provoke their societies in politically and aesthetically important ways ("Keimende"). Müller's interest in Shakespeare arises in part from the fact that Shakespeare lived in a time of incipient European exploration and capitalist expansion; see Müller, "Form" 148 and "Geschichtspessimismus" 207.

19. The opinion of the play as unworthy of its author was reiterated in East Germany by Schlösser, who denounced the drama as monstrous and tasteless. For a catalog of insults the play has endured, see Reese 77; Tricomi 103–04n; Waith, "Metamorphosis" 39. All three offer a defense of Shakespeare. For a general discussion of *Titus Andronicus*, including the issue of authorship, see Waith, Introduction.

20. Müller's comment is a response to Hensel's characterization of *Der Auftrag*. Munkelt provides excerpts from reviews of the play (224–25); her discussion offers another example of the denigration and subsequent misreading of Müller's text on moral grounds.

21. This is true of Rome even in Shakespeare's play, although the political background is not made explicit; see the excerpt from "The Tragical History of Titus Andronicus, etc." (Shakespeare 137).

22. For Müller Rome epitomizes the institution of the state: "Rome is the primordial cell of the state and its imperial structure" (*"Jenseits"* 77). Its form as well as its demise, furthermore, reflect Müller's vision of present-day Western Europe: "Western Europe is being devoured from within; the tidal wave of the Third World is crashing over Europe. . . . The analogy for this internal erosion of Western Europe is found in the decline of the Roman Empire, which in the end was gradually taken over by the slaves. Today the guest workers and immigrants in the metropolises have the same status as the slaves in ancient Rome" (*"Zur Lage"* 27).

23. Cf. the first descriptions of Titus in Shakespeare's text: "[a] nobler man, a braver warrior, / Lives not this day within the city walls" (I.i.25–26); Titus is "[t]he good Andronicus, / Patron of virtue, Rome's best champion" (I.i.64–65).

24. On the contrast between barbarian Goths and civilized Romans in Shakespeare's text, see Sommers; Tricomi. For alternative arguments, see Broude; Pearson.

25. In an earlier publication in *Theater Heute* the line reads "AND A CROWN FITS ON ANY BLOCKHEAD" (44). The same viewpoint is expressed by the servants and peasants in Müller's *Macbeth*. There the identity of Duncan's successor is of no interest to one servant, who explains, "The king is the king. And / If it's not him, it's another. This one or that" (204). Kott argues that Shakespeare's plays present history as a "Grand Mechanism" of violent repetition, an amoral struggle for power in which "there are no bad kings, or good kings; kings are only kings" (10, 17). Scholars have suggested that Kott's book, published in Polish in 1964, provided the basis for Müller's adaptation of *Macbeth*; see Fuhrmann 65–66 on this point. Kott's influence is perceptible in Müller's reworking of *Titus Andronicus* as well.

26. For more on the "subaltern optic" in Müller, see Botterman, esp. chap. 4.

27. Shakespeare's *Titus Andronicus* ends, notably, with imperial instructions regarding the burial (or nonburial) of Saturnius, Titus, Lavinia, and Tamora.

28. This is the historical continuity affirmed by the Hamlet figure in scene 1, "Familienalbum" ("Family Scrapbook") of *Hamletmaschine*. The connection to *Hamlet* is made in the passage just quoted from *Anatomie Titus*, which alludes to the final line of Shakespeare's play: "[t]he rest is silence."

29. The hunt of the African Aaron is defined in terms that clash with those of the "civilized" Europeans. Compare Aaron's "WITH TOOTH AND

CLAW INSTEAD OF HORN AND HOUND" with Titus's view of the hunt, rendered in the words of the play's commentator, as the killing sanctioned by the forms and manners of the upper class: "WITH HORN AND HOUND AGAINST THE BEAST OF THE FORESTS / A LITTLE BLOODSHED IN FINE SOCIETY" (136). Fiebach makes the point that the Third World represented by Aaron does not signify "the good Other" in contrast to the exploitive Roman (European) world: "[o]n the level of moral practice and humanism—or, rather, the absence of humanism—there are no significant differences. . . . Aaron's revenge is as bloody and egoistic as the acts of the Romans" (164). The consensus among scholars of Shakespeare is that Aaron plays the part of the Elizabethan villain, representing a diabolic principle of evil directed against morality and order; see, for example, Price; Spivack, chap. 2, chap. 11; Tricomi. Both Bryant and Williams, in contrast, argue that Aaron's evil is socially conditioned; cf. Bartels.

30. Cf. Eke, who argues that Aaron is not a model of the Third World revolutionary subject ("Neger" 312).

31. As Weimann puts it, "The social achievements of the present . . . just where the victory columns proclaim their eternity, are assailed by the victims they left behind" (119). In *Krieg ohne Schlacht* Müller describes *Anatomie Titus* as "a text with current relevance about the incursion of the Third World into the First World" (324), thus identifying with the position of the play's internal commentator. Elsewhere he speaks of the "dream of the incursion of the horse-trodden steppes into the world of established German manufacturing: . . . death comes from Asia" (*"Jenseits"* 65). The difference of the "Third World" is indicated by its unique treatment of its dead, in contrast to the monumentalizing burial rituals of Rome: "[t]he grave of Genghis Khan cannot be found: the Mongols had the habit of riding over the graves of their chiefs until they could no longer be distinguished from the ground" (*"Jenseits"* 65). Cf. *"Jenseits"* 78, where Müller claims that the Mongols, pursuing a lifestyle of mobility rather than stability, sought only to destroy empires, never to found them. As such they represent the very antinomy of the (European) state and of state control. See Raddatz on the relationships to death that characterize the European and the Third World figures in Müller's texts (17, 148, 151–54).

32. The continuity extends even into the next generation, as Lucius's son, also named Lucius, seeks to emulate his father (176).

33. For differing discussions of laughter in Müller's works, see Domdey; Greiner, "Jetzt." As Fiebach puts it, "In the story of the black slave, in his attitudes, his actions, and his commentaries . . . the dissecting anatomy, the implosion, the devastation of Rome and therefore of the rich metropolises,

is prepared and explained through their past victims" (164). Greiner presents an opposing argument that interprets the dismembered bodies in *Macbeth*, "Medeamaterial," and *Anatomie Titus* as "signifiers of emptiness" ("Jetzt" 46–47). Eke too sees in the last scene the "final shut-down of history" ("Neger" 306). For Weimann, Aaron's loyalty to his black son—what I would see as part of his tie to the Third World—leads to the failure of his plan of revenge and to the impossibility of an alternative to Rome (120).

34. Jason is crushed by his ship; thus the European explorer, conqueror, colonialist, man is killed by the instrument of his conquest and oppression ("Landschaft" 135). Müller comments: "[t]he fact that the vehicle of colonization kills the colonizer is an anticipation of its end. This is the threat of the end that we are facing. The 'end of growth' " ("Deutschland" 196). The Bochum program volume (Schauspielhaus) provides a wealth of source material for this scene, including excerpts on actual and fictional voyages from works by Homer, Verne, Poe, Conrad, Columbus, and Cook.

35. Schulz ("Heiner Müllers") offers an analysis of Müller's highly self-conscious language in these texts; see also Eke, *Heiner Müller* 216–25.

36. As Birringer puts it, "If 'Ophelia/Elektra' speaks in the name of difference . . . she is limited to a vision of death within the horizon of Jason's territory" (100). Birringer speaks of the "brutal contempt and masochistic guilt" of Müller's vision, in which political options lie in a realm "removed from the imagination and the rhetoric with which our Western intellectual and aesthetic representations could describe them" (111). But consider Kuzniar's suggestion that the woman's voice in a male author's text can articulate an alternative: "[a male author] can—like a female writer—design interventionary constructs based on the assumption of woman's specificity or difference. . . . Unique female paradigms in canonical male-authored works may challenge the dominant androcentric model" (1196).

37. Müller, speaking of *Anatomie Titus*, identifies "the dubious position of the author as a perpetrator behind a desk, or as someone between the victims and the perpetrators" (*Krieg* 324).

38. Munkelt provides details on Müller's deletions (226–27).

39. "THE NEGRO WRITES A DIFFERENT ALPHABET / PATIENCE OF THE KNIFE AND VIOLENCE OF THE AXES" (156) recalls Sasportas's statement about "whips our hands will use to write a new alphabet on other bodies" (*Auftrag* 89) and repeats the line "[t]he patience of the knife and the power of the axe [violence of the axes]" from Müller's *Zement* (39). The "EXCURSUS ON THE SLUMBER OF THE METROPOLISES" (*Anatomie* 140–41) incorporates motifs from Müller's essay on Robert Wilson ("Taube"); cf. Müller, "New York," and the text quoted in Fuchs and Leverett 63. I do not

wish to imply an identification between "author" and the person named Heiner Müller, only with specific themes and discursive features (a particular voice) within his works. The commentary is, according to Müller's endnote to *Anatomie Titus*, "a means to bring the reality of the author into play" (224). Cf. the quote in Bogumil, "Theoretische" 7; Müller, *Krieg* 324.

40. Müller has spoken of the priority of form over content; see his "Ich weiß" 97, "Ruth Berghaus" 116, "Weltuntergang" 162–63. Here I am proposing a yet higher priority: that of strategy, of attitude, over form. Another term might be "method," as Müller suggests when he implies that Brecht's work methods are more important than his results ("Man" 26).

41. Cf. Said, *Culture* 212–14 and Retamar, who discuss the efforts of Latin American and Caribbean writers to reclaim cultural authority by rewriting Shakespeare's *Tempest*.

42. On social and political issues cloaked in moral guise, see Müller's "Gespräch mit Bernard Umbrecht" 120; and the comments by Tragelehn regarding Müller's *Macbeth* adaptation (qtd. in Müller, "Shakespeares Stücke" 37).

43. Fiebach writes, "The anatomy of Titus—the epitome of social greatness, of nobility, of arrogant virtue—is the dismantling of an apparently immovable and eternal monumentality, of the myth of the unsurpassable civilization of Rome, of the (white) European world" (163). For Müller the motif reflects a dramaturgical principle: "[t]o demonstrate the amputations and deaths, monuments can be used, larger or smaller than life, on which the degree of devastation is marked" (*Anatomie* 225).

44. Titus is described as "A STONE" (132); his flesh and blood are transformed into "A WATERWORKS" (156); Lavinia is a "sculpture" (158); Titus's brother Marcus is a "stone relief" (165). The image of Titus monumentalized by the excrement of eagles symbolizes the process of European (Roman) history, whose victories are founded on waste: "ROME'S EAGLES SHIT ON THE BUTCHER OF THE GOTHS / UNTIL HE SHRIVELS INTO A MONUMENT OF HIMSELF" (155). There are numerous images as well of the destruction of monuments: the "EXCURSUS ON THE SLUMBER OF THE METROPOLISES" describes the crumbling of the monuments (churches, banks, statues) of the First World (140–41); Titus with his archers causes a "RAIN OF MARBLE STATUES," signifying the loss of virtue and justice in Rome (192); Lavinia becomes a "RUIN" (219). Domdey also discusses a process of monumentalization in Müller's works in which revolutionary figures become identified with landscapes, continents, or angels (226–27); see also Greiner on immobilization ("Jetzt" 41).

45. Analphabetism bears threatening cultural and political connotations.

Lucius claims that the Goths must become literate (217), thus promising to impose Roman letters and Roman thought on another race. Müller discusses his text in terms of the "resistance" of the Goths "against the imposition of a foreign alphabet" (*Krieg* 324–25).

46. Here I draw on arguments developed in Teraoka, "Writing" 191–93. Formulations of theater as "a conjuring up of the dead" fill Müller's essays and interviews: see his afterword to *Anatomie Titus* (224–25), "Für ein Theater" 136, "Shakespeare eine" 229, "Vorwärts" 25, *"Zur Lage"* 87. Müller connects the idea of resurrection to the idea of Communism (qtd. in Bittorf 178); he speaks of the resurrection of the young comrade from Brecht's *Die Maßnahme* in *"Ich bin"* 15, "Wunde" 105. Robert Wilson's theater is important because it includes the dead; see Müller, "Brief an Robert Wilson," *Krieg* 330, "Taube."

47. N.B. In Müller's view European theater began in Rome (*"Zur Lage"* 38).

48. Thus the words of the commentator: "YOUR MURDERER WILLIAM SHAKESPEARE IS MY MURDERER / . . . / MY NAME AND YOUR NAME GLOW IN THE BLOOD / THAT HE SPILLED WITH OUR INK" (153). Shakespeare's play thematizes the oppressive power of literary (mythological) models and the need to break through, to rewrite, their limits and distortions. See Fawcett; Kendall.

49. The possibility of the privileged author of a dominant language writing from the perspective of those dominated is argued for in theoretical terms by Deleuze and Guattari (*Kafka*) and, in terms specifically related to the theater, by Deleuze ("Manifest"). Müller attests to the importance of their work for his writing in *Krieg* 295, 316; for a discussion, see chap. 1 of my *Silence*. On the white author becoming (writing as) a black man, see Müller, *"Ich bin"* 28, *"Jenseits"* 55.

5. TALKING "TURK"

1. Former Chancellor Helmut Schmidt, for example, sees Turkey, the country of origin of the largest minority group, as belonging to a culture rooted in Asia and Africa, not Europe. Rudolf Augstein, editor of *Der Spiegel*, arguing against dual citizenship for Turks in Germany, also emphasized their non-European culture. Şenocak responds critically to both Schmidt and Augstein; see also Adelson, "Opposing" 309.

2. Räthzel suggests that the image of the other as Turkish may be dissolving in the wake of German reunification, as mounting tensions and social and cultural differences between West Germans, East Germans, and

Eastern European ethnic Germans destabilize Germanness as a biological concept (46–47).

3. From 1945 to the mid-1970s, some 30 million people entered Western European countries as workers or as workers' dependents, creating immigrant populations numbering over 16 million (Castles et al. 1–2). For the first fifteen years after the war, West Germany's economy absorbed close to 10 million ethnic Germans from former eastern territories of the Third Reich and nearly 3 million East Germans. These refugees constituted 90% of the population growth of the FRG between 1950 and 1960; in this decade, West Germany's gross national product doubled (Herbert 195). My introductory information for this chapter is drawn from Bischoff and Teubner; Castles et al.; Herbert; Räthzel; Wilpert.

4. There were twenty-three hundred documented crimes of violence against foreigners in 1991, ten times the number of incidents in 1990 (cf. Nandlinger). Two cases that received widespread attention were the firebombing murders of eight Turkish women and children in Mölln and Solingen in November 1992 and May 1993.

5. Räthzel makes the tie between fascist legislation of the 1930s and current German citizenship laws and foreigners laws (32, 41–42); cf. Herbert 207–08.

6. New legislation in 1990 eased naturalization requirements for second- and third-generation residents but, as Wilpert argues, did not challenge the principle of *jus sanguinis*, the right of citizenship by "blood" (75n).

7. All three authors engage in some form of participant observation, which Dithmar identifies as a feature of postwar workers literature (676–78). Zimmermann offers further comments on the technique (408–11). Participant observation in this context should not be confused with the method of the same name in Anglo-American anthropology (for the classic formulation, see Malinowski); as both Jell-Bahlsen and Kramer explain, there is no tradition of participant observation in German anthropology. On literary works by German authors dealing with Turkish workers, see Baudach; Scheuer; Sölcün.

8. Harbsmeier discusses the figure of the "speaking Other" in European literature; Wallraff, he suggests, offers a recent example of the strategy of seeing the world from the other's point of view.

9. "[The] focus on text making and rhetoric," Clifford says, "serves to highlight the constructed, artificial nature of cultural accounts" ("Introduction" 2). My analysis in this chapter especially is influenced by theoretical reflection in the field of anthropology; key contributions are Clifford, "On Ethnographic Authority"; Clifford and Marcus; Marcus and Cushman.

See also Asad; Dwyer; Fernandez; Pratt, "Fieldwork" and "Scratches"; Rabinow; Webster. For critiques of Clifford and Marcus, see Gordon; hooks, "Culture to Culture: Ethnography and Cultural Studies as Critical Intervention" (*Yearning* 123–33); Mascia-Lees et al. For discussions of the relevance of anthropology to literary study, see Daniel and Peck; the essays by Peck; Teraoka, "Is Culture."

10. Chiellino cites von der Grün as one of the few authors who have found "the right way to approach the everyday life of guest workers, to represent their experiences in their host country" (109). According to Sölcün, Gürlük is an actual person whom von der Grün knows well (79).

11. The observation about water makes sense from the perspective of rural life in Turkey, just as the patterns of the Turk's speech can be understood as part of an oral tradition of storytelling. My concern is for the way in which his narrative text is placed into a cultural context in which the reader is led to draw inappropriate conclusions. Baudach takes a different view of the Turk's speech: "in my view, Osman Gürlük's account belongs to the best German prose today. In the editor's rendering there is still a glimmer of the tradition of storytelling, the tradition of oral literature, which enjoys high standing in Turkey" (320).

12. This pattern holds true but is less blatant in the other portraits. My reading challenges that of Kircher, who sees "in the minimally edited interviews a seemingly very authentic reportage technique. . . . These semi-documentary portraits convince us with their realism" (148–49). Kircher does not recognize the constructed nature of von der Grün's documentary text. This is also true of Sperr, who emphasizes the author's objectivity (168).

13. On the use of the present tense as a form of "othering," see Pratt, "Scratches" 120–21; and Fabian's discussion of the "ethnographic present" (80–87).

14. This is true of each of the guest workers portrayed in the volume. While all reflect the stereotypes held by Germans, all are set apart in distinct ways from the (perceived) majority of their fellow countrymen—by linguistic skill in German, contact with West Germans, liberal or leftist political views, or sexual preferences. The Italian, for example, "looks the way German girls who read nothing but magazines imagine an Italian gigolo" (81), but he is also a former member of the Italian Communist Party (84).

15. The narrator claims later that Turkish workers who have lived in the FRG for some years "have come to think differently, they no longer think and act according to the criteria of the Orient, they have begun, without being conscious of it in Germany, to regard German values as definitive"

(20). Von der Grün of course implies that there is an essential "Turkish" or "Oriental" identity that is slowly being eroded. Scheuer feels that the guest workers wanted to flatter von der Grün by speaking favorably of Germans and Germany and critically of their own native cultures; he then asks the pertinent question, "Did Max von der Grün provoke such distortions because the foreigners sensed in him a representative of the ideology of prosperity?" (65). See Paredes for an analysis of ethnographic subjects pulling the leg of their Anglo ethnographer.

16. Von der Grün purportedly visited the villages he describes (Sperr 168). The author claims to have traveled "20,000 kilometers from one end of Europe to the other" in researching his book in 1974 (qtd. in Reinhardt 179).

17. The Italian echoes the words of the Turk; the separation between natal village and West German city is three thousand kilometers and three thousand years (15). See Fabian on the construction of the other in terms of spatial and temporal distance. The denial of coevalness, he argues, precludes the possibility of genuine communication between ethnographer and interlocutor.

18. Von der Grün was a member of the SPD until the Grand Coalition in 1966 but continued to support the party in elections; see his remarks in "Gespräch," *Deutsche* 175–76 and "Gespräch," *Gespräche* 156–57. Von der Grün states in the latter interview that socialism in the Federal Republic is attainable only through reform (187). This belief in slow change is supported by the lives of the guest workers depicted in his book.

19. This is not to say that all things are better in Germany. Germans are criticized for their coldness (7), their hypercritical arrogance (57), and their subservience to authority (113–14).

20. Scheuer reaches the same conclusion: "[i]n the final analysis existing prejudices are confirmed rather than dismantled" (66). Von der Grün's portraits present not only evidence of a "civilizing" process among guest workers but also a continuum of foreignness from the (German) norm. Gradations of acceptability and "civility" among guest worker groups are reflected, for example, in the language spoken by their representatives: the linguistic and stylistic discrepancy between the German of the guest worker and the German of the commentator, and the controlling role given to the voice of the native German, are greatest for the Turk and minimal for the Frenchwoman.

21. On the scandal regarding the experiences attributed to "Ali" and the authorship of *Ganz unten*, see *Der Spiegel* 15 June 1987: 182–200;

6 July 1987: 154–60; 12 October 1987: 294–301. Kuhn discusses the work's reception in Germany.

22. In fact, it is only Wallraff who has a definite identity and a definite history, which show through the thin disguise of "Ali." We see Wallraff, not Ali, for example, interacting with the politician Franz Josef Strauß (13–14).

23. Peters makes the point that Wallraff as Ali "has become not a real Turk" but rather "a 'Turk' . . . in the eyes of his German environment" (1008). I would push this further: *Ganz unten* offers a fragmentary figure that exists (is seen by Germans) only in very limited, well-defined situations.

24. Peters points out "how little Wallraff in his disguise maintains the role of a passive, suffering observer: he enters . . . into active, almost chemical interplay with his environment" (1012). In his view Wallraff reactivates "archetypes of good and evil, sacrifice and innocence, villain and hero," while playing the role of "James Bond" or "Zorro" (1012). Peters's point—that Wallraff's documentary is a self-styled heroic epic—is a good one, but he loses sight of the specific political and ideological dimensions of the project when he compares it to everything from the *Odyssey* and *Parzival* to Hegel's *Phenomenology of Mind* (1014).

25. *Ganz unten* (German orig.) 217. This is the chapter's subtitle, missing from the English translation. Theatrical metaphors are common in the book. Wallraff tests his disguise in a "dress rehearsal" (4–5); at times the text follows the literary conventions of drama, with sets, scene directions, and spoken parts, as in the chapter "The Baptism" (34–58). Wallraff describes his work generally as "a new art form that originates in action and represents a mixed genre. In it I am simultaneously director and actor" ("Ich bin" 160). The documentary, in other words, is deliberately enacted. Elsewhere Wallraff speaks of "role reportages, in which I slipped temporarily into other existences and then staged something on the spot" ("Deutsche" 1).

26. The provocative bracketed material in the following quotes has been deleted from the English translation. Where necessary, page references are also provided to the original German.

27. See the stories of "Alfi" (30), "Fritz" (30–31), "Hinrich" (31), "Helmut" (71), "Hermann T." (79–80), "Jürgen K." (157–65), "Frank M." (170–72), and "Horst T." (173–74).

28. Likewise, Peters sees Wallraff's "'Turk' as a mere cipher for absolutely subordinate, disposable, subaltern labor" (1008). According to Wallraff, "[The author] should try to put himself in the service of oppressed groups, of segments of society that otherwise would not have a say, that otherwise would not be represented" ("Gespräch," *Gespräche* 211).

29. Özakin criticizes Wallraff for presenting Ali as a "symbol of suffering" (7). In her view, Turks are not recognized as (or allowed to be) individuals but are seen by even progressive Germans as "member[s] of an oppressed, destitute and uneducated mass" (6), as objects of pity in need of protection. I would suggest that Wallraff is not so much presenting Turks as downtrodden and oppressed as he is taking their experience as paradigmatic of oppression. Özakin's criticism finds support in Elschenbroich, who sees in *Ganz unten* the stereotype of Turkish guest workers as "beaten figures" (47), projected from a stance of "pity" and "nostalgic concern" that is "the old position of social superiority" (46). Elschenbroich also notes Wallraff's blatant stereotyping of the Germans (47). Again, my point is that Wallraff is not presenting the behavior of Germans in *Ganz unten* as typical of Germans so much as paradigmatic of attitudes of oppression.

30. For the explicit connection to National Socialism, see 200 and the footnote, omitted in the English translation, in *Ganz unten* (German orig.) 244–45. Wallraff's book ends with the warning that "[n]othing would be more mistaken than to make a monster of [Adler]. He is one of many thousands who help to maintain and benefit from a system of boundless exploitation of, and disregard for, human beings" (208).

31. Geiersbach's work was followed by a second, similar, and equally interesting study (*Wie Mutlu*). My comments are restricted to Geiersbach's first book, although many of my points are applicable to the second as well. I analyze two later novels by Geiersbach (*Gott*; *Warten*) in "Turks."

32. Nonetheless, Geiersbach lists ways in which the Yorulmazes are "typical." These include their political views and interactions with Germans, their methods of childrearing, their handling of money, the furnishings of their apartment, "and much more" (8).

33. As a result, the Turkish voices are highly differentiated in their use of German—unlike the homogeneous German speech of the guest workers in *Leben im gelobten Land*.

34. This is not to suggest that the Turkish voices are seen as basically competent in German. To the contrary, Geiersbach claims that the Yorulmaz family members, like the majority of Turks in the FRG, "have an inadequate command of the language of this country and are therefore handicapped everywhere when it comes to looking after their interests, wishes, or social responsibilities" (8).

35. Geiersbach's statement of his project is accepted without question by Wallraff ("Zu diesem Buch" 6).

36. The German use of indirect discourse is lost in English translation.

Readers should imagine an implied "He says" before each of the last three sentences of this passage.

37. Geiersbach's cultural biases are further evident in his view that the problems of the foreign youth arise from their struggle for "more emancipation than is traditionally granted them" (9), or where he claims that the "outbreaks of raw violence" in foreign families can be made "transparent and comprehensible in sociological and social-psychiatric terms" (11). Whether the categories of Western sociology, psychiatry, or the European Enlightenment are applicable to members of another culture is never open to question. Geiersbach also notes the fact that the Yorulmazes are Alevis (31n, 44n) but does not consider to what extent this may affect their actions. But see Mandel on the importance of distinguishing between Alevi and Sunni Muslims.

38. Geiersbach edits his voice out of the conversations he records, thereby emphasizing his (questionably) passive role. Often his responses are present in the transcribed text only in the form of ellipses (e.g., 190–96, 213–20). When we do "hear" Geiersbach, it is always in indirect discourse.

39. Geiersbach is mediator, moral authority, and the ultimate voice of reason: "I try to make Alda understand her father's position. . . . I ask her to consider that Hoppa also probably went too far" (221); similarly, he attempts repeatedly to bring Hoppa back to a sense of "reality" (254). Like von der Grün, he also possesses superior knowledge and information—we see this when he is the only one who can recognize fake pearls (262), or when he supposedly enables Param, a shrewd businessman, to understand the concept of inflation (45).

40. Thus Geiersbach's work can be read as a reflexive ethnography in which "the proper referent . . . is not a represented 'world'; [but rather] specific instances of discourse. . . . [T]he principle of dialogical textual production . . . obliges writers to find diverse ways of rendering negotiated realities as multisubjective, power-laden, and incongruent. In this view, 'culture' is always relational, an inscription of communicative processes that exist, historically, *between* subjects in relations of power" (Clifford, "Introduction" 14–15). For amplification, see Crapanzano; Pratt, "Fieldwork"; Rosaldo.

41. Wallraff speaks of his work as "a standing call to others to do the same" ("Gespräch," *Gespräche* 243).

42. Cf. Clifford's comments on a shift from a visual to a discursive paradigm in anthropology ("Introduction" 11–12). On the "vitalities and vicissitudes of discourse," see also Fernandez. Fabian discusses the epis-

temological and political implications of a visual orientation toward the other and argues for the primacy of hearing over sight (105–31, 162–64).

43. JanMohamed in another context reaches a similar conclusion: "[i]n the final analysis, [the author's] success in comprehending or appreciating alterity will depend on his ability to bracket the values and bases of his culture" (74). See Dwyer for a trenchant epistemological analysis of the subject needing to put itself at stake in anthropological fieldwork.

Works Cited

Abusch, Alexander. "Landung und Kampf unter Mexikos Sonne." *Sinn und Form* 32 (1980): 547–72.

Adelson, Leslie A. *Making Bodies, Making History: Feminism and German Identity*. Lincoln: U of Nebraska P, 1993.

——. "Opposing Oppositions: Turkish-German Questions in Contemporary German Studies." *German Studies Review* 17 (1994): 305–30.

——. "Racism and Feminist Aesthetics: The Provocation of Anne Duden's *Opening of the Mouth*." *Signs* 13 (1988): 234–52. Rpt. in *Feminist Theory in Practice and Process*. Ed. Micheline R. Malson et al. Chicago: U of Chicago P, 1989. 163–81.

Alarcón, Norma. "The Theoretical Subject(s) of *This Bridge Called My Back* and Anglo-American Feminism." *Making Face, Making Soul/ Haciendo Caras: Creative and Critical Perspectives by Feminists of Color*. Ed. Gloria Anzaldúa. San Francisco: Aunt Lute, 1990. 356–69.

Alcoff, Linda. "The Problem of Speaking for Others." *Cultural Critique* 20 (winter 1991–92): 5–32.

Amin, Samir. *Eurocentrism*. Trans. Russell Moore. New York: Monthly Review, 1989. Trans. of *L'Eurocentrisme: critique d'une ideologie*. Paris: Anthropos, 1988.

Angress, R. K. "Kleist's Treatment of Imperialism: *Die Hermannsschlacht* and 'Die Verlobung in St. Domingo.'" *Monatshefte* 69 (1977): 17–33.

Arendt, Hannah, and Hans Magnus Enzensberger. "Ein Briefwechsel." *Über Hans Magnus Enzensberger*. Ed. Joachim Schickel. Frankfurt am Main: Suhrkamp, 1970. 172–80.

Asad, Talal, ed. *Anthropology and the Colonial Encounter*. London: Ithaca, 1973.

Augstein, Rudolf. "Heilmittel 'Doppelbürger'?" *Der Spiegel* 7 June 1993: 18.

Baker, Houston A., Jr. "Caliban's Triple Play." *Critical Inquiry* 13 (autumn 1986): 182–96. (Rpt. in *"Race," Writing, and Difference*. Ed. Henry Louis Gates Jr. Chicago: U of Chicago P, 1986. 381–95.)

Barnet, Sylvan. Introduction. *The Tragedy of Titus Andronicus*. By William Shakespeare. Ed. Sylvan Barnet. *The Two Noble Kinsmen; The Tragedy of Titus Andronicus; Pericles, Prince of Tyre*. Signet Classic Shakespeare. Ed. Sylvan Barnet. New York: NAL, 1977. xxi–xxxiv.

Bartels, Emily C. "Making More of the Moor: Aaron, Othello, and Renaissance Refashionings of Race." *Shakespeare Quarterly* 41 (1990): 433–54.

Bathrick, David. "'The Theater of the White Revolution Is Over': The Third World in the Works of Peter Weiss and Heiner Müller." *Blacks and German Culture*. Ed. Reinhold Grimm and Jost Hermand. Monatshefte Occasional Volumes 4. Madison: U of Wisconsin P, 1986. 135–49.

Batt, Kurt. *Anna Seghers: Versuch über Entwicklung und Werke*. Frankfurt am Main: Röderberg, 1973.

——. "Die Jahre in Mexiko." *Neue Deutsche Literatur* October 1973: 16–29.

Baudach, Katharina. "Mehmet spielt nur die Rolle des Schattens: In der deutschen Gegenwartsliteratur sind türkische Arbeitnehmer fast nur in Kinderbüchern bekannt." *Zeitschrift für Kulturaustausch* 31 (1981): 319–21.

Baumgart, Reinhard. "In die Moral entwischt? Der Weg des politischen Stückeschreibers Peter Weiss." *Text und Kritik* 37 (January 1973): 8–18.

Becker, Peter von. "Shakespearekasperle: Zur Bochumer Uraufführung von Heiner Müllers *Anatomie Titus Fall of Rome: Ein Shakespearekommentar*." *Theater Heute* March 1985: 41–42.

Behn-Liebherz, Manfred. "Der Schriftsteller als Gedächtnis der Revolution: Die *Karibischen Geschichten*." *Text und Kritik* 38 (September 1982): 87–95.

Berghahn, Klaus L. "Es genügt nicht die einfache Wahrheit: Hans Magnus Enzensbergers *Verhör von Habana* als Dokumentation und als Theaterstück." *Hans Magnus Enzensberger*. Ed. Reinhold Grimm. Frankfurt am Main: Suhrkamp, 1984. 279–93.

Birringer, Johannes. "*Medea*—Landscapes beyond History." *New German Critique* 50 (spring–summer 1990): 85–112.

Bischof, Henrik. "Lateinamerika (außer Kuba)." *Drei Jahrzehnte Außenpolitik der DDR: Bestimmungsfaktoren, Instrumente, Aktionsfelder*. Ed. Hans-Adolf Jacobsen et al. Schriften des Forschungsinstituts der Deutschen Gesellschaft für Auswärtige Politik e.V., Reihe Internationale Politik und Wirtschaft 44. München: Oldenbourg, 1979. 641–55.

Bischoff, Detlef, and Werner Teubner. *Zwischen Einbürgerung und Rückkehr: Ausländerpolitik und Ausländerrecht der Bundesrepublik Deutschland: Eine Einführung*. 3rd ed. Berlin: Hitit, 1992.

Bittorf, Wilhelm. "'Mein Platz wäre auf beiden Seiten der Front.'" *Der Spiegel* 15 February 1988: 166–78.

Blumer, Arnold. *Das dokumentarische Theater der sechziger Jahre in der Bundesrepublik Deutschland*. Meisenheim am Glan: Hain, 1977.

Works Cited

Bogumil, Sieghild. "Poesie und Gewalt: Heiner Müller, Jean Genet, Tankred Dorst." *Neue Rundschau* 96.1 (1985): 52–77.

———. "Theoretische und praktische Aspekte der Klassiker-Rezeption auf der zeitgenössischen Bühne: Heiner Müllers *Anatomie Titus Fall of Rome Ein Shakespearekommentar.*" *Forum Modernes Theater* 5.1 (1990): 3–17.

Böhme, Irene. "Metamorphose eines Dramatikers: Stationen bei der Eroberung der sozialistischen Wirklichkeit." *Weimarer Beiträge* 15 (1969): 337–54.

Bohrer, Karl Heinz. "Getarnte Anarchie: Zu Hans Magnus Enzensbergers *Untergang der Titanic.*" *Merkur* 32 (1978): 1275–79.

———. "Revolution als Metapher." *Die gefährdete Phantasie, oder Surrealismus und Terror.* München: Hanser, 1970. 89–105.

———. "Die Tortur: Peter Weiss' Weg ins Engagement—Die Geschichte eines Individualisten." *Die gefährdete Phantasie, oder Surrealismus und Terror.* München: Hanser, 1970. 62–88. Rpt. in *Peter Weiss.* Ed. Rainer Gerlach. Frankfurt am Main: Suhrkamp, 1984. 182–207.

Botterman, John Charles. "Hegemony and the Subaltern: End of History in Heiner Müller's Theater." Diss. U of Washington, 1987.

Brady, Philip. "Watermarks on the Titanic: Hans Magnus Enzensberger's Defence of Poesy." *Papers Read before the [English Goethe] Society, 1987–88.* Ed. Jeremy D. Adler et al. Leeds: Maney & Son, 1989. 3–26.

Braun, Volker. *Guevara oder Der Sonnenstaat. Stücke 2.* Frankfurt am Main: Suhrkamp, 1981. 39–97.

———. "Literatur und Geschichtsbewußtsein." *Neue Deutsche Literatur* February 1974: 129–34.

Brecht, Bertolt. *Das Badener Lehrstück vom Einverständnis. Gesammelte Werke.* Vol. 2. Frankfurt am Main: Suhrkamp, 1967. 587–612. 20 vols.

———. *Die Maßnahme. Gesammelte Werke.* Vol. 2. Frankfurt am Main: Suhrkamp, 1967. 631–64. 20 vols. *The Measures Taken.* Trans. Carl R. Mueller. *The Measures Taken and Other Lehrstücke.* By Bertolt Brecht. London: Eyre Methuen, 1977. 7–34.

Broude, Ronald. "Roman and Goth in *Titus Andronicus.*" *Shakespeare Studies* 6 (1970): 27–34.

Bryant, J. A., Jr. "Aaron and the Pattern of Shakespeare's Villains." *Renaissance Papers 1984.* Ed. Dale B. J. Randall and Joseph A. Porter. Durham NC: Southeastern Renaissance Conference, 1985. 29–36.

Bürger, Christa. "Mythos vom Weltuntergang—Ästhetik des Widerstands." *Tradition und Subjektivität.* Frankfurt am Main: Suhrkamp, 1980. 17–23.

Castles, Stephen, Heather Booth, and Tina Wallace. *Here for Good: Western Europe's New Ethnic Minorities*. London: Pluto, 1984.

Chiarloni, Anna. "La Lumière de l'histoire et le ciel de la trahison: Anna Seghers et Heiner Müller, ou deux générations face à face." *Connaissance de la RDA* 22 (1986): 79–89.

Chiellino, Carmine. "Zwischen Solidarität und Klischee." *Kürbiskern*, 1983, no. 1: 107–12.

Claas, Herbert, and Karl-Heinz Götze. "Ästhetik und Politik bei Hans Magnus Enzensberger und Peter Weiss." *Das Argument* 115 (1979): 369–81.

Clifford, James. "Introduction: Partial Truths." *Writing Culture: The Poetics and Politics of Ethnography*. Ed. James Clifford and George E. Marcus. Berkeley: U of California P, 1986. 1–26.

———. "On Ethnographic Authority." *Representations* 1 (1983): 118–46. Rpt. in *Predicament of Culture* 21–54.

———. *The Predicament of Culture: Twentieth-Century Ethnography, Literature, and Art*. Cambridge: Harvard UP, 1988.

Clifford, James, and George E. Marcus, eds. *Writing Culture: The Poetics and Politics of Ethnography*. Berkeley: U of California P, 1986.

Cohen, Robert. *Understanding Peter Weiss*. Columbia: U of South Carolina P, 1993.

Cosentino, Christine. "Volker Brauns roter Empedokles: *Guevara oder Der Sonnenstaat*." *Monatshefte* 71 (1979): 41–48.

Crapanzano, Vincent. "Hermes' Dilemma: The Masking of Subversion in Ethnographic Description." *Writing Culture: The Poetics and Politics of Ethnography*. Ed. James Clifford and George E. Marcus. Berkeley: U of California P, 1986. 51–76.

Daniel, E. Valentine, and Jeffrey M. Peck, eds. *Culture/Contexture: Explorations in Anthropology and Literary Study*. Berkeley: U of California P, forthcoming.

De Bopp, Marianne O. "Die Exilsituation in Mexiko." *Die deutsche Exilliteratur 1933–1945*. Ed. Manfred Durzak. Stuttgart: Reclam, 1973. 175–82.

Delacampagne, Christian. "Racism and the West: From Praxis to Logos." *Anatomy of Racism*. Ed. David Theo Goldberg. Minneapolis: U of Minnesota P, 1990. 83–88.

De Lauretis, Teresa. "Displacing Hegemonic Discourses: Reflections on Feminist Theory in the 1980's." *Inscriptions* 3–4 (1988): 127–44.

Deleuze, Gilles. "Ein Manifest weniger." *Kleine Schriften*. Trans. K. D. Schacht. Berlin: Merve, 1980. 37–74. Trans. of "Un manifesto di meno."

Sovrapposizioni. By Carmelo Bene and Gilles Deleuze. Milan: Feltrinelli, 1978. 67–92.

Deleuze, Gilles, and Félix Guattari. *Kafka: Toward a Minor Literature*. Trans. Dana Polan. Theory and History of Literature 30. Minneapolis: U of Minnesota P, 1986. *Kafka: Für eine kleine Literatur*. Trans. Burkhart Kroeber. Frankfurt am Main: Suhrkamp, 1976. Trans. of *Kafka: Pour une littérature mineure*. Paris: Minuit, 1975.

Demetz, Peter. *After the Fires: Recent Writing in the Germanies, Austria, and Switzerland*. San Diego: Harcourt, 1986.

Detje, Robin, Iris Radisch, and Christian Wernicke. "Des Müllers falsche Kleider." *Die Zeit* 15 January 1993: 2.

Dietschreit, Frank, and Barbara Heinze-Dietschreit. *Hans Magnus Enzensberger*. Stuttgart: Metzler, 1986.

Dithmar, Reinhard. "'Arbeiterliteratur' nach 1945." *Frankfurter Hefte* 29 (1974): 667–79.

Domdey, Horst. "'Ich lache über den Neger': Das Lachen des Siegers in Heiner Müllers Stück *Der Auftrag*." *Die Schuld der Worte*. Ed. Paul Gerhard Klussmann and Heinrich Mohr. *Jahrbuch zur Literatur in der DDR* 6 (1987): 220–34.

Domdey, Horst, and Richard Herzinger. "Byzanz gegen Rom: Heiner Müllers Manichäismus." *Literatur in der DDR: Rückblicke*. Ed. Heinz Ludwig Arnold and Frauke Meyer-Gosau. Text und Kritik Sonderband. München: Text und Kritik, 1991. 246–57.

Dwyer, Kevin. "The Dialogic of Ethnology." *Dialectical Anthropology* 4 (1979): 205–24.

Eke, Norbert Otto. *Heiner Müller: Apokalypse und Utopie*. Paderborn: Schöningh, 1989.

——. "'Der Neger schreibt ein andres Alphabet': Anmerkungen zu Heiner Müllers dialektischem Denk-Spiel *Anatomie Titus Fall of Rome Ein Shakespearekommentar*." *Zeitschrift für deutsche Philologie* 110 (1991): 294–315.

Ellis, Roger. *Peter Weiss in Exile: A Critical Study of His Works*. Ann Arbor: UMI Research, 1987.

Elschenbroich, Donata. "Die festgeschriebenen Opfer." *Pflasterstrand* February 1986: 46–47.

Emmerich, Wolfgang. *Kleine Literaturgeschichte der DDR 1945–1988*. Erweiterte Ausgabe. Frankfurt am Main: Luchterhand, 1989.

Enzensberger, Hans Magnus. "A. v. H. (1769–1859)." *Mausoleum: Siebenunddreißig* 62–65. "A. von H. (1769–1859)." *Mausoleum: Thirty-seven* 62–66.

———. "Berliner Gemeinplätze." *Palaver* 7–40. "Berlin Commonplaces." Trans. Michael Roloff. *Critical Essays* 138–56.

———. "Bildnis einer Partei: Vorgeschichte, Struktur und Ideologie der PCC." *Palaver* 55–90. "Portrait of a Party: Prehistory, Structure and Ideology of the PCC." Trans. Michael Roloff. *Politics and Crime.* By Hans Magnus Enzensberger. Ed. Michael Roloff. New York: Continuum-Seabury, 1974. 126–55.

———. *Critical Essays.* Ed. Reinhold Grimm and Bruce Armstrong. German Library 98. New York: Continuum, 1982.

———. *Deutschland, Deutschland unter anderm: Äußerungen zur Politik.* Frankfurt am Main: Suhrkamp, 1967.

———. "Das Ende der Konsequenz." *Politische Brosamen* 7–30. "Second Thoughts on Consistency." *Political Crumbs* 1–15.

———. "Entrevista con Hans Magnus Enzensberger." *Hans Magnus Enzensberger.* Ed. Reinhold Grimm. Frankfurt am Main: Suhrkamp, 1984. 106–16.

———. "Erste Glosse: Über die Geschichte als kollektive Fiktion." *Der kurze Sommer* 12–16.

———. "Europäische Peripherie." *Kursbuch* 2 (August 1965): 154–73. Rpt. in *Deutschland, Deutschland* 152–76.

———. "Eurozentrismus wider Willen: Ein politisches Vexierbild." *Politische Brosamen* 31–52. "Reluctant Eurocentrism: A Political Picture Puzzle." *Political Crumbs* 17–33.

———, ed. *Freisprüche: Revolutionäre vor Gericht.* Frankfurt am Main: Suhrkamp, 1970.

———. "Gemeinplätze, die Neueste Literatur betreffend." *Palaver* 41–54. "Commonplaces on the Newest Literature." Trans. Michael Roloff. *Critical Essays* 35–45.

———. "Gespräch mit Hans Magnus Enzensberger." *Hans Magnus Enzensberger.* Ed. Reinhold Grimm. Frankfurt am Main: Suhrkamp, 1984. 116–35.

———, ed. *Gespräche mit Marx und Engels.* Frankfurt am Main: Insel, 1973.

———. "Interview mit Hans Magnus Enzensberger." *Weimarer Beiträge* 17.5 (1971): 73–93.

———. "Klare Entscheidungen und trübe Aussichten." *Über Hans Magnus Enzensberger.* Ed. Joachim Schickel. Frankfurt am Main: Suhrkamp, 1970. 225–32.

———. *Der kurze Sommer der Anarchie: Buenaventura Durrutis Leben und Tod.* Frankfurt am Main: Suhrkamp, 1972.

———. "Las Casas oder Ein Rückblick in die Zukunft." *Kurzgefaßter*

Bericht von der Verwüstung der Westindischen Länder. By Bartolomé de
Las Casas. Ed. Hans Magnus Enzensberger. Frankfurt am Main: Insel,
1966. 124–50. *Deutschland, Deutschland* 123–51. "Las Casas, or A Look
Back into the Future." Trans. Michael Roloff. *Critical Essays* 116–37.

———. *Mausoleum: Siebenunddreißig Balladen aus der Geschichte des
Fortschritts.* Frankfurt am Main: Suhrkamp, 1975. *Mausoleum: Thirty-seven
Ballads from the History of Progress.* Trans. Joachim Neugroschel. New
York: Urizen, 1976.

———. "On Leaving America." (English orig.) *New York Review of Books* 29
February 1968: 31–32. "Offener Brief." *Über Hans Magnus Enzensberger.*
Ed. Joachim Schickel. Frankfurt am Main: Suhrkamp, 1970. 233–38.

———. *Palaver: Politische Überlegungen (1967–1973).* Frankfurt am Main:
Suhrkamp, 1974.

———. "Peter Weiss und andere." *Kursbuch* 6 (July 1966): 171–76. Rpt. in
Über Hans Magnus Enzensberger. Ed. Joachim Schickel. Frankfurt am
Main: Suhrkamp, 1970. 246–51.

———. *Politische Brosamen.* Frankfurt am Main: Suhrkamp, 1982. *Political
Crumbs.* Trans. Martin Chalmers. London: Verso, 1990.

———. "Revolutions-Tourismus." *Palaver* 130–68. "Tourists of the Revolution." Trans. Michael Roloff. *Critical Essays* 159–85.

———. "Unsere weißen Hände: Eine Nacherinnerung." *Persien, Modell
eines Entwicklungslandes oder Die Diktatur der Freien Welt.* By Bahman
Nirumand. Reinbek bei Hamburg: Rowohlt, 1967. 149–54. "Afterword: Our White Hands." *Iran: The New Imperialism in Action.* By
Bahman Nirumand. Trans. Leonard Mins. New York: Monthly Review,
1969. 183–89.

———. *Der Untergang der Titanic: Eine Komödie.* Frankfurt am Main:
Suhrkamp, 1978. *The Sinking of the Titanic: A Poem.* Trans. Hans Magnus
Enzensberger. Boston: Houghton, 1980.

———. *Das Verhör von Habana.* Frankfurt am Main: Suhrkamp, 1970. *The
Havana Inquiry.* Trans. Peter Mayer. Introduction by Martin Duberman.
New York: Holt, 1974.

———. *Der Weg ins Freie: Fünf Lebensläufe.* Frankfurt am Main: Suhrkamp, 1975.

———. "Zum *Hessischen Landboten*: Zwei Kontexte." *Deutschland,
Deutschland* 99–122.

———. "Zur Kritik der politischen Ökologie." *Palaver* 169–232. "A Critique of Political Ecology." Trans. Stuart Hood. *Critical Essays* 186–223.

———. "Zwei Randbemerkungen zum Weltuntergang." *Politische Brosa-*

men 225–36. "Two Notes on the End of the World." *Political Crumbs* 151–60.

Enzensberger, Hans Magnus, et al., eds. *Klassenbuch: Ein Lesebuch zu den Klassenkämpfen in Deutschland*. 3 vols. Darmstadt: Luchterhand, 1972.

Fabian, Johannes. *Time and the Other: How Anthropology Makes Its Object*. New York: Columbia UP, 1983.

Fanon, Frantz. *Les Damnés de la terre*. Paris: Maspero, 1961. *Die Verdammten dieser Erde*. Trans. Traugott König. Frankfurt am Main: Suhrkamp, 1966. *The Wretched of the Earth*. Trans. Constance Farrington. Preface by Jean-Paul Sartre. New York: Grove, 1968.

——. "Von der Gewalt." Trans. Traugott König. *Kursbuch* 2 (August 1965): 1–55.

Fawcett, Mary Laughlin. "Arms/Words/Tears: Language and the Body in *Titus Andronicus*." ELH 50 (1983): 261–77.

Fehervary, Helen. "Autorschaft, Geschlechtsbewußtsein und Öffentlichkeit: Versuch über Heiner Müllers *Die Hamletmaschine* und Christa Wolfs *Kein Ort. Nirgends*." *Entwürfe von Frauen in der Literatur des 20. Jahrhunderts*. Ed. Irmela von der Lühe. Literatur im historischen Prozeß, Neue Folge 5. Berlin: Argument, 1982. 132–53.

——. "Die erzählerische Kolonisierung des weiblichen Schweigens: Frau und Arbeit in der DDR-Literatur." *Arbeit als Thema in der deutschen Literatur vom Mittelalter bis zur Gegenwart*. Ed. Reinhold Grimm and Jost Hermand. Königstein: Athenäum, 1979. 171–95.

——. "The Gender of Authorship: Heiner Müller and Christa Wolf." *Studies in Twentieth Century Literature* 5.1 (1980): 41–58.

Fernandez, James W. "Exploded Worlds: Text as a Metaphor for Ethnography (and Vice Versa)." *Dialectical Anthropology* 10 (1985): 15–26.

Fiebach, Joachim. *Inseln der Unordnung: Fünf Versuche zu Heiner Müllers Theatertexten*. Berlin: Henschel, 1990.

Fischborn, Gottfried. *Stückeschreiben: Claus Hammel, Heiner Müller, Armin Stolper*. Berlin: Akademie, 1981.

Fischer, Gerhard. "Emanzipation, Entfremdung und der Mythos der Medea: Zur Darstellung der Geschlechterbeziehungen bei Heiner Müller." *Connaissance de la RDA* 16 (June 1983): 33–58.

Franz, Michael. "Hans Magnus Enzensberger: *Mausoleum*." *Hans Magnus Enzensberger*. Ed. Reinhold Grimm. Frankfurt am Main: Suhrkamp, 1984. 294–311.

Fromm, Harold. "The Hegemonic Form of Othering; or, The Academic's Burden." *Critical Inquiry* 13 (autumn 1986): 197–200. (Rpt. in *"Race,"*

Writing, and Difference. Ed. Henry Louis Gates Jr. Chicago: U of Chicago P, 1986. 396–99.)

Frye, Marilyn. "On Being White: Thinking toward a Feminist Understanding of Race and Race Supremacy." *The Politics of Reality: Essays in Feminist Theory*. Freedom CA: Crossing, 1983. 110–27.

Fuchs, Elinor, and James Leverett. "A Taxi Ride with Wilson with Müller in the Trunk." *Village Voice* 18 December 1984: 62–63.

Fuhrmann, Helmut. "'Where Violent Sorrow Seems a Modern Ecstasy': Über Heiner Müllers *Macbeth nach Shakespeare*." *Arcadia* 13 (1978): 55–71.

Gates, Henry Louis, Jr. "Critical Remarks." *Anatomy of Racism*. Ed. David Theo Goldberg. Minneapolis: U of Minnesota P, 1990. 319–29.

——. "Editor's Introduction: Writing 'Race' and the Difference It Makes." *Critical Inquiry* 12 (autumn 1985): 1–20. (Rpt. in *"Race," Writing, and Difference*. Ed. Henry Louis Gates Jr. Chicago: U of Chicago P, 1986. 1–20.)

——. "'Ethnic and Minority' Studies." *Introduction to Scholarship in Modern Languages and Literatures*. Ed. Joseph Gibaldi. 2nd ed. New York: MLA, 1992. 288–302.

——. "Talkin' That Talk." *Critical Inquiry* 13 (autumn 1986): 203–10. (Rpt. in *"Race," Writing, and Difference*. Ed. Henry Louis Gates Jr. Chicago: U of Chicago P, 1986. 402–09.)

Geiersbach, Paul. *Bruder, muß zusammen Zwiebel und Wasser essen! Eine türkische Familie in Deutschland*. Berlin: Dietz, 1982.

——. *Gott auch in der Fremde dienen*. Foreword by Bahman Nirumand. Berlin: Mink, 1990. Vol. 2 of *Ein Türkenghetto in Deutschland*. 2 vols. 1989–90.

——. *Warten bis die Züge wieder fahren*. Foreword by Günter Wallraff. 2nd ed. Berlin: Mink, 1990. Vol. 1 of *Ein Türkenghetto in Deutschland*. 2 vols. 1989–90.

——. *Wie Mutlu Öztürk schwimmen lernen muß: Ein Lebenslauf*. Foreword by Günter Wallraff. Berlin: Dietz, 1983.

Gerlach, Rainer, and Matthias Richter, eds. *Peter Weiss im Gespräch*. Frankfurt am Main: Suhrkamp, 1986.

Gnüg, Hiltrud. "Hans Magnus Enzensberger: 'A. v. H. (1769-1859).'" *Geschichte im Gedicht: Texte und Interpretationen: Protestlied, Bänkelsang, Ballade, Chronik*. Ed. Walter Hinck. Frankfurt am Main: Suhrkamp, 1979. 295–301.

Gökberk, Ülker. "Understanding Alterity: *Ausländerliteratur* between Relativism and Universalism." *Theoretical Issues in Literary History*. Ed.

David Perkins. Harvard English Studies 16. Cambridge: Harvard UP, 1991. 143–72.

Goldberg, David Theo. *Racist Culture: Philosophy and the Politics of Meaning*. Oxford: Blackwell, 1993.

Gordon, Deborah. "Writing Culture, Writing Feminism: The Poetics and Politics of Experimental Ethnography." *Inscriptions* 3–4 (1988): 7–24.

Gould, Stephen Jay. "Measuring Bodies: Two Case Studies on the Apishness of Undesirables." *The Mismeasure of Man*. New York: Norton, 1981. 113–45.

Greiner, Bernhard. "Der Bann der Zeichen: Anna Seghers' Entwürfe der Identitätsfindung." *Probleme deutscher Identität*. Ed. Paul Gerhard Klussmann and Heinrich Mohr. *Jahrbuch zur Literatur in der DDR* 3 (1983): 131–55.

———. "'Jetzt will ich sitzen wo gelacht wird': Über das Lachen bei Heiner Müller." *Dialektik des Anfangs*. Ed. Paul Gerhard Klussmann and Heinrich Mohr. *Jahrbuch zur Literatur in der DDR* 5 (1986): 29–63.

Grimm, Reinhold. "Bildnis Hans Magnus Enzensberger: Struktur, Ideologie und Vorgeschichte eines Gesellschaftskritikers." *Hans Magnus Enzensberger*. Ed. Reinhold Grimm. Frankfurt am Main: Suhrkamp, 1984. 139–88.

———. "Eiszeit und Untergang: Zu einem Motivkomplex in der deutschen Gegenwartsliteratur." *Texturen: Essays und anderes zu Hans Magnus Enzensberger*. New York University Ottendorfer Series, Neue Folge 19. New York: Lang, 1984. 174–217.

———. "Enzensberger, Kuba und *La Cubana*." *Texturen: Essays und anderes zu Hans Magnus Enzensberger*. New York University Ottendorfer Series, Neue Folge 19. New York: Lang, 1984. 97–111.

———. "Germans, Blacks, and Jews; or Is There a German Blackness of Its Own?" *Blacks and German Culture*. Ed. Reinhold Grimm and Jost Hermand. Monatshefte Occasional Volumes 4. Madison: U of Wisconsin P, 1986. 150–84.

———. "An Introduction to Enzensberger." *Texturen: Essays und anderes zu Hans Magnus Enzensberger*. New York University Ottendorfer Series, Neue Folge 19. New York: Lang, 1984. 12–20.

———. "Das Messer im Rücken: Utopisch-dystopische Bildlichkeit bei Hans Magnus Enzensberger." *Texturen: Essays und anderes zu Hans Magnus Enzensberger*. New York University Ottendorfer Series, Neue Folge 19. New York: Lang, 1984. 148–68.

Große, Anneliese, and Brigitte Thurm. "Gesellschaftliche Irrelevanz und manipulierbare Subjektivität." *Weimarer Beiträge* 16.2 (1970): 151–81.

Gugelberger, Georg M. "Rethinking *Germanistik*: *Germanistik*, the Canon, and Third World Literature." *Monatshefte* 83 (1991): 45–58.

———. "Them in Our Literature and We in Theirs: Geo-Thematics Reconsidered and Reversed." *Blacks and German Culture*. Ed. Reinhold Grimm and Jost Hermand. Monatshefte Occasional Volumes 4. Madison: U of Wisconsin P, 1986. 87–112.

Gutzmann, Gertraud. "Eurozentristisches Welt- und Menschenbild in Anna Seghers' *Karibischen Geschichten*." *Frauen—Literatur—Politik*. Ed. Annegret Pelz et al. Literatur im historischen Prozeß, Neue Folge 21–22. Hamburg: Argument, 1988. 189–204.

———. "Der lateinamerikanische Kontinent in Anna Seghers' publizistischen Schriften." *"Neue Welt"/"Dritte Welt": Interkulturelle Beziehungen Deutschlands zu Lateinamerika und der Karibik*. Ed. Sigrid Bauschinger and Susan L. Cocalis. Tübingen: Francke, 1994. 155–83.

Haase, Horst, et al. *Literatur der Deutschen Demokratischen Republik*. Ed. Hans-Günther Thalheim et al. 2nd ed. Berlin: Volk und Wissen, 1977. Vol. 11 of *Geschichte der deutschen Literatur von den Anfängen bis zur Gegenwart*. 12 vols. 1960–90.

Hacks, Peter. *Die Fische. Ausgewählte Dramen*. Vol. 3. Berlin: Aufbau, 1981. 167–230. 3 vols. 1972–81.

———. "Noten zum Schauspiel *Die Fische*." *Die Maßgaben der Kunst: Gesammelte Aufsätze*. Düsseldorf: Claassen, 1977. 401–03.

Haiduk, Manfred. *Der Dramatiker Peter Weiss*. Berlin: Henschel, 1977.

———. "Peter Weiss' *Gesang vom Lusitanischen Popanz*." *Gesang vom Lusitanischen Popanz: Mit Materialien*. By Peter Weiss. Frankfurt am Main: Suhrkamp, 1974. 77–82.

Hammel, Claus. "Gespräch mit Claus Hammel." *Theater der Zeit* 34.8 (1979): 56–57.

———. *Humboldt und Bolívar oder Der Neue Continent*. Berlin: Aufbau, 1980.

———. *Humboldt und Bolívar oder Der Neue Continent*. *Theater der Zeit* 34.8 (1979): 58–71.

———. "Interview mit Claus Hammel." With Irene Böhme. *Weimarer Beiträge* 15 (1969): 325–36.

———. "Zu diesem Stück." *Humboldt und Bolívar oder Der Neue Continent*. Berlin: Aufbau, 1980. 138–44.

———. "Zu diesem Stück." *Theater der Zeit* 34.8 (1979): 72.

Haraway, Donna. "Situated Knowledges: The Science Question in Feminism and the Privilege of Partial Perspective." *Feminist Studies* 14 (1988): 575–99.

Harbsmeier, Michael. "Beyond Anthropology." *Folk* 28 (1986): 33-59.

Hegel, G. W. F. *Phenomenology of Spirit*. Trans. A. V. Miller. Oxford: Oxford UP, 1977.

Heidelberger-Leonard, Irene. "Der Stellenwert der *Divina Commedia* in der Werkgeschichte von Peter Weiss." *Orbis Litterarum* 44 (1989): 252–66.

Heitz, Raymond. "Zu Peter Hacks' dramatischem Werk: Die Weltsicht des Dichters im Spiegel der Form." *Revue d'Allemagne* 14 (1982): 543–80.

Hempel, Wido. "Zur Nachwirkung der Divina Commedia in der Literatur des 20. Jahrhunderts." *Italia Viva: Studien zur Sprache und Literatur Italiens: Festschrift für Hans Ludwig Scheel*. Ed. Willi Hirdt and Reinhard Klesczewski. Tübingen: Narr, 1983. 169–83.

Hensel, Georg. "Gelächter auf der Fleischbank: Heiner Müllers *Titus*-Version als Uraufführung in Bochum." *Frankfurter Allgemeine Zeitung* 16 February 1985: 21.

Herbert, Ulrich. *Geschichte der Ausländerbeschäftigung in Deutschland 1880 bis 1980: Saisonarbeiter, Zwangsarbeiter, Gastarbeiter*. Berlin: Dietz, 1986. *A History of Foreign Labor in Germany, 1880–1980: Seasonal Workers, Forced Laborers, Guest Workers*. Trans. William Templer. Ann Arbor: U of Michigan P, 1990.

Herting, Helga. *Geschichte für die Gegenwart: Historische Belletristik in der Literatur der DDR*. Berlin: Dietz, 1979.

Hodges, Carolyn R. "The Power of the Oppressed: The Evolution of the Black Character in Anna Seghers' Caribbean Fiction." *Studies in GDR Culture and Society* 7 (1987): 185–97.

Hofer, Hermann. "Befreien französische Autoren des 18. Jahrhunderts die schwarzen Rebellen und die Sklaven aus ihren Ketten? oder Versuch darüber, wie man den Guten Wilden zur Strecke bringt." *Die andere Welt: Studien zum Exotismus*. Ed. Thomas Koebner and Gerhart Pickerodt. Frankfurt am Main: Athenäum, 1987. 137–70.

Holthusen, Hans Egon. *Utopie und Katastrophe: Der Lyriker Hans Magnus Enzensberger 1957–1978. Sartre in Stammheim: Zwei Themen aus den Jahren der großen Turbulenz*. Stuttgart: Klett-Cotta, 1982. 7–97.

Hölzel, Horst. "Für Tiefe und Breite ein Beispiel." Review of *Das Licht auf dem Galgen*, by Anna Seghers. *Neue Deutsche Literatur* November 1961: 124–28.

hooks, bell. *Feminist Theory: From Margin to Center*. Boston: South End, 1984.

——. *Yearning: Race, Gender, and Cultural Politics*. Boston: South End, 1990.

Horkheimer, Max, and Theodor W. Adorno. *Dialektik der Aufklärung: Philosophische Fragmente*. Frankfurt am Main: Fischer, 1969. *Dialectic of Enlightenment*. Trans. John Cumming. New York: Continuum, 1982.

Hörnigk, Frank. "Erinnerungen an Revolutionen: Zu Entwicklungstendenzen in der Dramatik Heiner Müllers, Peter Hacks' und Volker Brauns am Ende der siebziger Jahre." *Tendenzen und Beispiele: Zur DDR-Literatur in den siebziger Jahren*. Ed. Hans Kaufmann. Leipzig: Reclam, 1981. 148–84.

Huettich, H. G. *Theater in the Planned Society: Contemporary Drama in the German Democratic Republic in Its Historical, Political, and Cultural Context*. Chapel Hill: U of North Carolina P, 1978.

Hügel, Ika, et al., eds. *Entfernte Verbindungen: Rassismus, Antisemitismus, Klassenunterdrückung*. Berlin: Orlanda, 1993.

Hulme, Peter. *Colonial Encounters: Europe and the Native Caribbean, 1492–1797*. London: Methuen, 1986.

Ihekweazu, Edith. "Ein neues Afrikabild in der deutschen Literatur—oder alter Wein in neuen Schläuchen?" *Etudes Germano-Africaines* 2–3 (1984–85): 196–212.

Ismayr, Wolfgang. *Das politische Theater in Westdeutschland*. Meisenheim am Glan: Hain, 1977.

James, C. L. R. *The Black Jacobins: Toussaint L'Ouverture and the San Domingo Revolution*. 2nd ed. New York: Vintage-Random, 1963.

JanMohamed, Abdul R. "The Economy of Manichaean Allegory: The Function of Racial Difference in Colonialist Literature." *Critical Inquiry* 12 (autumn 1985): 59–87. (Rpt. in *"Race," Writing, and Difference*. Ed. Henry Louis Gates Jr. Chicago: U of Chicago P, 1986. 78–106.)

JanMohamed, Abdul R., and David Lloyd. "Introduction: Minority Discourse—What Is to Be Done?" *Cultural Critique* 7 (fall 1987): 5–17. (Rpt. in *The Nature and Context of Minority Discourse*. Ed. Abdul R. JanMohamed and David Lloyd. New York: Oxford UP, 1990. 1–16.)

——. "Introduction: Toward a Theory of Minority Discourse." *Cultural Critique* 6 (spring 1987): 5–12. (Rpt. in *The Nature and Context of Minority Discourse*. Ed. Abdul R. JanMohamed and David Lloyd. New York: Oxford UP, 1990. 1–16.)

Jardine, Alice. "Woman in Limbo: Deleuze and His Br(others)." *SubStance* 44–45 (1984): 46–60.

Jehser, Werner. "Zur Dialektik von Ideal und Wirklichkeit in den Stücken von Peter Hacks seit Mitte der siebziger Jahre." *Weimarer Beiträge* 29 (1983): 1729–52.

Jell-Bahlsen, Sabine. "Ethnology and Fascism in Germany." *Dialectical Anthropology* 9 (1985): 313–35.

Kaiser, Joachim. *Erlebte Literatur: Vom "Doktor Faustus" zum "Fettfleck": Deutsche Schriftsteller in unserer Zeit.* München: Piper, 1988.

Kant, Hermann. "Unsere Worte wirken in der Klassenauseinandersetzung." *Neue Deutsche Literatur* February 1974: 23–47.

Kant, Immanuel. *Critique of Pure Reason.* Trans. Norman Kemp Smith. New York: St. Martin's, 1965.

——. *Prolegomena to Any Future Metaphysics.* Ed. Lewis White Beck. Indianapolis: Liberal Arts-Bobbs, 1950.

——. "What Is Enlightenment?" Trans. Lewis White Beck. *On History.* By Immanuel Kant. Ed. Lewis White Beck. Indianapolis: Liberal Arts-Bobbs, 1963. 3–10.

Kaplan, Caren. "Deterritorializations: The Rewriting of Home and Exile in Western Feminist Discourse." *Cultural Critique* 6 (spring 1987): 187–98. (Rpt. in *The Nature and Context of Minority Discourse.* Ed. Abdul R. JanMohamed and David Lloyd. New York: Oxford UP, 1990. 357–68.)

Karnick, Manfred. "Peter Weiss' dramatische Collagen: Vom Traumspiel zur Agitation." *Peter Weiss.* Ed. Rainer Gerlach. Frankfurt am Main: Suhrkamp, 1984. 208–48.

Kassé, Maguèye. "Heinrich von Kleist—Anna Seghers: La Révolution française et le thème de la révolte dans les Antilles françaises." *Etudes Germano-Africaines* 2 (1983): 57–71.

Kaufmann, Hans. "Veränderte Literaturlandschaft." *Tendenzen und Beispiele: Zur DDR-Literatur in den siebziger Jahren.* Ed. Hans Kaufmann. Leipzig: Reclam, 1981. 7–40.

Kehn, Wolfgang. *Von Dante zu Hölderlin: Traditionswahl und Engagement im Werk von Peter Weiss.* Köln: Böhlau, 1975.

Kendall, Gillian Murray. "'Lend me thy hand': Metaphor and Mayhem in *Titus Andronicus.*" *Shakespeare Quarterly* 40 (1989): 299–316.

Kerndl, Rainer. *Nacht mit Kompromissen. Stücke.* Berlin: Henschel, 1983. 79–138.

Khamis, Yousri. "Der *Popanz* zwischen Kairo/Bagdad/Damaskus." *Gesang vom Lusitanischen Popanz: Mit Materialien.* By Peter Weiss. Frankfurt am Main: Suhrkamp, 1974. 101–08.

Kießling, Wolfgang. *Exil in Lateinamerika.* Frankfurt am Main: Röderberg, 1981. Vol. 4 of *Kunst und Literatur im antifaschistischen Exil 1933–1945.* 7 vols. 1979–81.

Kircher, Hartmut. "Max von der Grün." *Deutsche Literatur der Gegenwart in Einzeldarstellungen*. Ed. Dietrich Weber. Vol. 2. Stuttgart: Kröner, 1977. 128–51. 2 vols. 1976–77.

Kleines Politisches Wörterbuch. Berlin: Dietz, 1985.

Koebner, Thomas. "'Am Kap der guten Hoffnungslosigkeit': Endzeit bei Hans Magnus Enzensberger und Günter Kunert." *Kontroversen, alte und neue: Akten des VII. Internationalen Germanisten-Kongresses, Göttingen 1985*. Ed. Albrecht Schöne. Vol. 10. Tübingen: Niemeyer, 1986. 225–33. 11 vols.

Köpf, Gerhard. "Der halbe Türke: Literatur und koloniale Wahrnehmung." *Literatur und Kolonialismus I: Die Verarbeitung der kolonialen Expansion in der europäischen Literatur*. Ed. Wolfgang Bader and János Riesz. Frankfurt am Main: Lang, 1983. 323–48.

Köpke, Wulf. "Das Wartesaal-Leben: Die Nicht-Erfahrung der Fremde im Exil nach 1933." *Begegnung mit dem "Fremden": Grenzen—Traditionen—Vergleiche: Akten des VIII. Internationalen Germanisten-Kongresses, Tokyo 1990*. Ed. Eijiro Iwasaki. Vol. 8. München: Iudicium, 1991. 35–43. 11 vols.

Kott, Jan. *Shakespeare Our Contemporary*. Trans. Boleslaw Taborski. New York: Norton, 1974. *Shakespeare heute*. Trans. Peter Lachmann. München: Langen-Müller, 1964. Trans. of *Szkice o Szekspirze*. Warsaw: Państwowe Wydawnictwo Naukowe, 1964.

Kramer, Fritz W. "Empathy—Reflections on the History of Ethnology in Pre-Fascist Germany: Herder, Creuzer, Bastian, Bachofen, and Frobenius." *Dialectical Anthropology* 9 (1985): 337–47.

Krause, Rolf D. *Faschismus als Theorie und Erfahrung: "Die Ermittlung" und ihr Autor Peter Weiss*. Frankfurt am Main: Lang, 1982.

Krueger, Merle Curtis. *Authors and the Opposition: West German Writers and the Social Democratic Party from 1945 to 1969*. Stuttgarter Arbeiten zur Germanistik 107. Stuttgart: Heinz, 1982.

Krüger, Kurt. "Solidarität der DDR mit den Völkern Asiens, Afrikas und Lateinamerikas." *Deutsche Außenpolitik* October 1979: 52–64.

Kuhn, Anna K. "Bourgeois Ideology and the (Mis)Reading of Günter Wallraff's *Ganz Unten*." *New German Critique* 46 (winter 1989): 191–202.

Künzel, Horst. "Vom Vergnügen in der Kunst: Enzensberger und die Alten Meister." *Die Horen* 4 (1980): 57–63.

Kuzniar, Alice. "Hearing Woman's Voices in *Heinrich von Ofterdingen*." *PMLA* 107 (1992): 1196–207.

LaBahn, Kathleen J. *Anna Seghers' Exile Literature: The Mexican Years (1941–1947)*. American University Studies, Series I 37. New York: Lang, 1986.

Lamping, Dieter. "Die Komödie des Weltuntergangs: Eine Anmerkung zu Hans Magnus Enzensbergers *Der Untergang der Titanic*." *Germanisch-Romanische Monatsschrift* 37 (1987): 229–31.

Lanser, Susan S. "Feminist Criticism, 'The Yellow Wallpaper,' and the Politics of Color in America." *Feminist Studies* 15 (1989): 415–41.

Lehmann, Hans-Thies. "Eisberg und Spiegelkunst: Notizen zu Hans Magnus Enzensbergers Lust am Untergang der Titanic." *Hans Magnus Enzensberger*. Ed. Reinhold Grimm. Frankfurt am Main: Suhrkamp, 1984. 312–34.

Lehmann, Hans-Thies, and Genia Schulz. "Anatomie de Shakespeare: Le Scalpel de Heiner Müller." *Théâtre en Europe* July 1985: 73–77.

Leistner, Bernd. "Nachwort." *Ausgewählte Dramen*. By Peter Hacks. Vol. 3. Berlin: Aufbau, 1981. 371–95. 3 vols. 1972–81.

Lennox, Sara. "Enzensberger, *Kursbuch*, and 'Third Worldism': The Sixties' Construction of Latin America." *"Neue Welt"/"Dritte Welt": Interkulturelle Beziehungen Deutschlands zu Lateinamerika und der Karibik*. Ed. Sigrid Bauschinger and Susan L. Cocalis. Tübingen: Francke, 1994. 185–200.

Lewis, Oscar. *The Children of Sánchez: Autobiography of a Mexican Family*. New York: Random, 1961. *Die Kinder von Sánchez: Selbstporträt einer mexikanischen Familie*. Trans. Margarete Bormann. Frankfurt am Main: Fischer, 1961. 6th ed. Göttingen: Lamuv, 1992.

Liebscher, Gertraud. "Die Politik der BRD gegenüber Entwicklungsländern." *Deutsche Außenpolitik* March 1980: 47–59.

Lorisika, Irene. *Frauendarstellungen bei Irmgard Keun und Anna Seghers*. Frankfurt am Main: Haag & Herchen, 1985.

Love, Joseph L. " 'Third World': A Response to Professor Worsley." *Third World Quarterly* 2 (1980): 315–17.

Lugones, Maria C., and Elizabeth V. Spelman. "Have We Got a Theory for You! Feminist Theory, Cultural Imperialism and the Demand for 'The Woman's Voice.' " *Women and Values: Readings in Recent Feminist Philosophy*. Ed. Marilyn Pearsall. 2nd ed. Belmont CA: Wadsworth, 1993. 18–29.

Maczewski, Johannes. " 'Parteigänger des sozialistischen Weges der Deutschen': Überlegungen zur Person und Dramatik des Claus Hammel." *Proceedings: Pacific Northwest Council on Foreign Languages* 29.1 (1978): 69–72.

Mader, Jakob. "Peripheres Europa?" *Kürbiskern*, 1966, no. 1: 142–57.

Malinowski, Bronislaw. "Introduction: The Subject, Method and Scope of This Inquiry." *Argonauts of the Western Pacific: An Account of Native*

Enterprise and Adventure in the Archipelagoes of Melanesian New Guinea. London: Routledge, 1922. 2–25.

Maltzan, Carlotta von. "'Der Tod ist eine Frau': Die Darstellung der Rolle der Frau bei Heiner Müller." *Acta Germanica* 16 (1983): 247–59.

Mandel, Ruth. "Turkish Headscarves and the 'Foreigner Problem': Constructing Difference through Emblems of Identity." *New German Critique* 46 (winter 1989): 27–46.

Marcus, George E., and Dick Cushman. "Ethnographies as Texts." *Annual Review of Anthropology* 11 (1982): 25–69.

Martin, Biddy, and Chandra Talpade Mohanty. "Feminist Politics: What's Home Got to Do with It?" *Feminist Studies/Critical Studies*. Ed. Teresa de Lauretis. Bloomington: Indiana UP, 1986. 191–212.

Mascia-Lees, Frances E., Patricia Sharpe, and Colleen Ballerino Cohen. "The Postmodernist Turn in Anthropology: Cautions from a Feminist Perspective." *Signs* 15 (1989): 7–33.

Mayer, Hans. *Außenseiter*. Frankfurt am Main: Suhrkamp, 1975. *Outsiders: A Study in Life and Letters*. Trans. Denis M. Sweet. Cambridge: MIT P, 1984.

McCall, Grant. "Four Worlds of Experience and Action." *Third World Quarterly* 2 (1980): 536–45.

Melin, Charlotte. "Autobiography and Epic in *Der Untergang der Titanic*." *Germanic Notes* 22.1–2 (1991): 14–16.

Melin, Charlotte, and Cecile Cazort Zorach. "Cuba as Paradise, Paradigm, and Paradox in German Literature." *Monatshefte* 78 (1986): 480–99.

Mennemeier, Franz Norbert. *Modernes deutsches Drama: Kritiken und Charakteristiken*. 2nd ed. 2 vols. München: Fink, 1975–79.

Milfull, John. "Juden, Frauen, Mulatten, Neger: Probleme der Emanzipation in Anna Seghers *Karibische Erzählungen*." *Frauenliteratur: Autorinnen — Perspektiven — Konzepte*. Ed. Manfred Jurgensen. Bern: Lang, 1983. 45–55.

Mitchell, Michael. *Peter Hacks: Theatre for a Socialist Society*. Glasgow: Scottish Papers in Germanic Studies, 1990.

Mittenzwei, Werner. "Revolution und Reform im westdeutschen Drama." *Sinn und Form* 23 (1971): 109–54.

Moeller, Hans-Bernhard, ed. *Latin America and the Literature of Exile: A Comparative View of the 20th-Century European Refugee Writers in the New World*. Reihe Siegen 47. Heidelberg: Winter, 1983.

Mohanty, Chandra Talpade. "Under Western Eyes: Feminist Scholarship and Colonial Discourses." *Third World Women and the Politics of Femi-*

nism. Ed. Chandra Talpade Mohanty et al. Bloomington: Indiana UP, 1991. 51–80.

Mohanty, S. P. "Us and Them: On the Philosophical Bases of Political Criticism." *Yale Journal of Criticism* 2.2 (1989): 1–31.

Moraga, Cherríe, and Gloria Anzaldúa, eds. *This Bridge Called My Back: Writings by Radical Women of Color*. 2nd ed. Latham NY: Kitchen Table, 1983.

Morrison, Toni. *Playing in the Dark: Whiteness and the Literary Imagination*. New York: Vintage-Random, 1993.

Mountjoy, Alan B. "Worlds without End." *Third World Quarterly* 2 (1980): 753–57.

Müller, Fred. *Peter Weiss: Drei Dramen*. München: Oldenbourg, 1973.

Müller, Götz. "*Der Untergang der Titanic*: Bemerkungen zu Enzensbergers Gedicht." *Zeitschrift für deutsche Philologie* 100 (1981): 254–74.

Müller, Heiner. *Anatomie Titus Fall of Rome Ein Shakespearekommentar*. *Shakespeare Factory 2* 125–225.

———. *Anatomie Titus Fall of Rome: Ein Shakespearekommentar*. *Theater Heute* March 1985: 44–59.

———. *Der Auftrag: Erinnerung an eine Revolution*. *Herzstück* 43-70. *The Task*. *Hamletmachine and Other Texts* 81–101.

———. *Bildbeschreibung*. *Shakespeare Factory 1* 7–14. *Explosion of a Memory/Description of a Picture*. *Explosion of a Memory* 93–102.

———. "Brief an den Regisseur der bulgarischen Erstaufführung von *Philoktet* am Dramatischen Theater Sofia." *Herzstück* 102–09.

———. "Brief an Robert Wilson." *Heiner Müller Material: Texte und Kommentare*. Ed. Frank Hörnigk. Göttingen: Steidl, 1989. 51–54. "A Letter to Robert Wilson." *Explosion of a Memory* 151–55.

———. "'Deutschland spielt noch immer die Nibelungen.'" *Der Spiegel* 9 May 1983: 196–207. (Rpt. as "Was ein Kunstwerk kann, ist Sehnsucht wecken nach einem anderen Zustand der Welt." *Gesammelte Irrtümer* 130–40.)

———. "Diskussionsbeitrag auf der 'Berliner Begegnung' vom 13. und 14. Dezember 1981." *Rotwelsch* 199–200.

———. *Explosion of a Memory: Writings by Heiner Müller*. Ed. and trans. Carl Weber. New York: Performing Arts Journal, 1989.

———. "'Die Form entsteht aus dem Maskieren.'" With Olivier Ortolani. *Theater 1985*. Ed. Peter von Becker et al. Jahrbuch der Zeitschrift *Theater Heute*. Zürich: Füssli & Friedrich, 1985. 88–93. Rpt. in *Gesammelte Irrtümer* 141–54.

———. "Für ein Theater, das an Geschichte glaubt: Gespräch mit Flavia Foradini." *Gesammelte Irrtümer 2* 130–36.

———. *Gesammelte Irrtümer: Interviews und Gespräche*. Frankfurt am Main: Verlag der Autoren, 1986.

———. *Gesammelte Irrtümer 2: Interviews und Gespräche*. Ed. Gregor Edelmann and Renate Ziemer. Frankfurt am Main: Verlag der Autoren, 1990.

———. "Geschichtspessimismus oder Geschichtsoptimismus, das sind nur zwei Begriffe für Geschichtsunkenntnis: Heiner Müller im Dialog." *Sprache im technischen Zeitalter* 103 (September 1987): 192–221.

———. "Gespräch mit Bernard Umbrecht." *Rotwelsch* 107–24.

———. "Gespräch mit Heiner Müller." With Ulrich Dietzel. *Sinn und Form* 37 (1985): 1193–217. (Rpt. as "Was gebraucht wird: mehr Utopie, mehr Phantasie und mehr Freiräume für Phantasie." *Gesammelte Irrtümer* 155–75.)

———. *Hamletmachine and Other Texts for the Stage*. Ed. and trans. Carl Weber. New York: Performing Arts Journal, 1984.

———. *Die Hamletmaschine. Mauser*. Berlin: Rotbuch, 1978. 89-97. *Hamletmachine. Hamletmachine and Other Texts* 49–58.

———. *Herzstück*. Berlin: Rotbuch, 1983.

———. *"Ich bin ein Neger": Diskussion mit Heiner Müller*. Darmstadt: Georg Büchner Buchhandlung, 1986.

———. "Ich scheiß auf die Ordnung." *Tip*, 1982, no. 7: 51–59. Rpt. as "Ich scheiße auf die Ordnung der Welt." *Gesammelte Irrtümer* 116–29.

———. "Ich weiß nicht, was Avantgarde ist." *Gesammelte Irrtümer 2* 94–104.

———. *"Jenseits der Nation": Heiner Müller im Interview mit Frank M. Raddatz*. Berlin: Rotbuch, 1991.

———. "Keimende Begabungen entdecken." *Theater der Zeit* February 1986: 26.

———. *Krieg ohne Schlacht: Leben in zwei Diktaturen*. Köln: Kiepenheuer & Witsch, 1992.

———. *Leben Gundlings Friedrich von Preussen Lessings Schlaf Traum Schrei: Ein Greuelmärchen. Herzstück* 9–41. *Gundling's Life Frederick of Prussia Lessing's Sleep Dream Scream: A Horror Story. Hamletmachine and Other Texts* 59–78.

———. Letter to Erich Wonder. *Explosion of a Memory Heiner Müller DDR: Ein Arbeitsbuch*. Ed. Wolfgang Storch. Berlin: Hentrich, 1988. 47.

———. *Macbeth (nach Shakespeare). Shakespeare Factory 1* 183–239.

———. "Man muß nach der Methode fragen." *Gesammelte Irrtümer 2* 26–32.

———. "Mich interessiert der Fall Althusser . . ." *Rotwelsch* 173–78. "The Case of Althusser Interests Me . . ." Trans. Arlene A. Teraoka. *Kairos* 1.4 (1985): 48–53.

———. "New York oder Das eiserne Gesicht der Freiheit." *Heiner Müller Material: Texte und Kommentare.* Ed. Frank Hörnigk. Göttingen: Steidl, 1989. 95–98.

———. *Rotwelsch.* Berlin: Merve, 1982.

———. "Ruth Berghaus und Heiner Müller im Gespräch." *Sinn und Form* 41 (1989): 114–31. (Rpt. in *Gesammelte Irrtümer 2* 71–93.)

———. "Der Schrecken die erste Erscheinung des Neuen." *Rotwelsch* 94–98. "Reflections on Post-Modernism." Trans. Jack Zipes and Betty Nance Weber. *New German Critique* 16 (winter 1979): 55–57.

———. "Shakespeare eine Differenz." *Shakespeare Factory 2* 227-30.

———. *Shakespeare Factory 1.* Berlin: Rotbuch, 1985.

———. *Shakespeare Factory 2.* Berlin: Rotbuch, 1989.

———. "Shakespeares Stücke sind komplexer als jede Aneignung—man braucht zu verschiedenen Zeiten verschiedene Übersetzungen: Ein Gespräch." *Theater Heute* July 1975: 32–37.

———. "Taube und Samurai." *Heiner Müller Material: Texte und Kommentare.* Ed. Frank Hörnigk. Göttingen: Steidl, 1989. 50.

———. *Verkommenes Ufer Medeamaterial Landschaft mit Argonauten. Herzstück* 91–101. *Despoiled Shore Medeamaterial Landscape with Argonauts. Hamletmachine and Other Texts* 123–35.

———. " 'Vorwärts zurück zu Shakespeare in einer auch von Brechts Theater mit veränderten Welt': Ein Gespräch zwischen Wolfgang Heise und Heiner Müller." *Theater der Zeit* February 1988: 22–26. (Rpt. as "Ein Gespräch zwischen Wolfgang Heise und Heiner Müller." *Gesammelte Irrtümer 2* 50–70.)

———. "Walls." (English orig.) *Rotwelsch* 9–48. "Mauern." Trans. Guntram Weber. *Rotwelsch* 49–86. Rpt. as "Ich glaube an Konflikt. Sonst glaube ich an nichts." *Gesammelte Irrtümer* 69–106.

———. "Der Weltuntergang ist zu einem modischen Problem geworden." *Gesammelte Irrtümer* 176–81. "The End of the World Has Become a Faddish Problem." *Explosion of a Memory* 157–63.

———. "Die Wunde Woyzeck." *Shakespeare Factory 2* 261–63. "The Wound Woyzeck." *Explosion of a Memory* 103–06.

———. *Zement. Geschichten aus der Produktion 2.* Berlin: Rotbuch, 1974. 65–133. *Cement.* Trans. Helen Fehervary, Sue-Ellen Case, and Marc D.

Silberman. New German Critique Publication 1. *New German Critique* 16 (winter 1979): Supplement.

——. *"Zur Lage der Nation": Heiner Müller im Interview mit Frank M. Raddatz*. Berlin: Rotbuch, 1990.

Muni, S. D. "The Third World: Concept and Controversy." *Third World Quarterly* 1.3 (1979): 119–28.

Munkelt, Marga. "*Titus Andronicus*: Metamorphoses of a Text in Production." *Shakespeare: Text, Language, Criticism: Essays in Honour of Marvin Spevack*. Ed. Bernhard Fabian and Kurt Tetzeli von Rosador. Hildesheim: Ohms-Weidmann, 1987. 212–34.

Nandlinger, Gabriele. "Chronik der Gewalt: Ausländerfeindliche Übergriffe in der Bundesrepublik Deutschland 1991/1992." *Die zweite Vertreibung: Fremde in Deutschland*. Ed. Klaus-Henning Rosen. Bonn: Dietz, 1992. 117–58.

Naumann, Heinrich. "Dante im deutschen Schrifttum des 19. Jahrhunderts." *Wirkendes Wort* 21 (1971): 38–59.

Negt, Oskar, and Alexander Kluge. "Die Geschichte von Jason." *Verkommenes Ufer Medea Material Landschaft mit Argonauten*. By Heiner Müller. Ed. Schauspielhaus Bochum. Stuttgart: Druckhaus Münster, 1983. 162–70.

Neugebauer, Heinz. *Anna Seghers: Leben und Werk*. Berlin: Das Europäische Buch, 1978.

Newton, Judith, and Judith Stacey. "Learning Not to Curse, or, Feminist Predicaments in Cultural Criticism by Men: Our Movie Date with James Clifford and Stephen Greenblatt." *Cultural Critique* 23 (winter 1992–93): 51–82.

Nirumand, Bahman. "Vorwort." *Gott auch in der Fremde dienen*. By Paul Geiersbach. Berlin: Mink, 1990. iii-vi. Vol. 2 of *Ein Türkenghetto in Deutschland*. 2 vols. 1989–90.

Ong, Aihwa. "Colonialism and Modernity: Feminist Re-presentations of Women in Non-Western Societies." *Inscriptions* 3–4 (1988): 79–93.

Özakin, Aysel. "Ali hinter den Spiegeln." *Literatur Konkret* 1986: 6–9.

"Panel Discussion 2." *Inscriptions* 3–4 (1988): 94–104.

Paredes, Américo. "On Ethnographic Work among Minority Groups: A Folklorist's Perspective." *New Scholar* 6 (1977): 1–32.

Parkes, K. Stuart. *Writers and Politics in West Germany*. New York: St. Martin's, 1986.

Pearson, Jacqueline. "Romans and Barbarians: The Structure of Irony in Shakespeare's Roman Tragedies." *Shakespearian Tragedy*. Ed. Malcolm

Bradbury and David Palmer. Stratford-upon-Avon Studies 20. London: Edward Arnold, 1984. 159–82.

Peck, Jeffrey M. "Advanced Literary Study as Cultural Study: A Redefinition of the Discipline." *Profession 85*. New York: MLA, 1985. 49–54.

——. "Going Native: Establishing Authority in German Studies." *German Studies Review* 13 (1990): 127–33.

——. "The Institution of *Germanistik* and the Transmission of Culture: The Time and Place for an Anthropological Approach." *Monatshefte* 79 (1987): 308–19.

——. "Methodological Postscript: What's the Difference? Minority Discourse in German Studies." *New German Critique* 46 (winter 1989): 203–08.

——. "There's No Place Like Home? Remapping the Topography of German Studies." *German Quarterly* 62 (1989): 178–87.

Peters, Paul. "Ritter von der wandelbaren Gestalt: Zu Günter Wallraffs *Ganz Unten.*" *Die Neue Gesellschaft/Frankfurter Hefte* 33 (1986): 1006–14.

Pickerodt, Gerhart. "Aufklärung und Exotismus." *Die andere Welt: Studien zum Exotismus*. Ed. Thomas Koebner and Gerhart Pickerodt. Frankfurt am Main: Athenäum, 1987. 121–36.

Polacco, Giorgio. "Unterentwickelte Länder und revolutionäre Welt: Eine Begegnung mit Peter Weiss." *Gesang vom Lusitanischen Popanz: Mit Materialien*. By Peter Weiss. Frankfurt am Main: Suhrkamp, 1974. 87–92. (Rpt. in *Peter Weiss im Gespräch*. Ed. Rainer Gerlach and Matthias Richter. Frankfurt am Main: Suhrkamp, 1986. 129–35.)

Porter, Dennis. "*Orientalism* and Its Problems." *The Politics of Theory*. Proc. of the Essex Conference on the Sociology of Literature, July 1982. Ed. Francis Barker et al. Colchester: U of Essex, 1983. 179–93.

Posharskaja, Genia. *Ein Morgen für die Blume Ngo. Neue Deutsche Literatur* December 1967: 14–41.

Das Präsidium des Deutschen Schriftstellerverbandes. "Solidarität mit dem chilenischen Volk!" *Neue Deutsche Literatur* November 1973: frontispiece.

Pratt, Mary Louise. "Fieldwork in Common Places." *Writing Culture: The Poetics and Politics of Ethnography*. Ed. James Clifford and George E. Marcus. Berkeley: U of California P, 1986. 27–50.

——. "A Reply to Harold Fromm." *Critical Inquiry* 13 (autumn 1986): 201–02. (Rpt. in *"Race," Writing, and Difference*. Ed. Henry Louis Gates Jr. Chicago: U of Chicago P, 1986. 400–01.)

——. "Scratches on the Face of the Country; or, What Mr. Barrow Saw in the Land of the Bushmen." *Critical Inquiry* 12 (autumn 1985):

119–43. (Rpt. in *"Race," Writing, and Difference*. Ed. Henry Louis Gates Jr. Chicago: U of Chicago P, 1986. 138–62.)

Price, H. T. "The Authorship of *Titus Andronicus*." *Journal of English and Germanic Philology* 42 (1943): 55–81.

Profitlich, Ulrich. "'Dialektische' Tragik im DDR-Drama?" *Drama und Theater im 20. Jahrhundert: Festschrift für Walter Hinck*. Ed. Hans Dietrich Irmscher and Werner Keller. Göttingen: Vandenhoeck, 1983. 317–32.

———. *Volker Braun: Studien zu seinem dramatischen und erzählerischen Werk*. München: Fink, 1985.

Rabinow, Paul. "Discourse and Power: On the Limits of Ethnographic Texts." *Dialectical Anthropology* 10 (1985): 1–13.

Raddatz, Frank-Michael. *Dämonen unterm Roten Stern: Zu Geschichtsphilosophie und Ästhetik Heiner Müllers*. Stuttgart: Metzler, 1991.

Räthzel, Nora. "Germany: One Race, One Nation?" *Race & Class* 32.3 (1991): 31–48.

Reese, Jack E. "The Formalization of Horror in *Titus Andronicus*." *Shakespeare Quarterly* 21 (1970): 77–84.

Reinhardt, Stephan. "Kurzbiographie Max von der Grün." *Max von der Grün: Materialienbuch*. Ed. Stephan Reinhardt. Darmstadt: Luchterhand, 1978. 174–80.

Reinhold, Ursula. "Geschichtliche Konfrontation und poetische Produktivität: Zu Hans Magnus Enzensberger in den siebziger Jahren." *Weimarer Beiträge* 27.1 (1981): 104–27.

———. "Literatur und Politik bei Enzensberger." *Weimarer Beiträge* 17.5 (1971): 94–113.

Retamar, Roberto Fernández. "Caliban: Notes toward a Discussion of Culture in Our America." *Caliban and Other Essays*. Trans. Edward Baker. Foreword by Fredric Jameson. Minneapolis: U of Minnesota P, 1989. 3–45. Trans. of "Caliban." *Casa de las Américas* 68 (September–October 1971).

Rischbieter, Henning. "*Gesang vom lusitanischen Popanz*." *Über Peter Weiss*. Ed. Volker Canaris. Frankfurt am Main: Suhrkamp, 1970. 97–105.

Rödel, Fritz. "Claus Hammel." *Literatur der DDR in Einzeldarstellungen*. Ed. Hans Jürgen Geerdts. Stuttgart: Kröner, 1972. 473–89.

Rohde, Gerhard. "Peter Hacks entdeckt das Missing Link." *Frankfurter Allgemeine Zeitung* 14 December 1978: 25.

Romero, Christiane Zehl. *Anna Seghers: Mit Selbstzeugnissen und Bilddokumenten*. Reinbek: Rowohlt, 1993.

——. "*Seghersmaterial* in Heiner Müller und Volker Braun." *Studies in GDR Culture and Society* 9 (1989): 57–83.

Rosaldo, Renato. "From the Door of His Tent: The Fieldworker and the Inquisitor." *Writing Culture: The Poetics and Politics of Ethnography.* Ed. James Clifford and George E. Marcus. Berkeley: U of California P, 1986. 77–97.

Rosellini, Jay. *Volker Braun.* Autorenbücher 31. München: Beck, 1983.

Rüdiger, Horst. "Dante als Erwecker geistiger Kräfte in der deutschen Literatur." *Festschrift für Richard Alewyn.* Ed. Herbert Singer and Benno von Wiese. Köln: Böhlau, 1967. 17–45.

Sadji, Amadou Booker. "Hans Magnus Enzensberger und die 'Dritte Welt.'" *Hans Magnus Enzensberger.* Ed. Reinhold Grimm. Frankfurt am Main: Suhrkamp, 1984. 258–75.

Said, Edward W. *Culture and Imperialism.* New York: Knopf, 1993.

——. *Orientalism.* New York: Vintage-Random, 1979.

——. "Orientalism Reconsidered." *Cultural Critique* 1 (fall 1985): 89–107.

——. "Representing the Colonized: Anthropology's Interlocutors." *Critical Inquiry* 15 (winter 1989): 205–25.

Salloch, Erika. "The *Divina Commedia* as Model and Anti-Model for *The Investigation* by Peter Weiss." *Modern Drama* 14.1 (1971): 1–12.

Sareika, Rüdiger. *Die Dritte Welt in der westdeutschen Literatur der sechziger Jahre.* Frankfurt am Main: R. G. Fischer, 1980.

——. "Peter Weiss' Engagement für die 'Dritte Welt': *Lusitanischer Popanz* und *Viet Nam Diskurs*." *Peter Weiss.* Ed. Rainer Gerlach. Frankfurt am Main: Suhrkamp, 1984. 249–67.

——. "Von der Systemkritik zur Ethnopoesie: Außereuropäische Kulturen in der deutschen Literatur." *Dieser Tag voller Vulkane: Ein Dritte-Welt-Lesebuch.* Ed. Christian Schaffernicht. Fischerhude: Atelier im Bauernhaus, 1983. 20–26.

Schauspielhaus Bochum, ed. *Verkommenes Ufer Medea Material Landschaft mit Argonauten.* By Heiner Müller. Stuttgart: Druckhaus Münster, 1983.

Scherpe, Klaus R. "Die *Ästhetik des Widerstands* als *Divina Commedia*: Peter Weiss' künstlerische Vergegenständlichung der Geschichte." *Peter Weiss: Werk und Wirkung.* Ed. Rudolf Wolff. Bonn: Bouvier, 1987. 88–99.

Scheuer, Helmut. "Der 'Gastarbeiter' in Literatur, Film und Lied deutscher Autoren." *Zeitschrift für Literaturwissenschaft und Linguistik* 56 (1984): 62–74.

Schlösser, Anselm. "*Titus Andronicus.*" *Shakespeare Jahrbuch* 104 (1968):

75–84. Rpt. with revisions as *"Titus Andronicus:* Eine Wüstenei, von Tigern voll." *Shakespeare: Analysen und Interpretationen.* Berlin: Aufbau, 1977. 95–105.

Schlunk, Jürgen E. "Auschwitz and Its Function in Peter Weiss' Search for Identity." *German Studies Review* 10 (1987): 11–30.

Schmidt, Helmut. "Der Teppich braucht keine neuen Flicken." *Die Zeit* 27 January 1989: 7.

Schmidt, Henry J. "What Is Oppositional Criticism? Politics and German Literary Criticism from Fascism to the Cold War." *Monatshefte* 79 (1987): 292–307.

Schmitt, Maria C. *Peter Weiss, "Die Ästhetik des Widerstands": Studien zu Kontext, Struktur und Kunstverständnis.* St. Ingbert: Röhrig, 1986.

Schmitz, Ingeborg. *Dokumentartheater bei Peter Weiss: Von der "Ermittlung" zu "Hölderlin."* Frankfurt am Main: Lang, 1981.

Schödel, Helmut. "Schlachtbeschreibung: Uraufführung in Bochum: *Anatomie Titus Fall of Rome Ein Shakespearekommentar* und andere Stücke in Ost-Berlin und München." *Die Zeit* 22 February 1985: 51–52.

Schöning-Kalender, Claudia. Review of *Bruder, muß zusammen Zwiebel und Wasser essen!* and *Wie Mutlu Öztürk schwimmen lernen muß,* by Paul Geiersbach. *Zeitschrift für Volkskunde* 81 (1985): 116–17.

Schuhmacher, Klaus. "Candides Untergang: Zu Hans Magnus Enzensbergers Ästhetik des Verschwindens." *Sprachkunst* 16 (1985): 43–65.

Schuhmann, Klaus. "Anmerkungen zu Volker Brauns *Guevara oder der Sonnenstaat.*" *Text und Kritik* 55 (July 1977): 27–34.

———. "Nachwort." *Stücke.* By Volker Braun. Berlin: Henschel, 1983. 355–75.

Schulz, Genia. "Abschied von Morgen: Zu den Frauengestalten im Werk Heiner Müllers." *Text und Kritik* 73 (January 1982): 58–70.

———. "'Ein Bier und vor dir steht ein Kommunist, Flint': Zur Dialektik des Anfangs bei Heiner Müller." *Dialektik des Anfangs.* Ed. Paul Gerhard Klussmann and Heinrich Mohr. *Jahrbuch zur Literatur in der DDR* 5 (1986): 15–28.

———. "Heiner Müllers Theater der Sprache(n)." *Vom Wort zum Bild: Das neue Theater in Deutschland und den USA.* Ed. Sigrid Bauschinger and Susan L. Cocalis. Bern: Francke, 1992. 199–217.

———. "Medea: Zu einem Motiv im Werk Heiner Müllers." *Weiblichkeit und Tod in der Literatur.* Ed. Renate Berger and Inge Stephan. Köln: Böhlau, 1987. 241–64.

Schumacher, Ernst. *"Gesang vom Lusitanischen Popanz." Gesang vom Lusi-*

tanischen Popanz: Mit Materialien. By Peter Weiss. Frankfurt am Main: Suhrkamp, 1974. 83–86.

——. *"Vietnam-Diskurs* in Rostock." *Über Peter Weiss.* Ed. Volker Canaris. Frankfurt am Main: Suhrkamp, 1970. 106–11.

Seeba, Hinrich C. "Der Untergang der Utopie: Ein Schiffbruch in der Gegenwartsliteratur." *German Studies Review* 4 (1981): 281–98.

Seghers, Anna. *Aufsätze, Ansprachen, Essays 1927–1953.* 2nd ed. Berlin: Aufbau, 1984. Vol. 13 of *Gesammelte Werke in Einzelausgaben.* 14 vols. 1977–80.

——. *Aufsätze, Ansprachen, Essays 1954–1979.* 2nd ed. Berlin: Aufbau, 1984. Vol. 14 of *Gesammelte Werke in Einzelausgaben.* 14 vols. 1977–80.

——. "Aufstand der Fischer von St. Barbara." *"Aufstand der Fischer von St. Barbara" und andere Erzählungen.* Darmstadt: Luchterhand, 1981. 7–66. *The Revolt of the Fishermen.* Trans. Margaret Goldsmith. New York: Longmans, 1930.

——. "Der Ausflug der toten Mädchen." *Der Ausflug der toten Mädchen: Erzählungen.* Darmstadt: Luchterhand, 1979. 33–52. *The Excursion of the Dead Young Girls.* Toronto: Coach House, 1995.

——. "Briefe an F. C. Weiskopf." *Neue Deutsche Literatur* November 1985: 5–46.

——. "Crisanta." *Crisanta; Das wirkliche Blau: Zwei Geschichten aus Mexiko.* Darmstadt: Luchterhand, 1981. 5–30.

——. *Drei Frauen aus Haiti.* Darmstadt: Luchterhand, 1980.

——. "Die Heimkehr des verlorenen Volkes." *Die Kraft der Schwachen: Neun Erzählungen.* Darmstadt: Luchterhand, 1983. 139–56. "The Return of the Lost Tribe." *Benito's Blue and Nine Other Stories.* Trans. Joan Becker. Berlin: Seven Seas, 1973. 250–70.

——. *Die Hochzeit von Haiti: Karibische Geschichten.* Darmstadt: Luchterhand, 1976.

——. *Überfahrt: Eine Liebesgeschichte.* Darmstadt: Luchterhand, 1982.

——. "Das wirkliche Blau." *Crisanta; Das wirkliche Blau: Zwei Geschichten aus Mexiko.* Darmstadt: Luchterhand, 1981. 31–110. "Benito's Blue." *Benito's Blue and Nine Other Stories.* Trans. Joan Becker. Berlin: Seven Seas, 1973. 9–93.

Şenocak, Zafer. "Prinz Augstein, der Gedankenritter." *War Hitler Araber? IrreFührungen an den Rand Europas.* Berlin: Babel, 1994. 93–94.

Shakespeare, William. *The Tragedy of Titus Andronicus.* Ed. Sylvan Barnet. *The Two Noble Kinsmen; The Tragedy of Titus Andronicus; Pericles, Prince of Tyre.* Signet Classic Shakespeare. Ed. Sylvan Barnet. New York: NAL, 1977.

Smith, Barbara, ed. *Home Girls: A Black Feminist Anthology*. New York: Kitchen Table, 1983.

Sodaro, Michael. "The GDR and the Third World: Supplicant and Surrogate." *Eastern Europe and the Third World: East vs. South*. Ed. Michael Radu. Studies of the Institute on East Central Europe, Columbia University. New York: Praeger, 1981. 106–41.

Sölcün, Sargut. "Türkische Gastarbeiter in der deutschen Gegenwartsliteratur." *Kürbiskern*, 1979, no. 3: 74–81.

Sommers, Alan. " 'Wilderness of Tigers': Structure and Symbolism in *Titus Andronicus*." *Essays in Criticism* 10 (1960): 275–89.

Sorg, Bernhard. "Komödie und Rechenschaftsbericht: Zu Hans Magnus Enzensbergers *Der Untergang der Titanic*." *Text und Kritik* 49 (March 1985): 44–51.

Spelman, Elizabeth V. *Inessential Woman: Problems of Exclusion in Feminist Thought*. Boston: Beacon, 1988.

Sperr, Monika. Review of *Leben im gelobten Land*, by Max von der Grün. *Die Tat* 5 July 1975. Rpt. in *Max von der Grün: Materialienbuch*. Ed. Stephan Reinhardt. Darmstadt: Luchterhand, 1978. 167–69.

Spivack, Bernard. *Shakespeare and the Allegory of Evil: The History of a Metaphor in Relation to His Major Villains*. New York: Columbia UP, 1958.

Spivak, Gayatri Chakravorty. "Can the Subaltern Speak?" *Marxism and the Interpretation of Culture*. Ed. Cary Nelson and Lawrence Grossberg. Urbana: U of Illinois P, 1988. 271–313. Rpt. in *Colonial Discourse and Post-Colonial Theory: A Reader*. Ed. Patrick Williams and Laura Chrisman. New York: Columbia UP, 1994. 66–111.

Staatliche Zentralverwaltung für Statistik, ed. *Statistisches Taschenbuch der Deutschen Demokratischen Republik 1985*. Berlin: Staatsverlag der DDR, 1985.

Stavrianos, L. S. *Global Rift: The Third World Comes of Age*. New York: Morrow, 1981.

Stern, Kurt. "Tätige, kampfbereite Solidarität!" *Neue Deutsche Literatur* February 1974: 63–65.

Streese, Konstanze. *"Cric?"—"Crac!" Vier literarische Versuche, mit dem Kolonialismus umzugehen*. New York University Ottendorfer Series, Neue Folge 38. Bern: Lang, 1991.

Streller, Siegfried. "Geschichte und Aktualität in Anna Seghers' Erzählung *Das Licht auf dem Galgen*." *Weimarer Beiträge* 8 (1962): 740–51.

——. "Von verborgener Größe." *Neue Deutsche Literatur* November 1980: 139–42.

———. "Zauber und Leid der Karibik: Lateinamerika im Werk von Anna Seghers." *Wortweltbilder: Studien zur deutschen Literatur*. Berlin: Aufbau, 1986. 187–97.

Teichmann, Klaus. *Der verwundete Körper: Zu Texten Heiner Müllers*. 2nd ed. Freiburg: Burg, 1989.

Teraoka, Arlene A. "*Der Auftrag* and *Die Maßnahme*: Models of Revolution in Heiner Müller and Bertolt Brecht." *German Quarterly* 59 (1986): 65–84.

———. "Is Culture to Us What Text Is to Anthropology? A Response to Jeffrey M. Peck's Paper." *German Quarterly* 62 (1989): 188–91.

———. *The Silence of Entropy or Universal Discourse: The Postmodernist Poetics of Heiner Müller*. New York University Ottendorfer Series, Neue Folge 21. New York: Lang, 1985.

———. "Subway Art and *Fantasia*: Heiner Müller on Resistance and Disorder in America." *Kairos* 1.4 (1985): 38–47.

———. "Turks as Subjects: The Ethnographic Novels of Paul Geiersbach." *Culture/Contexture: Explorations in Anthropology and Literary Study*. Ed. E. Valentine Daniel and Jeffrey M. Peck. Berkeley: U of California P, forthcoming.

———. "Writing and Violence in Heiner Müller's *Bildbeschreibung*." *Vom Wort zum Bild: Das neue Theater in Deutschland und den USA*. Ed. Sigrid Bauschinger and Susan L. Cocalis. Bern: Francke, 1992. 179–98.

Thurm, Brigitte. "Gesellschaftliche Relevanz und künstlerische Subjektivität: Zur Subjekt-Objekt-Problematik in den Dramen von Peter Weiss." *Weimarer Beiträge* 15 (1969): 1091–102.

Timm, Hans-Jürgen. "Geschichte als Erfahrungsraum: Zu Aspekten der Dramatik Volker Brauns." *Weimarer Beiträge* 35 (1989): 1506–30.

Todorov, Tzvetan. "'Race,' Writing, and Culture." *Critical Inquiry* 13 (autumn 1986): 171–81. (Rpt. in *"Race," Writing, and Difference*. Ed. Henry Louis Gates Jr. Chicago: U of Chicago P, 1986. 370–80.)

Tricomi, Albert H. "The Mutilated Garden in *Titus Andronicus*." *Shakespeare Studies* 9 (1977): 85–105.

Trilse, Christoph. *Peter Hacks: Das Werk*. 2nd ed. Berlin: Das Europäische Buch, 1981.

Trinh T. Minh-ha. *When the Moon Waxes Red: Representation, Gender, and Cultural Politics*. New York: Routledge, 1991.

———. *Woman, Native, Other: Writing Postcoloniality and Feminism*. Bloomington: Indiana UP, 1989.

Tulasiewicz, W. F. Introduction. *Die Hochzeit von Haiti*. By Anna Seghers. Ed. W. F. Tulasiewicz and K. Scheible. London: Macmillan, 1970. 7–69.

Turner, Henry Ashby, Jr. *The Two Germanies since 1945.* New Haven: Yale UP, 1987.

Ullrich, Peter. "'Ein neuer Mensch beginnend mit dem Ende . . .'" *Theater der Zeit* March 1984: 50–52.

Uschner, Manfred. "Neue revolutionäre Erschütterungen in Lateinamerika." *Deutsche Außenpolitik* December 1979: 42–55.

Vaßen, Florian. "Die entfremdete und die fremde Revolution: Reflexionen über Heiner Müllers Revolutionsstücke." *Begegnung mit dem "Fremden": Grenzen—Traditionen—Vergleiche: Akten des* VIII. *Internationalen Germanisten-Kongresses, Tokyo 1990.* Ed. Eijiro Iwasaki. Vol. II. München: Iudicium, 1991. 313–23. II vols.

——. "Der Tod des Körpers in der Geschichte: Tod, Sexualität und Arbeit bei Heiner Müller." *Text und Kritik* 73 (January 1982): 45–57.

Vodoz, Isabelle. "Deux lettres de Jamaïque sur la Révolution: Anna Seghers: *La Lumière sur le gibet,* Heiner Müller: *La Mission.*" *Germanica* 6 (1989): 181–94.

von der Grün, Max. "Gespräch mit Max von der Grün." *Deutsche Bücher* 12 (1982): 165–83.

——. "Gespräch mit Max von der Grün." *Gespräche mit Schriftstellern: Max Frisch, Günter Grass, Wolfgang Koeppen, Max von der Grün, Günter Wallraff.* Ed. Heinz Ludwig Arnold. München: Beck, 1975. 142–97.

——. *Leben im gelobten Land: Gastarbeiterporträts.* Darmstadt: Luchterhand, 1975.

Vormweg, Heinrich. *Peter Weiss.* München: Beck; Text und Kritik, 1981.

Wagner, Frank. "Selbstbehauptung und ihr geschichtliches Maß: Aus Anlaß der Geschichten *Drei Frauen aus Haiti* von Anna Seghers." *Zeitschrift für Germanistik* 2 (1981): 37–47.

Wais, Kurt. "Die *Divina Commedia* als dichterisches Vorbild im XIX. und XX. Jahrhundert." *Arcadia* 3 (1968): 27–47.

Waith, Eugene M. Introduction. *Titus Andronicus.* By William Shakespeare. Ed. Eugene M. Waith. Oxford Shakespeare. Oxford: Oxford UP, 1984. 1–69.

——. "The Metamorphosis of Violence in *Titus Andronicus.*" *Shakespeare Survey* 10 (1957): 39–49.

Wallace, Ian. "Das Dennoch und der Triumph der Selbstbehauptung: Identitätssuche und Zivilisationskrise bei Volker Braun." *Probleme deutscher Identität.* Ed. Paul Gerhard Klussmann and Heinrich Mohr. *Jahrbuch zur Literatur in der DDR* 3 (1983): 185–208.

Wallraff, Günter. "Deutsche Linke im Beißkrampf." *Taz* 8 October 1987: 1–2.

———. *Ganz unten*. Köln: Kiepenheuer & Witsch, 1985. *Lowest of the Low*. Trans. Martin Chalmers. Introduction by A. Sivanandan. London: Methuen, 1988.

———. "Gespräch mit Günter Wallraff." *Gespräche mit Schriftstellern: Max Frisch, Günter Grass, Wolfgang Koeppen, Max von der Grün, Günter Wallraff*. Ed. Heinz Ludwig Arnold. München: Beck, 1975. 198–243.

———. "Ich bin eine Antwort auf diese Gesellschaft." *Der Spiegel* 6 July 1987: 154–60.

———. *The Undesirable Journalist*. Trans. Steve Gooch and Paul Knight. Woodstock NY: Overlook, 1979.

———. "Zu diesem Buch." *Wie Mutlu Öztürk schwimmen lernen muß: Ein Lebenslauf*. By Paul Geiersbach. Berlin: Dietz, 1983. 5–7.

Warneken, Bernd Jürgen. "Kritik am *Viet Nam Diskurs*." *Über Peter Weiss*. Ed. Volker Canaris. Frankfurt am Main: Suhrkamp, 1970. 112–30.

Wasmund, Klaus. "The Political Socialization of West German Terrorists." *Political Violence and Terror: Motifs and Motivations*. Ed. Peter H. Merkl. Berkeley: U of California P, 1986. 191–228.

Weber, Carl. Preface. *Hamletmachine and Other Texts for the Stage*. By Heiner Müller. Ed. and trans. Carl Weber. New York: Performing Arts Journal, 1984. 9–10.

Weber, Heinz-Dieter. "Die Wiederkehr des Tragischen in der Literatur der DDR." *Der Deutschunterricht* 30.2 (1978): 79–99.

Webster, Steven. "Dialogue and Fiction in Ethnography." *Dialectical Anthropology* 7 (1982): 91–114.

Weigel, Sigrid. "Die nahe Fremde—das Territorium des 'Weiblichen': Zum Verhältnis von 'Wilden' und 'Frauen' im Diskurs der Aufklärung." *Die andere Welt: Studien zum Exotismus*. Ed. Thomas Koebner and Gerhart Pickerodt. Frankfurt am Main: Athenäum, 1987. 171–99.

———. "'Ein neues Alphabet schreiben auf andre Leiber': Fremde Kultur und Weiblichkeit in den 'Karibischen Geschichten' von Anna Seghers, Hans Christoph Buch und Heiner Müller." *Begegnung mit dem "Fremden": Grenzen—Traditionen—Vergleiche: Akten des* VIII. *Internationalen Germanisten-Kongresses, Tokyo 1990*. Ed. Eijiro Iwasaki. Vol. II. München: Iudicium, 1991. 296–304. II vols.

Weimann, Gundula. "Zur Funktion des Antihelden im Text *Anatomie Titus Fall of Rome Ein Shakespearekommentar* von Heiner Müller: Aarons Welttheater im Kunstwerk der tatsächlichen Schlacht ein lebendiges Erbe." *Shakespeare Jahrbuch* 125 (1989): 116–20.

Weiss, Peter. "10 Arbeitspunkte eines Autors in der geteilten Welt." *Rapporte 2* 14–23.

——. "'Amerika will den Völkermord.'" *Der Spiegel* 5 August 1968: 66–74. Rpt. in *Peter Weiss im Gespräch*. Ed. Rainer Gerlach and Matthias Richter. Frankfurt am Main: Suhrkamp, 1986. 158–69.

——. "Antwort auf eine Kritik zur Stockholmer Aufführung der *Ermittlung*." *Rapporte 2* 45–50.

——. *Die Ästhetik des Widerstands*. 3 vols. Frankfurt am Main: Suhrkamp, 1983.

——. "Aus den *Notizbüchern*." *Hans Magnus Enzensberger*. Ed. Reinhold Grimm. Frankfurt am Main: Suhrkamp, 1984. 101–05.

——. "Che Guevara!" *Rapporte 2* 82–90. "Che Guevara!" (English trans.) *Notizbücher 1960–1971* 555–61.

——. "Enzensbergers Illusionen." *Kursbuch* 6 (July 1966): 165-70. (Rpt. in *Über Hans Magnus Enzensberger*. Ed. Joachim Schickel. Frankfurt am Main: Suhrkamp, 1970. 239–45.) Rpt. as "Brief an H. M. Enzensberger." *Rapporte 2* 35–44.

——. *Die Ermittlung: Oratorium in 11 Gesängen. Stücke I*. Frankfurt am Main: Suhrkamp, 1976. 257–449. *The Investigation*. Trans. Jon Swan and Ulu Grosbard. New York: Atheneum, 1966.

——. *Gesang vom Lusitanischen Popanz: Stück mit Musik in 2 Akten. Stücke II* 1: 7–71. *Song of the Lusitanian Bogey*. Trans. Lee Baxandall. *Two Plays*. By Peter Weiss. New York: Atheneum, 1970. 1–63.

——. "Gespräch über Dante." *Rapporte* 142–69.

——. "I Come Out of My Hiding Place." (English orig.) *The Nation* 30 May 1966: 652+. "Rede in englischer Sprache gehalten an der Princeton University USA am 25. April 1966, unter dem Titel: 'I Come Out of My Hiding Place.'" *Über Peter Weiss*. Ed. Volker Canaris. Frankfurt am Main: Suhrkamp, 1970. 9–14.

——. "Interview mit Peter Weiss." With Volker Canaris. *Der andere Hölderlin: Materialien zum "Hölderlin"-Stück von Peter Weiss*. Ed. Thomas Beckermann and Volker Canaris. Frankfurt am Main: Suhrkamp, 1972. 142–48.

——. "Die Luftangriffe der USA am 21.11.1970 auf die Demokratische Republik Viet Nam." *Rapporte 2* 132–51.

——. "Meine Ortschaft." *Rapporte* 113–24. "My Place." Trans. Christopher Middleton. *German Writing Today*. Ed. Christopher Middleton. Harmondsworth, England: Penguin, 1967. 20–28.

——. *Notizbücher 1960–1971*. 2 vols. Frankfurt am Main: Suhrkamp, 1982.

——. *Notizbücher 1971–1980*. 2 vols. Frankfurt am Main: Suhrkamp, 1981.

——. "Notizen zum dokumentarischen Theater." *Rapporte 2* 91–104. *Stücke II* 2: 598–606. "The Material and the Models: Notes towards a Definition of Documentary Theatre." Trans. Heinz Bernard. *Theatre Quarterly* 1.1 (1971): 41–43.

——. *Notizen zum kulturellen Leben in der Demokratischen Republik Viet Nam*. Frankfurt am Main: Suhrkamp, 1968. *Notes on the Cultural Life of the Democratic Republic of Vietnam*. London: Calder & Boyars, 1971.

——. "Peter Weiss dramatisiert Vietnam: Gespräch mit dem Autor nach der Uraufführung seines neuen Stückes *Gesang vom lusitanischen Popanz*." With Henning Rischbieter. *Theater Heute* March 1967: 6–7.

——. *Rapporte*. Frankfurt am Main: Suhrkamp, 1968.

——. *Rapporte 2*. Frankfurt am Main: Suhrkamp, 1971.

——. "'. . . ein ständiges Auseinandersetzen mit den Fehlern und mit den Mißgriffen . . . ': Heinz Ludwig Arnold im Gespräch mit Peter Weiss (19. September 1981)." *Die Ästhetik des Widerstands*. Ed. Alexander Stephan. Frankfurt am Main: Suhrkamp, 1983. 11–58.

——. *Stücke II*. 2 vols. Frankfurt am Main: Suhrkamp, 1977.

——. "Vietnam!" *Rapporte 2* 51–62.

——. "Vietnam bleibt unsere Sache." With Michael Opperskalski. *Peter Weiss im Gespräch*. Ed. Rainer Gerlach and Matthias Richter. Frankfurt am Main: Suhrkamp, 1986. 239–42.

——. *Viet Nam Diskurs*. (*Diskurs über die Vorgeschichte und den Verlauf des lang andauernden Befreiungskrieges in Viet Nam als Beispiel für die Notwendigkeit des bewaffneten Kampfes der Unterdrückten gegen ihre Unterdrücker sowie über die Versuche der Vereinigten Staaten von Amerika die Grundlagen der Revolution zu vernichten.*) *Stücke II* 1: 73–264. *Discourse on the Progress of the Prolonged War of Liberation in Viet Nam and the Events Leading Up to It as Illustration of the Necessity for Armed Resistance against Oppression and on the Attempts of the United States of America to Destroy the Foundations of Revolution*. Trans. Geoffrey Skelton. *Two Plays*. By Peter Weiss. New York: Atheneum, 1970. 65–229.

——. "Vorübung zum dreiteiligen Drama divina commedia." *Rapporte* 125–41.

——. "Weiss in Nordvietnam: Die Bomben der USA zwingen die Bevölkerung unter die Erde." *Peter Weiss im Gespräch*. Ed. Rainer Gerlach and Matthias Richter. Frankfurt am Main: Suhrkamp, 1986. 154–57.

Weiss, Peter, and Gunilla Palmstierna-Weiss. *Bericht über die Angriffe der US-Luftwaffe und -Marine gegen die Demokratische Republik Viet Nam nach der Erklärung Präsident Johnsons über die "begrenzte Bombardierung" am 31. März 1968*. Voltaire Flugschriften 23. Frankfurt am Main: Voltaire, 1968. *"Limited Bombing" in Vietnam: Report on the Attacks against the Democratic Republic of Vietnam by the US Air Force and the Seventh Fleet*, *after the Declaration of "Limited Bombing" by President Lyndon B. John-son on March 31, 1968*. Trans. Anna Björkwall and Davis Jones. London: Bertrand Russell Peace Foundation, 1969.

——. "'Büffel und Schweine kamen um': Aus dem Bericht des Peter Weiss über die Angriffe der US-Luftwaffe auf die Provinz Quang Binh." *Der Spiegel* 5 August 1968: 67.

Wiedemann-Wolf, Barbara. "Die Rezeption Dantes und Ungarettis in Enzensbergers *Untergang der Titanic*." *Arcadia* 19 (1984): 252–68.

Williams, Jimmy Lee. "Thematic Links in Shakespeare's *Titus Andronicus* and *Othello*: Sex, Racism and Exoticism, Point and Counterpoint." *Identity and Awareness in the Minority Experience: Selected Proceedings of the 1st and 2nd Annual Conferences on Minority Studies*. Ed. George E. Carter and Bruce L. Mouser. La Crosse: Institute for Minority Studies, U of Wisconsin-La Crosse, 1975. 157–90.

Wilpert, Czarina. "Ideological and Institutional Foundations of Racism in the Federal Republic of Germany." *Racism and Migration in Western Europe*. Ed. John Wrench and John Solomos. Oxford: Berg, 1993. 67–81.

Wolf, Christa. "Glauben an Irdisches." *Lesen und Schreiben: Neue Samm-lung: Essays, Aufsätze, Reden*. Darmstadt: Luchterhand, 1980. 115–43.

Wolf-Phillips, Leslie. "Why Third World?" *Third World Quarterly* 1.1 (1979): 105–13.

Worsley, Peter. "How Many Worlds?" *Third World Quarterly* 1.2 (1979): 100–08.

——. *The Three Worlds: Culture and World Development*. Chicago: U of Chicago P, 1984.

Young, Robert. *White Mythologies: Writing History and the West*. London: Routledge, 1990.

Zantop, Susanne. "Verlobung, Hochzeit und Scheidung in St. Domingo: Die haitianische Revolution in zeitgenössischer deutscher Literatur (1792–1817)." *"Neue Welt"/"Dritte Welt": Interkulturelle Beziehungen Deutschlands zu Lateinamerika und der Karibik*. Ed. Sigrid Bauschinger and Susan L. Cocalis. Tübingen: Francke, 1994. 29–52.

Ziermann, Horst. "Eine Schwäche für überflüssige Tugenden." *Die Welt* 28 November 1978: 27.

Zimmermann, Peter. "Günter Wallraff." *Deutsche Literatur der Gegenwart in Einzeldarstellungen*. Ed. Dietrich Weber. Vol. 2. Stuttgart: Kröner, 1977. 402–24. 2 vols. 1976–77.

Index

Index

European intellectuals (*cont.*)
olution in Hammel, 92–93. *See also*
revolutionaries, white

Fabian, Johannes, 203 n.17, 206 n.42
Fanon, Frantz, 31, 110
fascism: and German crisis of identity, 163, 165; German heritage of,
5; in Weiss, 37. *See also* Auschwitz;
National Socialism
Federal Republic of Germany (FRG):
citizenship, 136; GDR critiques of,
82, 187 n.4; immigration to, 136,
201 n.3; and Latin America, 80;
recruitment of foreign labor, 135;
student movement, 27–28, 29; and
Vietnam, 28
Fehervary, Helen, 193 n.9
feminism, 172 n.8 n.9
Fernandez, James W., 206 n.42
Fiebach, Joachim, 193 n.5, 195 n.17,
196 n.29, 197 n.33, 199 n.43
Freies Deutschland (Free Germany), 9,
173 n.1

Gates, Henry Louis, Jr., 26, 172 n.9,
177 n.27
GDR drama, 83–84, 103–4, 105. *See also*
individual writers
GDR writers: and Latin America, 83–85;
and the Third World, 79, 83–85. *See*
also individual writers
GDR Writers Association, 7, 83, 86, 105,
187 n.3, 188 n.9
Geiersbach, Paul: authorial role in,
152–55, 156–57; background information, 138; and difference, 166–67;
humanism in, 155–56; plurivocality
in, 159, 160; and reflexive ethnography, 206 n.40; self-reflection in,
167–68; social reality as contested
in, 159, 160; on Turkish diversity,
152–53; voice of the Turk in, 152,
153–55, 157–59. Works: *Bruder, muß*
zusammen Zwiebel und Wasser essen!
Eine türkische Familie in Deutsch-
land, 139–40, 151–59; *Wie Mutlu*

Öztürk schwimmen lernen muß: Ein
Lebenslauf, 205 n.31
gender: and colonialism in Müller,
194 n.11
German Democratic Republic (GDR):
and antifascism, 82; and Chile, 80–81,
83–84, 187 n.2; and German human-
ism, 82; and Latin America, 80–81,
82–84, 91–92, 187 n.2; liberalization
in the 1970s, 81–82; national identity
of, 79, 81; and the Third World, 80,
82, 84, 85, 91–92, 93, 101, 187 n.2 n.3;
and Vietnam, 187 n.3
Germany. *See* Federal Republic of
Germany; German Democratic
Republic
Gökberk, Ülker, 3, 172 n.8
Grass, Günter, 28
Greiner, Bernhard, 197 n.33
Grimm, Reinhold, 176 n.22,
184 n.47 n.48
Group 47, 28, 36
Group 61, 137
Guadeloupe, 10
Guattari, Félix, 3, 200 n.49
Guevara, Che: in Braun, 101, 103
Gugelberger, Georg M., 179 n.14,
180 n.19
Gutzmann, Gertraud, 26, 174 n.6,
176 n.18 n.20

Hacks, Peter: biography, 86; the civilizing mission in, 95–96; and difference,
166–67; the European intellectual
and the Third World in, 93–96,
100–104, 167; language, European
vs. Mexican use of, 97–98; Mexican
cultural identity in, 97–99; Mexico
in, 93–100. Works: *Die Fische*, 84, 85,
86, 93–101, 102, 103; *Moritz Tassow*,
86; *Die Sorgen und die Macht*, 86
Haiti, 8, 25, 26
Hallstein doctrine, 79, 80
Hammel, Claus: biography, 85–86;
compared with Seghers, 92; and
difference, 166–67; the European intellectual in, 92–93, 100–101, 102–3,
167; humanism and revolution in,

245